Trends in Functional Programming
Volume 6

Edited by
Marko van Eekelen
Radboud University, Nijmegen

intellect Bristol, UK / Chicago, USA

First Published in the UK in 2007 by
Intellect Books, PO Box 862, Bristol BS99 1DE, UK

First published in the USA in 2007 by
Intellect Books, The University of Chicago Press, 1427 E. 60th Street, Chicago,
IL 60637, USA

A catalogue record for this book is available from the British Library.

Cover Design: Gabriel Solomons

ISBN 978–1-84150–176-5

Printed and bound by Gutenberg Press, Malta.

Contents

Preface

This book contains selected papers from the proceedings presented at the Sixth Symposium on Trends in Functional Programming (TFP05). Continuing the TFP series with its previous instances held in Stirling (1999), St. Andrews (2000), Stirling (2001), Edinburgh (2003) and Munich (2004) the symposium was held in Tallinn, Estland in co-location with ICFP 2005 and GPCE 2005.

TFP (www.tifp.org) aims to combine a lively environment for presenting the latest research results with a formal post-symposium refereeing process leading to the publication by Intellect of a high-profile volume containing a selection of the best papers presented at the symposium. Compared to the earlier events in the TFP sequence the sixth symposium in 2005 was proud to host more participants than ever. This was partly due to the financial support given to many participants via the APPSEM II Thematic Network.

The 2005 Symposium on Trends in Functional Programming (TFP05) was an international forum for researchers with interests in all aspects of functional programming languages, focusing on providing a broad view of current and future trends in Functional Programming. Via the submission of abstracts admission to the symposium was made possible upon acceptance by the program chair. The Tallinn proceedings contain 30 full papers based on these abstracts.

After the Symposium *all authors* were given the opportunity to improve their papers incorporating *personal feedback* given at the symposium. These improved papers were refereed according to academic peer-review standards by the TFP05 programme committee. Finally, all submitted papers (student and non-student) were reviewed according to the same criteria. Out of 27 submitted papers the best 14 papers were selected for this book. These papers all fulfill the criteria for academic publication as laid down by the programme committee.

Evaluation of extra student feedback round

In order to enhance the quality of student submissions, *student papers* were given the option of an extra *programme committee review feedback* round based upon their submission to the symposium proceedings. This feedback in advance of the post-symposium refereeing process is intended for authors who are less familiar with a formal publication process. It provides general qualitative feedback on the submission, but it does not give a grade or ranking. This extra student feedback round was a novelty for the TFP-series suggested by the programme chair and approved by the programme committee.

Since the effort of an extra student feedback round performed by the PC was novel, it was decided to evaluate it. Fifteen students used the feedback round. Twelve of them still decided to submit after the extra feedback round. The others decided to work more on their paper and submit to another venue later. The feedback round included comments from at least 3 pc-members. At the final submission a letter was attached by the student author explaining how the feedback was incorporated in the final paper. Then, the student papers were reviewed again by the original reviewers according to the standard criteria.

In the final submission the acceptance rates for the students (0.42) were a bit lower than the overall acceptance rate (0.52). This is a significant improvement compared to earlier TFP-events where the acceptance rates for students were much lower.

It is also important to note that the grades that were given by the reviewers to student papers were on average at the same level as the overall average (2.903 vs 2.898 on a decreasing scale from 1 to 5).

As part of the evaluation we sent round a questionnaire to the students asking 13 different questions evaluating the feedback round. Ten out of 15 returned the questionnaire. The answers were very positive. For some students the advantages were mainly in improving technical details or in improving the motivation of the work. For most students the advantages were in improving the structure or the presentation of the work. Overall, the students gave on average 4.5 on an increasing scale from 1 to 5 to the questions regarding the usefulness and the desirability of the feedback round.

It was decided by the TFP-advisory committee to continue this feedback round in later TFP-events.

New paper categories

Upon proposal of the TFP05 programme chair, the TFP05 programme committee introduced besides the usual research papers three other paper categories reflecting the focus of the symposium on trends in functional programming: *Project Start* papers (acknowledging that new projects fit in or create a new trend), *Project Evaluation* papers (acknowledging that evaluations of finished projects may greatly influence the direction and the creation of new trends) and *Position* papers (acknowledging that an academically motivated position may create a new trend in itself).

This book contains papers from two out of three of these new categories. The criteria for each category are given on page viii of this book.

Best student paper award

TFP traditionally pays special attention to research students, acknowledging that students are almost by definition part of new subject trends. As part of the post-symposium refereeing process the TFP05 **best student paper**

award (i.e. for the best paper with a student as first author) acknowledges more formally the special attention TFP has for students.

The best student paper award of TFP05 was awarded to **Kevin Millikin** from the University of Aarhus for his paper entitled '*A New Approach to One-Pass Transformations*'.

It is certainly worth noticing that for this paper the grades that were given by the reviewers were the best of *all* the papers that were submitted.

Acknowledgements

As TFP05 programme chair I would like to thank all those who provided help in making the 2005 TFP symposium work.

First of all, of course, I want to thank the full programme committee (for a full list of members see page x) for their effort in providing the peer-reviewing resulting in this selection of papers.

Secondly, I want to thank Ando Saabas and Ronny Wichers Schreur for their excellent technical assistance. Thirdly, I thank organisational chair Tarmo Uustalu for the enormous amount of local organisation work. Without Tarmo nothing would have happened.

Last but in no way least, I would like to thank the TFP2005 general chair Kevin Hammond who excellently kept me on track by providing direction, support and advice and by sending me 'just in time' messages where needed.

Nijmegen,

Marko van Eekelen

TFP05 Programme Chair
Editor of Trends in Functional Programming Volume 6

TFP Review Criteria

These are the TFP05 review criteria as used by the programme committee to decide upon academic publication.

General Criteria For All Papers

- Formatted according to the TFP-rules;
- The number of submitted pages is less or equal to 16 (the programme committee may ask the authors to elaborate a bit on certain aspects, allowing a few extra pages);
- Original, technically correct, previously unpublished, not submitted elsewhere;
- In English, well written, well structured, well illustrated;
- Abstract, introduction, conclusion;
- Clearly stated topic, clearly indicated category (student/non-student; research, project, evaluation, overview, position);
- Relevance as well as methodology are well motivated;
- Proper reference to and comparison with relevant related work.

Student Paper

- Exactly the same as for non-student papers; just extra feedback!

Research Paper

- Leading-edge;
- Technical Contribution;
- Convincing motivation for the relevance of the problem and the approach taken to solve it;
- Clear outline of approach to solve the problem, the solution and how the solution solves the problem;
- Conclusion: summarise the problem, the solution and how the work solves the problem.

Project Start Paper

- Description of recently started new project, likely part of a new trend;
- Convincing motivation for relevance of the project;
- Motivated overview of project methodology;
- Expected academic benefits of the results;

- Technical content.

Project Evaluation Paper

- Overview of a finished project, its goals and its academic results;
- Description and motivation of the essential choices that were made during the project; evaluation of these choices;
- Reflection on the achieved results in relation to the aims of the project;
- Clear, well-motivated description of the methodological lessons that can be drawn from a finished project;
- A discussion on how this may influence new trends;
- Technical Content.

Position Paper

- A convincing academic motivation for what should become a new trend;
- Academic arguments, convincing examples;
- Motivation why there are academically realistic prospects;
- Technical Content.

TFP2005 COMMITTEE

Programme Committee

Andrew Butterfield	Trinity College Dublin (Ireland)
Gaetan Hains	Université d'Orleans (France)
Therese Hardin	Université Paris VI (France)
Kevin Hammond	St Andrews University (UK)
John Hughes	Chalmers University (Sweden)
Graham Hutton	University of Nottingham (UK)
Hans-Wolfgang Loidl	Ludwig-Maximilians-University Munich (Germany)
Rita Loogen	Philipps-University Marburg (Germany)
Greg Michaelson	Heriot-Watt University Edinburgh (UK)
John O'Donnell	University of Glasgow (UK)
Ricardo Peña	Universidad Complutense de Madrid (Spain)
Rinus Plasmeijer	Radboud University Nijmegen (The Netherlands)
Claus Reinke	University of Kent at Canterbury (UK)
Sven Bodo Scholz	University of Hertfordshire (UK)
Doaitse Swierstra	Utrecht University (The Netherlands)
Phil Trinder	Heriot-Watt University Edinburgh (UK)
Tarmo Uustalu	Institute of Cybernetics, Tallinn (Estonia)

Local Organisation

Tarmo Uustalu	Institute of Cybernetics, Tallinn (Estonia)

Treasurer

Greg Michaelson	Heriot-Watt University Edinburgh (UK)

Programme Chair

Marko van Eekelen	Radboud University Nijmegen (The Netherlands)

General Chair

Kevin Hammond	St Andrews University (UK)

Chapter 1

Best Student Paper: A New Approach to One-Pass Transformations

Kevin Millikin[1]

Abstract: We show how to construct a one-pass optimizing transformation by fusing a non-optimizing transformation with an optimization pass. We state the transformation in build form and the optimization pass in cata form, i.e., as a catamorphism; and we use cata/build fusion to combine them. We illustrate the method by fusing Plotkin's call-by-value and call-by-name CPS transformations with a reduction-free normalization function for the λ-calculus, thus obtaining two new one-pass CPS transformations.

1.1 INTRODUCTION

Compiler writers often face a choice between implementing a simple, non-optimizing transformation pass that generates poor code which will require subsequent optimization, and implementing a complex, optimizing transformation pass that avoids generating poor code in the first place. A two-pass strategy is compelling because it is simpler to implement correctly, but its disadvantage is that the intermediate data structures can be large and traversing them unnecessarily can be costly. In a system performing just-in-time compilation or run-time code generation, the costs associated with a two-pass compilation strategy can render it impractical. A one-pass optimizing transformation is compelling because it avoids generating intermediate data structures requiring further optimization, but its disadvantage is that the transformation is more difficult to implement.

The specification of a one-pass transformation is that it is extensionally equal to the composition of a non-optimizing transformation and an optimization pass.

---

[1] Department of Computer Science, University of Aarhus, IT-parken, Aabogade 34, DK-8200 Aarhus N, Denmark; Email: `kmillikin@brics.dk`

A one-pass transformation is not usually constructed this way, however, but is instead constructed as a separate artifact which must then be demonstrated to match its specification. Our approach is to construct one-pass transformations directly, as the fusion of passes via shortcut deforestation [GLJ93, TM95], thus maintaining the explicit connection to both the non-optimizing transformation and the optimization pass.

Shortcut deforestation relies on a simple but powerful program transformation rule known as cata/build fusion. This rule requires both the transformation and optimization passes to be expressed in a stylized form. The first pass, the transformation, must be written as a *build*, abstracted over the constructors of its input. The second pass, the optimization, must be a *catamorphism*, defined by compositional recursive descent over its input.

The non-optimizing CPS transformation generates terms that contain *administrative redexes* which can be optimized away by β-reduction. A one-pass CPS transformation [DF90, DF92] generates terms that do not contain administrative redexes, in a single pass, by contracting these redexes at transformation time. Thus β-reduction is the notion of optimization for the CPS transformation. The normalization function we will use for reduction of CPS terms, however, contracts all β-redexes, not just administrative redexes. In Section 1.6 we describe how to contract only the administrative redexes.

When using a metalanguage to express normalization in the object language, as we do here, the evaluation order of the metalanguage is usually important. However, because CPS terms are insensitive to evaluation order [Plo75], evaluation order is not a concern.

This work. We present a systematic method to construct a one-pass transformation, based on the fusion of a non-optimizing transformation with an optimization pass. We demonstrate the method by constructing new one-pass CPS transformations as the fusion of non-optimizing CPS transformations with a catamorphic normalization function.

The rest of the paper is organized as follows. First, we briefly review catamorphisms, builds, and cata/build fusion in Section 1.2. Then, in Section 1.3 we restate Plotkin's call-by-value CPS transformation [Plo75] with build, and in Section 1.4 we restate a reduction-free normalization function for the untyped λ-calculus to use a catamorphism. We then present a new one-pass CPS transformation obtained by fusion, in Section 1.5. In Section 1.6 we describe how to modify the transformation to contract only the administrative redexes. We compare our new CPS transformation to the one-pass transformation of Danvy and Filinski [DF92] in Section 1.7. In Section 1.8 we repeat the method for Plotkin's call-by-name CPS transformation. We present related work and conclude in Section 1.9.

Prerequisites. The reader should be familiar with reduction in the λ-calculus, and the CPS transformation [Plo75]. Knowledge of functional programming, particularly catamorphisms (i.e., the higher-order function *fold*) [MFP91] is expected. We use a functional pseudocode that is similar to Haskell.

1.2   CATA/BUILD FUSION FOR λ-TERMS

The familiar datatype of λ-terms is defined by the following context-free grammar (assuming the metavariable x ranges over a set *Ident* of identifiers):

$$Term \ni m ::= \text{var } x \mid \text{lam } x\, m \mid \text{app } m\, m$$

A catamorphism [GLJ93, MFP91, TM95] (or fold) over λ-terms captures a common pattern of recursion. It recurs on all subterms and replaces each of the constructors var, lam, and app in a λ-term with functions of the appropriate type. We use the combinator $fold_\lambda$, with type $\forall A.(Ident \to A) \to (Ident \to A \to A) \to (A \to A \to A) \to Term \to A$, to construct a catamorphism over λ-terms:

$$
\begin{aligned}
fold_\lambda \ vr \ lm \ ap \ (\text{var } x) &= vr \ x \\
fold_\lambda \ vr \ lm \ ap \ (\text{lam } x\, m) &= lm \ x \ (fold_\lambda \ vr \ lm \ ap \ m) \\
fold_\lambda \ vr \ lm \ ap \ (\text{app } m_0 \ m_1) &= ap \ (fold_\lambda \ vr \ lm \ ap \ m_0) \ (fold_\lambda \ vr \ lm \ ap \ m_1)
\end{aligned}
$$

We use the combinator $build_\lambda$ to systematically construct λ-terms. It takes a polymorphic function f which uses arbitrary functions (of the appropriate types) instead of the λ-term constructors to transform an input into an output, and then applies f to the λ-term constructors, producing a function that transforms an input into a λ-term. It has type $\forall A.(\forall B.(Ident \to B) \to (Ident \to B \to B) \to (B \to B \to B) \to A \to B) \to A \to Term$:

$$build_\lambda \ f = f \text{ var lam app}$$

Cata/build fusion [GLJ93, TM95] is a simple program transformation that fuses a catamorphism with a function that produces its output using build. For λ-terms, cata/build fusion consists of the rewrite rule:

$$(fold_\lambda \ vr \ lm \ ap) \circ (build_\lambda \ f) \Rightarrow f \ vr \ lm \ ap$$

The fused function produces its output without constructing intermediate data structures.

1.3   THE CALL-BY-VALUE CPS TRANSFORMATION USING BUILD

The non-optimizing call-by-value CPS transformation [Plo75] is given in Figure 1.1. We assume the ability to choose fresh identifiers when needed; the identifiers k, v_0, and v_1 are chosen fresh.

Fusion with a catamorphic normalization function requires that the transformation is written using build, i.e., parameterized over the constructors used to

3

$$
\begin{aligned}
&transform & &: Term \rightarrow Term \\
&transform\ (\text{var } x) & &= \text{lam } k\ (\text{app } (\text{var } k)\ (\text{var } x)) \\
&transform\ (\text{lam } x\ m) & &= \text{lam } k\ (\text{app } (\text{var } k)\ (\text{lam } x\ (transform\ m))) \\
&transform\ (\text{app } m_0\ m_1) & &= \text{lam } k\ (\text{app } (transform\ m_0) \\
& & & \qquad (\text{lam } v_0\ (\text{app } (transform\ m_1) \\
& & & \qquad\qquad (\text{lam } v_1\ (\text{app } (\text{app } (\text{var } v_0)\ (\text{var } v_1))\ (\text{var } k))))))
\end{aligned}
$$

FIGURE 1.1. **Plotkin's non-optimizing call-by-value CPS transformation**

produce its output. The transformation using build thus constructs a Church encoding of the original output.[2] The non-optimizing transformation in build form is shown in Figure 1.2. As before, the identifiers k, v_0, and v_1 are chosen fresh.

$$
\begin{aligned}
&f & &: \forall B.(Ident \rightarrow B) \rightarrow (Ident \rightarrow B \rightarrow B) \\
& & & \quad \rightarrow (B \rightarrow B \rightarrow B) \rightarrow Term \rightarrow B \\
&f\ vr\ lm\ ap\ (\text{var } x) & &= lm\ k\ (ap\ (vr\ k)\ (vr\ x)) \\
&f\ vr\ lm\ ap\ (\text{lam } x\ m) & &= lm\ k\ (ap\ (vr\ k)\ (lm\ x\ (f\ vr\ lm\ ap\ m))) \\
&f\ vr\ lm\ ap\ (\text{app } m_0\ m_1) & &= lm\ k\ (ap\ (f\ vr\ lm\ ap\ m_0) \\
& & & \qquad (lm\ v_0\ (ap\ (f\ vr\ lm\ ap\ m_1) \\
& & & \qquad\qquad (lm\ v_1\ (ap\ (ap\ (vr\ v_0)\ (vr\ v_1))\ (vr\ k)))))) \\
\\
&transform & &: Term \rightarrow Term \\
&transform & &= build_\lambda\ f
\end{aligned}
$$

FIGURE 1.2. **Non-optimizing CPS transformation as a build**

The transformation is non-optimizing because it produces terms that contain extraneous administrative redexes. Transforming the simple term $\lambda x.\lambda y.y\ x$ (written with the usual notation for λ-terms) produces the term

$$\lambda k.k\ (\lambda x.\lambda k.((\lambda k.k\ (\lambda y.\lambda k.k\ y))\ (\lambda x_0.((\lambda k.k\ x)\ (\lambda x_1.x_0\ x_1\ k)))))$$

containing administrative redexes (for simplicity, we have used only a single continuation identifier).

1.4 A CATAMORPHIC NORMALIZATION FUNCTION

Normalization by evaluation (NBE) is a reduction-free approach to normalization that is not based on the transitive closure of a single-step reduction function. Instead, NBE uses a non-standard evaluator to map a term to its denotation in a

---

[2]Placing the last argument first in the definition of f in Figure 1.2 yields a function that constructs a Church encoding of the output of *transform* in Figure 1.1

residualizing model. The residualizing model has the property that a denotation in the model can be reified into a syntactic representation of a term, and that reified terms are in normal form. A *reduction-free* normalization function is then constructed as the composition of evaluation and reification.

NBE has been used in the typed λ-calculus, combinatory logic, the free monoid, and the untyped λ-calculus [DD98]. We adopt the traditional normalization function for the untyped λ-calculus as our optimizer for CPS terms. We show it in Figure 1.3. Just as in the CPS transformation, we assume the ability to choose a fresh identifier when needed. We note, however, that our approach works equally well with other methods of name generation such as using de Bruijn levels or threading a source of fresh names through the evaluator. We opt against the former approach here because we want to compare our resulting one-pass transformation with existing one-pass transformations. The latter approach goes through without a hitch, but we opt against it here because the extra machinery involved with name generation distracts from the overall example without contributing anything essential.

$$
\begin{array}{lll}
Norm \ni n & ::= \mathsf{atom_N}\, a \mid \mathsf{lam_N}\, x\, n \\
Atom \ni a & ::= \mathsf{var_N}\, x \mid \mathsf{app_N}\, a\, n \\
\\
Val & = Atom + (Val \to Val) \\
Val \ni v & ::= \mathsf{res}\, a \mid \mathsf{fun}\, f \\
\\
Env & = Ident \to Val \\
\\
eval & : \ Term \to Env \to Val \\
eval\, (\mathsf{var}\, x)\, \rho & = \rho\, x \\
eval\, (\mathsf{lam}\, x\, m)\, \rho & = \mathsf{fun}\, (\lambda v.eval\, m\, (\rho\{x \mapsto v\})) \\
eval\, (\mathsf{app}\, m_0\, m_1)\, \rho & = apply\, (eval\, m_0\, \rho)\, (eval\, m_1\, \rho) \\
\\
\downarrow & : \ Val \to Norm \\
\downarrow (\mathsf{res}\, a) & = \mathsf{atom_N}\, a \\
\downarrow (\mathsf{fun}\, f) & = \mathsf{lam_N}\, x\, (\downarrow (f\, (\mathsf{res}\, (\mathsf{var_N}\, x)))), \text{ where } x \text{ is fresh} \\
\\
apply & : \ Val \to Val \to Val \\
apply\, (\mathsf{res}\, a)\, v & = \mathsf{res}\, (\mathsf{app_N}\, a\, (\downarrow v)) \\
apply\, (\mathsf{fun}\, f)\, v & = f\, v \\
\\
normalize & : \ Term \to Norm \\
normalize\, m & = \downarrow (eval\, m\, \rho_{init})
\end{array}
$$

FIGURE 1.3. Reduction-free normalization function

The normalization function maps terms to their β-normal form. Normal forms are given by the grammar for *Norm* in Figure 1.3. Elements *Val* of the residualizing model are either atoms (terms that are not abstractions, given by the grammar for *Atom*), or else functions from *Val* to *Val*.

Environments are somewhat unusual in that the initial environment maps each identifier to itself as an element of the residualizing model, which allows us to handle open terms:

$$\rho_{init}\, x \qquad = \text{res}\,(\text{var}_N\, x)$$
$$(\rho\{x \mapsto v\})\, x = v$$
$$(\rho\{y \mapsto v\})\, x = \rho\, x,\ \text{if}\ x \neq y$$

Abstractions denote functions from *Val* to *Val*. The recursive function reify ($\downarrow$) extracts a normal term from an element of the residualizing model. The function *apply* dispatches on the value of the operator of an application to determine whether to build a residual atom or to apply the function. Normalization is then the composition of evaluation (in the initial environment) followed by reification.

Because the evaluation function is compositional, we can rewrite it as a catamorphism over λ-terms, given in Figure 1.4. The domains of terms, atoms, values, and environments do not change, nor do the auxiliary functions $\downarrow$ and *apply*.

$$
\begin{aligned}
vr &\quad : Ident \to Env \to Val \\
vr\, x\, \rho &\quad = \rho\, x \\[6pt]
lm &\quad : Ident \to (Env \to Val) \to Env \to Val \\
lm\, x\, m\, \rho &\quad = \text{fun}\,(\lambda v.m\,(\rho\{x \mapsto v\})) \\[6pt]
ap &\quad : (Env \to Val) \to (Env \to Val) \to Env \to Val \\
ap\, m_0\, m_1\, \rho &= apply\,(m_0\, \rho)\,(m_1\, \rho) \\[6pt]
eval &\quad : Term \to Env \to Val \\
eval &\quad = fold_\lambda\, vr\, lm\, ap
\end{aligned}
$$

FIGURE 1.4.   Evaluation as a catamorphism

Using this normalization function to normalize the example term from Section 1.3 produces $\lambda x_2.x_2\,(\lambda x_3.\lambda x_4.x_4\, x_3)$, where all the β-redexes have been contracted (and fresh identifiers have been generated for all bound variables).

1.5   A NEW ONE-PASS CALL-BY-VALUE CPS TRANSFORMATION

We fuse the non-optimizing CPS transformation $build_\lambda\, f : Term \to Term$ of Section 1.3 and the catamorphic evaluation function $fold_\lambda\, vr\, lm\, ap : Term \to Env \to Val$ of Section 1.4 to produce a one-pass transformation from λ-terms into the residualizing model. This one-pass transformation is simply $f\, vr\, lm\, ap : Term \to Env \to Val$. We then extract β-normal forms from the residualizing model by applying to the initial environment and reifying, as before.

6

Inlining the definitions of f, vr, lm and ap, performing β-reduction, and simplifying environment operations (namely, replacing environment applications that yield a known value with their value and trimming bindings that are known to be unneeded) yields the simplified specification of the one-pass transformation shown in Figure 1.5. The domains of normal terms, atoms, values, and environments as well as the auxiliary functions $\downarrow$ and *apply* are the same as in Figure 1.3.

$$
\begin{aligned}
&\textit{xform} &&: \textit{Term} \rightarrow \textit{Env} \rightarrow \textit{Val} \\
&\textit{xform}\ (\mathsf{var}\ x)\ \rho &&= \mathsf{fun}\ (\lambda k.\textit{apply}\ k\ (\rho\ x)) \\
&\textit{xform}\ (\mathsf{lam}\ x\ m)\ \rho &&= \mathsf{fun}\ (\lambda k.\textit{apply}\ k\ (\mathsf{fun}\ (\lambda v.\textit{xform}\ m\ (\rho\{x \mapsto v\})))) \\
&\textit{xform}\ (\mathsf{app}\ m_0\ m_1)\ \rho &&= \mathsf{fun}\ (\lambda k.\textit{apply}\ (\textit{xform}\ m_0\ \rho) \\
&&&\qquad\quad (\mathsf{fun}\ (\lambda v_0.\textit{apply}\ (\textit{xform}\ m_1\ \rho) \\
&&&\qquad\qquad\quad (\mathsf{fun}\ (\lambda v_1.\textit{apply}\ (\textit{apply}\ v_0\ v_1)\ k)))))) \\
\\
&\textit{transform} &&: \textit{Term} \rightarrow \textit{Norm} \\
&\textit{transform}\ m &&= \downarrow (\textit{xform}\ m\ \rho_{\textit{init}})
\end{aligned}
$$

FIGURE 1.5.   A new one-pass call-by-value CPS transformation

We have implemented this one-pass transformation in Standard ML and Haskell, letting the type inferencer act as a theorem prover to verify that the transformation returns a β-normal form if it terminates [DRR01].

1.6   SUPPRESSING CONTRACTION OF SOURCE REDEXES

Compared to traditional one-pass CPS transformations, our transformation is over-zealous. The normalization function we use contracts all β-redexes; it cannot tell which ones are administrative redexes. Therefore our CPS transformation does not terminate for terms that do not have a β-normal form (e.g., $(\lambda x.x\ x)\ (\lambda x.x\ x)$). Of course, if we restricted the input to simply-typed λ-terms, then the transformation would always terminate because the corresponding normalization function does.

We can modify the new CPS transformation to contract only the administrative redexes. We modify the datatype of intermediate terms (and the associated catamorphism operator) to contain two types of applications, corresponding to source and administrative redexes. This is an example of a general technique of embedding information known to the first pass in the structure of the intermediate language, for use by the second pass.

$$Term \ni m ::= \mathsf{var}\ x \mid \mathsf{lam}\ x\ m \mid \mathsf{app}\ m\ m \mid \mathsf{srcapp}\ m\ m$$

We then modify the non-optimizing CPS transformation to preserve source applications (by replacing the app (var v_0) (var v_1) with srcapp (var v_0) (var v_1) in the clause for applications) and we modify the normalization function (to always reify both the operator and operand of source applications). The datatype of normal forms now includes source redexes:

$$Norm \ni n ::= atom_N \ a \mid lam_N \ x \ n$$
$$Atom \ni a ::= var_N \ x \mid app_N \ a \ n \mid srcapp_N \ n \ n$$

The result of fusing the modified call-by-value CPS transformation with the modified normalization function is shown in Figure 1.6. Again, the domains of values and environments, and the auxiliary functions $\downarrow$ and *apply* are the same as in Figure 1.3.

$xform$: $Term \rightarrow Env \rightarrow Val$

$xform$ (var x) ρ = fun ($\lambda k.apply \ k \ (\rho \ x)$)

$xform$ (lam $x \ m$) ρ = fun ($\lambda k.apply \ k$ (fun ($\lambda v.xform \ m \ (\rho\{x \mapsto v\})$))))

$xform$ (app $m_0 \ m_1$) ρ = fun ($\lambda k.apply$ ($xform \ m_0 \ \rho$)
                            (fun ($\lambda v_0.apply$ ($xform \ m_1 \ \rho$)
                                (fun ($\lambda v_1.apply$ (res ($srcapp_N$ ($\downarrow v_0$) ($\downarrow v_1$))) k)))))

$transform$: $Term \rightarrow Norm$

$transform \ m$ = $\downarrow$ ($xform \ m \ \rho_{init}$)

FIGURE 1.6. A call-by-value CPS transformation that does not contract source redexes

---

Given the term from Section 1.3, the modified transformation produces

$$\lambda x_0.x_0 \ (\lambda x_1.\lambda x_2.(((\lambda x_3.\lambda x_4.x_4 \ x_3) \ x_1) \ x_2))$$

(i.e., it does not contract the source redex).

1.7   COMPARISON TO DANVY AND FILINSKI'S ONE-PASS CPS TRANSFORMATION

Danvy and Filinski [DF92] obtained a one-pass CPS transformation by anticipating which administrative redexes would be built and contracting them at transformation time. They introduced a binding-time separation between static and dynamic constructs in the CPS transformation (static constructs are represented here by metalanguage variables, abstractions, and applications; and dynamic constructs by the constructors var, lam, and app). Static β-redexes are contracted at transformation time and dynamic redexes are residualized. We present their transformation in Figure 1.7.

In our transformation, the binding-time separation is present as well. Residualized atoms are dynamic and functions from values to values are static. This distinction arises naturally as a consequence of the residualizing model of the nor-

$$
\begin{aligned}
&\textit{xform} &&: \textit{Term} \to (\textit{Term} \to \textit{Term}) \to \textit{Term} \\
&\textit{xform} \ (\text{var } x) &&= \lambda\kappa.\kappa \ (\text{var } x) \\
&\textit{xform} \ (\text{lam } x \ m) &&= \lambda\kappa.\kappa \ (\text{lam } x \ (\text{lam } k \ (\textit{xform}' \ m \ (\text{var } k)))) \\
&\textit{xform} \ (\text{app } m_0 \ m_1) &&= \lambda\kappa.\textit{xform} \ m_0 \\
& && \quad (\lambda v_0.\textit{xform} \ m_1 \\
& && \qquad (\lambda v_1.\text{app} \ (\text{app} \ (\text{var } v_0) \ (\text{var } v_1)) \ (\text{lam } x \ (\kappa \ (\text{var } x))))))
\end{aligned}
$$

$$
\begin{aligned}
&\textit{xform}' &&: \textit{Term} \to \textit{Term} \to \textit{Term} \\
&\textit{xform}' \ (\text{var } x) &&= \lambda k.\text{app} \ k \ (\text{var } x) \\
&\textit{xform}' \ (\text{lam } x \ m) &&= \lambda k.\text{app} \ k \ (\text{lam } x \ (\text{lam } k' \ (\textit{xform}' \ m \ (\text{var } k')))) \\
&\textit{xform}' \ (\text{app } m_0 \ m_1) &&= \lambda k.\textit{xform} \ m_0 \\
& && \quad (\lambda v_0.\textit{xform} \ m_1 \\
& && \qquad (\lambda v_1.\text{app} \ (\text{app} \ (\text{var } v_0) \ (\text{var } v_1)) \ k))
\end{aligned}
$$

$$
\begin{aligned}
&\textit{transform} &&: \textit{Term} \to \textit{Term} \\
&\textit{transform } m &&= \text{lam } k \ (\textit{xform}' \ m \ (\text{var } k))
\end{aligned}
$$

FIGURE 1.7.   Danvy and Filinski's one-pass CPS transformation

malization function. Dynamic abstractions are only constructed by the auxiliary function $\downarrow$, and dynamic applications are only constructed by *apply*.

Both CPS transformations are properly tail recursive: they do not generate η-redexes as the continuations of tail calls. In order to avoid generating this η-redex, Danvy and Filinski employ a pair of transformation functions, one for terms in tail position and one for terms in non-tail position. Our transformation uses a single transformation function for both terms in tail position and terms in non-tail position. The *apply* function determines whether the operand of an application will be reified or not (reification will construct an η-expanded term if its argument is not already a normal-form atom).

1.8   A NEW ONE-PASS CALL-BY-NAME CPS TRANSFORMATION

The same fusion technique can be used with the CPS transformations for other evaluation orders [HD94]. For instance, we can start with Plotkin's call-by-name CPS transformation [Plo75] shown in Figure 1.8.

After fusion and simplification, we obtain the one-pass call-by-name CPS transformation of Figure 1.9.

The evaluation order of the normalization function is the same as that of the metalanguage. Due to the indifference theorems for both the call-by-value and call-by-name CPS transformations [Plo75], the evaluation order of the normalization function is irrelevant here.

$$
\begin{aligned}
&\textit{transform} &&: \textit{Term} \rightarrow \textit{Term} \\
&\textit{transform } (\text{var } x) &&= \text{var } x \\
&\textit{transform } (\text{lam } x\, m) &&= \text{lam } k\ (\text{app } (\text{var } k)\ (\text{lam } x\ (\textit{transform } m))) \\
&\textit{transform } (\text{app } m_0\, m_1) &&= \text{lam } k\ (\text{app } (\textit{transform } m_0) \\
&&&\qquad\qquad (\text{lam } v\ (\text{app } (\text{app } (\text{var } v)\ (\textit{transform } m_1))\ (\text{var } k))))
\end{aligned}
$$

FIGURE 1.8. Plotkin's non-optimizing call-by-name CPS transformation

$$
\begin{aligned}
&\textit{xform} &&: \textit{Term} \rightarrow \textit{Env} \rightarrow \textit{Val} \\
&\textit{xform } (\text{var } x)\ \rho &&= \rho\, x \\
&\textit{xform } (\text{lam } x\, m)\ \rho &&= \text{fun } (\lambda k.\textit{apply } k\ (\text{fun } (\lambda v.\textit{xform } m\ (\rho\{x \mapsto v\})))) \\
&\textit{xform } (\text{app } m_0\, m_1)\ \rho &&= \text{fun } (\lambda k.\textit{apply } (\textit{xform } m_0\ \rho) \\
&&&\qquad\qquad (\text{fun } (\lambda v.\textit{apply } (\textit{apply } v\ (\textit{xform } m_1\ \rho))\ k))) \\
\\
&\textit{transform} &&: \textit{Term} \rightarrow \textit{Norm} \\
&\textit{transform } m &&= {\downarrow}\, (\textit{xform } m\ \rho_{init})
\end{aligned}
$$

FIGURE 1.9. A new one-pass call-by-name CPS transformation

1.9   RELATED WORK AND CONCLUSION

This work brings together two strands of functional-programming research: program fusion and normalization by evaluation. It combines them to construct new one-pass CPS transformations based on NBE. The method should be applicable to constructing one-pass transformations from a pair of transformations where the second (optimization) pass is compositional (i.e., a catamorphism).

Program fusion.   Techniques to eliminate intermediate data structures from functional programs are an active area of research spanning three decades [Bur75]. Wadler coined the term "deforestation" to describe the elimination of intermediate trees [Wad90], and Gill et al. introduced the idea of using repeated application of the foldr/build rule for "shortcut" deforestation of intermediate lists [GLJ93]. Takano and Meijer extended shortcut deforestation to arbitrary polynomial datatypes [TM95]. Ghani et al. give an alternative semantics for programming with catamorphism and build [GUV04], which is equivalent to the usual initial algebra semantics but has the cata/build fusion rule as a simple consequence. Our contribution is the use of program-fusion techniques to construct one-pass transformations

Normalization by evaluation.   The idea behind normalization by evaluation, that the metalanguage can be used to express normalization in the object language, is due to Martin Löf [ML75]. This idea is present in Danvy and Filinski's one-pass CPS transformation [DF90, DF92], which is therefore an instance of NBE. Other examples include the free monoid [BD95], the untyped lambda-calculus and combinatory logic [Gol96a, Gol96b, Gol00], the simply-typed λ-calculus [Ber93, BS91], and type-directed partial evaluation [Dan96b]. The term "normalization by evaluation" was coined by Schwichtenberg in 1998 [BES98]. Many people have discovered the same type-directed normalization function for the typed λ-calculus, using reify and reflect auxiliary functions [DD98]. The normalization function for the untyped λ-calculus has also been multiply discovered (e.g., by Coquand in the setting of dependent types [SPG03]). It has recently been investigated operationally by Aehlig and Joachimski [AJ04] and denotationally by Filinski and Rohde [FR02]. Our contribution is to factor Danvy and Filinski's early example of NBE—the one-pass CPS transformation—into Plotkin's original CPS transformation and the normalization function for the untyped λ-calculus. The factorization scales to other CPS transformations [HD94] and more generally to other transformations on the λ-calculus.

NBE and the CPS transformation. Two other works combine normalization by evaluation with the CPS transformation. Danvy uses type-directed partial evaluation to residualize values produced by a continuation-passing evaluator for the λ-calculus [Dan96a], producing CPS terms in β-normal form; he does this for both call-by-value and call-by-name evaluators, yielding call-by-value and call-by-name CPS transformations. Filinski defines a (type-directed) extensional CPS transformation from direct-style values to CPS values and its inverse [Fil01]; he composes this extensional CPS transformation with a type-directed reification function for the typed λ-calculus to obtain a transformation from direct-style values to CPS terms. We are not aware, however, of any other work combining the CPS transformation and reduction-free normalization using program fusion.

Acknowledgements. I wish to thank Olivier Danvy for his encouragement, his helpful discussions regarding normalization by evaluation, and for his comments. Thanks are due to the anonymous reviewers of TFP 2005 for their helpful suggestions. This work was partly carried out while the author visited the TOPPS group at DIKU.

REFERENCES

[AJ04]   Klaus Aehlig and Felix Joachimski. Operational aspects of untyped normalization by evaluation. *Mathematical Structures in Computer Science*, 14:587–611, 2004.

[BD95]   Ilya Beylin and Peter Dybjer. Extracting a proof of coherence for monoidal categories from a proof of normalization for monoids. In Stefano Berardi and Mario Coppo, editors, *Types for Proofs and Programs, International Workshop TYPES'95*, number 1158 in Lecture Notes in Computer Science, pages 47–61, Torino, Italy, June 1995. Springer-Verlag.

[Ber93]   Ulrich Berger. Program extraction from normalization proofs. In Marc Bezem and Jan Friso Groote, editors, *Typed Lambda Calculi and Applications*, number 664 in Lecture Notes in Computer Science, pages 91–106, Utrecht, The Netherlands, March 1993. Springer-Verlag.

[BES98]   Ulrich Berger, Matthias Eberl, and Helmut Schwichtenberg. Normalization by evaluation. In Bernhard Möller and John V. Tucker, editors, *Prospects for hardware foundations (NADA)*, number 1546 in Lecture Notes in Computer Science, pages 117–137, Berlin, Germany, 1998. Springer-Verlag.

[BS91]   Ulrich Berger and Helmut Schwichtenberg. An inverse of the evaluation functional for typed λ-calculus. In Gilles Kahn, editor, *Proceedings of the Sixth Annual IEEE Symposium on Logic in Computer Science*, pages 203–211, Amsterdam, The Netherlands, July 1991. IEEE Computer Society Press.

[Bur75]   William H. Burge. *Recursive Programming Techniques*. Addison-Wesley, 1975.

[Dan96a]   Olivier Danvy. Décompilation de lambda-interprètes. In Guy Lapalme and Christian Queinnec, editors, *JFLA 96 – Journées francophones des langages applicatifs*, volume 15 of *Collection Didactique*, pages 133–146, Val-Morin, Québec, January 1996. INRIA.

[Dan96b]   Olivier Danvy. Type-directed partial evaluation. In Guy L. Steele Jr., editor, *Proceedings of the Twenty-Third Annual ACM Symposium on Principles of Programming Languages*, pages 242–257, St. Petersburg Beach, Florida, January 1996. ACM Press.

[DD98]   Olivier Danvy and Peter Dybjer, editors. *Proceedings of the 1998 APPSEM Workshop on Normalization by Evaluation (NBE 1998)*, BRICS Note Series NS-98-8, Gothenburg, Sweden, May 1998. BRICS, Department of Computer Science, University of Aarhus.

[DF90]   Olivier Danvy and Andrzej Filinski. Abstracting control. In Mitchell Wand, editor, *Proceedings of the 1990 ACM Conference on Lisp and Functional Programming*, pages 151–160, Nice, France, June 1990. ACM Press.

[DF92]   Olivier Danvy and Andrzej Filinski. Representing control, a study of the CPS transformation. *Mathematical Structures in Computer Science*, 2(4):361–391, 1992.

[DRR01]   Olivier Danvy, Morten Rhiger, and Kristoffer Rose. Normalization by evaluation with typed abstract syntax. *Journal of Functional Programming*, 11(6):673–680, 2001.

[Fil01]   Andrzej Filinski. An extensional CPS transform (preliminary report). In Amr Sabry, editor, *Proceedings of the Third ACM SIGPLAN Workshop on Continuations*, Technical report 545, Computer Science Department, Indiana University, pages 41–46, London, England, January 2001.

[FR02]   Andrzej Filinski and Henning Korsholm Rohde. A denotational account of untyped normalization by evaluation. In Igor Walukiewicz, editor, *Foundations of Software Science and Computation Structures, 7th International Conference, FOSSACS 2004*, number 2987 in Lecture Notes in Computer Science, pages 167–181, Barcelona, Spain, April 2002. Springer-Verlag.

[GLJ93]   Andrew J. Gill, John Launchbury, and Simon L. Peyton Jones. A short cut to deforestation. In Arvind, editor, *Proceedings of the Sixth ACM Conference on Functional Programming and Computer Architecture*, pages 223–232, Copenhagen, Denmark, June 1993. ACM Press.

[Gol96a]   Mayer Goldberg. Gödelization in the λ-calculus. Technical Report BRICS RS-96-5, Computer Science Department, Aarhus University, Aarhus, Denmark, March 1996.

[Gol96b]   Mayer Goldberg. *Recursive Application Survival in the λ-Calculus*. PhD thesis, Computer Science Department, Indiana University, Bloomington, Indiana, May 1996.

[Gol00]   Mayer Goldberg. Gödelization in the λ-calculus. *Information Processing Letters*, 75(1-2):13–16, 2000.

[GUV04]   Neil Ghani, Tarmo Uustalu, and Varmo Vene. Build, augment and destroy, universally. In Wei-Ngan Chin, editor, *APLAS*, volume 3302 of *Lecture Notes in Computer Science*, pages 327–347. Springer, 2004.

[HD94]   John Hatcliff and Olivier Danvy. A generic account of continuation-passing styles. In Hans-J. Boehm, editor, *Proceedings of the Twenty-First Annual ACM Symposium on Principles of Programming Languages*, pages 458–471, Portland, Oregon, January 1994. ACM Press.

[MFP91]   Erik Meijer, Maarten M. Fokkinga, and Ross Paterson. Functional programming with bananas, lenses, envelopes and barbed wire. In John Hughes, editor, *FPCA*, volume 523 of *Lecture Notes in Computer Science*, pages 124–144. Springer, 1991.

[ML75]   Per Martin-Löf. About models for intuitionistic type theories and the notion of definitional equality. In *Proceedings of the Third Scandinavian Logic Symposium (1972)*, volume 82 of *Studies in Logic and the Foundation of Mathematics*, pages 81–109. North-Holland, 1975.

[Plo75]   Gordon D. Plotkin. Call-by-name, call-by-value and the λ-calculus. *Theoretical Computer Science*, 1:125–159, 1975.

[SPG03]   Mark R. Shinwell, Andrew M. Pitts, and Murdoch Gabbay. FreshML: programming with binders made simple. In Olin Shivers, editor, *Proceedings of the 2003 ACM SIGPLAN International Conference on Functional Programming*, pages 263–274, Uppsala, Sweden, August 2003. ACM Press.

[TM95]   Akihiko Takano and Erik Meijer. Shortcut deforestation in calculational form. In *Proceedings of the Seventh ACM Conference on Functional Programming and Computer Architecture*, pages 306–313, 1995.

[Wad90]   Philip Wadler. Deforestation: Transforming programs to eliminate trees. *Theoretical Computer Science*, 73(2):231–248, 1990.

Chapter 2

A Static Checker for Safe Pattern Matching in Haskell

Neil Mitchell and Colin Runciman [2.1]

Abstract: A Haskell program may fail at runtime with a pattern-match error if the program has any incomplete (non-exhaustive) patterns in definitions or case alternatives. This paper describes a static checker that allows non-exhaustive patterns to exist, yet ensures that a pattern-match error does not occur. It describes a constraint language that can be used to reason about pattern matches, along with mechanisms to propagate these constraints between program components.

2.1 INTRODUCTION

Often it is useful to define pattern matches which are incomplete, for example head fails on the empty list. Unfortunately programs with incomplete pattern matches may fail at runtime.

Consider the following example:

```
risers :: Ord a => [a] -> [[a]]
risers [] = []
risers [x] = [[x]]
risers (x:y:etc) = if x <= y then (x:s):ss else [x]:(s:ss)
    where (s:ss) = risers (y:etc)
```

A sample execution of this function would be:

```
> risers [1,2,3,1,2]
[[1,2,3],[1,2]]
```

In the last line of the definition, (s:ss) is matched against the output of risers. If risers (y:etc) returns an empty list this would cause a pattern

---

[2.1]University of York, UK. http://www.cs.york.ac.uk/~ndm and http://www.cs.york.ac.uk/~colin

15

match error. It takes a few moments to check this program manually – and a few more to be sure one has not made a mistake!

GHC [The05] 6.4 has a warning flag to detect incomplete patterns, which is named `-fwarn-incomplete-patterns`. Adding this flag at compile time reports:[2.2]

```
Warning: Pattern match(es) are non-exhaustive
```

But the GHC checks are only local. If the function `head` is defined, then it raises a warning. No effort is made to check the *callers* of `head` – this is an obligation left to the programmer.

Turning the `risers` function over to the checker developed in this paper, the output is:

```
> (risers (y:etc)){:}
> True
```

The checker first decides that for the code to be safe the recursive call to `risers` must always yield a non-empty list. It then notices that if the argument in a `risers` application is non-empty, then so will the result be. This satisfies it, and it returns True, guaranteeing that no pattern-match errors will occur.

2.1.1 Roadmap

This paper starts by introducing a reduced language similar to Haskell in §2.2. Next a constraint language is introduced in §2.3 and algorithms are given to manipulate these constraints in §2.4. A worked example is given in §2.5, followed by a range of small examples and a case study in §2.6. This paper is compared to related work in §2.7. Finally conclusions are given in §2.8, along with some remaining tasks – this paper reports on work in progress.

2.2 REDUCED HASKELL

The full Haskell language is a bit unwieldy for analysis. In particular the syntactic sugar complicates analysis by introducing more types of expression to consider. The checker works instead on a simplified language, a core to which other Haskell programs can be reduced. This core language is a functional language, making use of case expressions, function applications and algebraic data types.

As shown in example 1, only one defining equation per function is permitted, pattern-matching occurs only in case expressions and every element within a constructor must be uniquely named by a selector (e.g. `hd` and `tl`). A convertor from a reasonable subset of Haskell to this reduced language has been written.

[2.2]The additional flag `-fwarn-simple-patterns` is needed, but this is due to GHC bug number 1075259

Example 2.1

```
data [] a = (:) {hd :: a, tl :: [] a} | []

head x = case x of (a:_) -> a

map f xs = case xs of
                []      -> []
                (a:as) -> f x : map f as

reverse xs = rev xs []

reverse2 x a = case x of
                []      -> a
                (y:ys) -> reverse2 ys (y:a)             □
```

2.2.1 Higher Order Functions

The current checker is not higher order, and does not allow partial application.

The checker tries to eliminate higher-order functions by specialization. A mutually recursive group of functions can be specialized in their nth argument if in all recursive calls this argument is invariant.

Examples of common functions whose applications can be specialized in this way include `map`, `filter`, `foldr` and `foldl`.

When a function can be specialized, the expression passed as the nth argument has all its free variables passed as extra arguments, and is expanded in the specialized version. All recursive calls within the new function are then renamed.

Example 2.2

```
map f xs = case xs of
                []      -> []
                (a:as) -> f a : map f as

adds x n = map (add n) x
```

is transformed into:

```
map_adds n xs = case xs of
                []      -> []
                (a:as) -> add n a : map_adds n as

adds x n = map_adds n x                                 □
```

Although this firstification approach is not complete by any means, it appears to be sufficient for a large range of examples. Alternative methods are available for full firstification, such as that detailed by Hughes [Hug96], or the defunctionalisation approach by Reynolds [Rey72].

17

2.2.2 Internal Representation

While the concrete syntax allows the introduction of new variable names, the internal representation does not. All variables are referred to using a *selector path* from an argument to the function.

For example, the internal representation of map is:

```
map f xs = case xs of
                [ ]     -> [ ]
                (_:_) -> f (xs·hd) : map f (xs·tl)
```

(Note that the infix · operator here is used to compose paths; it is *not* the Haskell function composition operator.)

2.3 A CONSTRAINT LANGUAGE

In order to implement a checker that can ensure unfailing patterns, it is useful to have some way of expressing properties of data values. A constraint is written as $\langle e, r, c \rangle$, where e is an expression, r is a regular expression over selectors and c is a set of constructors. Such a constraint asserts that any well-defined application to e of a path of selectors described by r must reach a constructor in the set c.

These constraints are used as atoms in a predicate language with conjunction and disjunction, so constraints can be about several expressions and relations between them. The checker does not require a negation operator. We also use the term constraint to refer to logical formulae with constraints as atoms.

Example 2.3

Consider the function minimum, defined as:

```
minimum xs = case xs of
                  [x]       -> x
                  (a:b:xs) -> minimum (min a b : xs)

min a b = case a < b of
                True  -> a
                False -> b
```

Now consider the expression minimum e. The constraint that must hold for this expression to be safe is $\langle e, \lambda, \{ : \} \rangle$. This says that the expression e must reduce to an application of :, i.e. a non-empty list. In this example the path was λ – the empty path. □

Example 2.4

Consider the expression map minimum e. In this case the constraint generated is $\langle e, \text{tl}^*·\text{hd}, \{ : \} \rangle$. If we apply any number (possibly zero) of tls to e,

18

then apply `hd`, we reach a : construction. Values satisfying this constraint include `[]` and `[[1],[2],[3]]`, but not `[[1],[]]`. The value `[]` satisfies this constraint because it is impossible to apply either `tl` or `hd`, and therefore the constraint does not assert anything about the possible constructors.

□

Constraints divide up into three parts – the *subject*, the *path* and the *condition*.

The subject in the above two examples was just *e*, representing any expression – including a call, a construction or even a `case`.

The path is a regular expression over selectors.

A regular expression is defined as:

$s+t$	union of regular expressions s and t
$s \cdot t$	concatenation of regular expressions s then t
s^*	any number (possibly zero) occurrences of s
x	a selector, such as `hd` or `tl`
λ	the language is the set containing the empty string
ϕ	the language is the empty set

The condition is a set of constructors which, due to static type checking, must all be of the same result type.

The meaning of a constraint is defined by:

$$\langle e, r, c \rangle \Leftrightarrow (\forall l \in L(r) \bullet \mathit{defined}(e, l) \Rightarrow \mathit{constructor}(e \cdot l) \in c)$$

Here $L(r)$ is the language represented by the regular expression r; *defined* returns true if a path selection is well-defined; and *constructor* gives the constructor used to create the data. Of course, since $L(r)$ is potentially infinite, this cannot be checked by enumeration.

If no path selection is well-defined then the constraint is vacuously true.

2.3.1 Simplifying the Constraints

From the definition of the constraints it is possible to construct a number of identities which can be used for simplification.

Path does not exist: in the constraint $\langle [], \mathrm{hd}, \{:\} \rangle$ the expression `[]` does not have a `hd` path, so this constraint simplifies to true.

Detecting failure: the constraint $\langle [], \lambda, \{:\} \rangle$ simplifies to false because the `[]` value is not the constructor :.

Empty path: in the constraint $\langle e, \phi, c \rangle$, the regular expression is ϕ, the empty language, so the constraint is always true.

Exhaustive conditions: in the constraint $\langle e, \lambda, \{\,:\,,\ [\,]\,\} \rangle$ the condition lists all the possible constructors, if e reaches weak head normal form then because of static typing e must be one of these constructors, therefore this constraint simplifies to true.

Algebraic conditions: finally a couple of algebraic equivalences:

$$\langle e, r_1, c \rangle \wedge \langle e, r_2, c \rangle = \langle e, (r_1 + r_2), c \rangle$$
$$\langle e, r, c_1 \rangle \wedge \langle e, r, c_2 \rangle = \langle e, r, c_1 \cap c_2 \rangle$$

2.4 DETERMINING THE CONSTRAINTS

This section concerns the derivation of the constraints, and the operations involved in this task.

2.4.1 The Initial Constraints

In general, a `case` expression, where $\vec{v}$ are the arguments to a constructor:

```
case e of C₁ v⃗ -> val₁;  ...;  Cₙ v⃗ -> valₙ
```

produces the initial constraint $\langle e, \lambda, \{C_1, \ldots, C_n\} \rangle$. If the case alternatives are exhaustive, then this can be simplified to true. All `case` expressions in the program are found, their initial constraints are found, and these are joined together with conjunction.

2.4.2 Transforming the constraints

For each constraint in turn, if the subject is x_f (i.e. the x argument to f), the checker searches for every application of f, and gets the expression for the argument x. On this expression, it sets the existing constraint. This constraint is then transformed using a backward analysis (see §2.4.3), until a constraint on arguments is found.

Example 2.5

Consider the constraint $\langle xs_{minimum}, \lambda, \{:\} \rangle$ – that is `minimum`'s argument xs must be a non-empty list. If the program contains the expression:

```
f x = minimum (g x)
```

then the derived constraint is $\langle (g\ x_f), \lambda, \{:\} \rangle$. $\qquad\square$

2.4.3 Backward Analysis

Backward analysis takes a constraint in which the subject is a compound expression, and derives a combination of constraints over arguments only. This process

$$\varphi\langle e \cdot s, r, c \rangle \rightarrow \varphi\langle e, s \cdot r, c \rangle \tag{sel}$$

$$\frac{\bigwedge_{i=1}^{\#\vec{e}} \varphi\langle e_i, \frac{\partial r}{\partial S(C,i)}, c \rangle \rightarrow P}{\varphi\langle C \ \vec{e}, r, c \rangle \rightarrow (\lambda \in L(r) \Rightarrow C \in c) \wedge P} \tag{con}$$

$$\varphi\langle f \ \vec{e}, r, c \rangle \rightarrow \varphi\langle \mathcal{D}(f, \vec{e}), r, c \rangle \tag{app}$$

$$\frac{\bigwedge_{i=1}^{\#\vec{e}} (\varphi\langle e_0, \lambda, C(C_i) \rangle \vee \varphi\langle e_i, r, c \rangle) \rightarrow P}{\varphi\langle \texttt{case} \ e_0 \ \texttt{of} \ \{C_1 \ \vec{v}\texttt{->}e_1; \cdots; C_n \ \vec{v}\texttt{->}e_n\}, r, c \rangle \rightarrow P} \tag{cas}$$

FIGURE 2.1. Specification of backward analysis, φ

is denoted by a function φ, which takes a constraint and returns a predicate over constraints. This function is detailed in Figure 2.1.

In this figure, C denotes a constructor, c is a set of constructors, f is a function, e is an expression, r is a regular expression over selectors and s is a selector.

The (sel) rule moves the composition from the expression to the path.

The (con) rule deals with an application of a constructor C. If λ is in the path language the C must be permitted by the condition. This depends on the *empty word property* (ewp) [Con71], which can be calculated structurally on the regular expression.

For each of the arguments to C, a new constraint is obtained from the derivative of the regular expression with respect to that argument's selector. This is denoted by $\partial r / \partial S(C, i)$, where $S(C, i)$ gives the selector for the ith argument of the constructor C. The differentiation method is based on that described by Conway [Con71]. It can be used to test for membership in the following way:

$$\begin{aligned} \lambda \in L(r) &= \text{ewp}(r) \\ s \cdot r' \in L(r) &= r' \in L(\partial r / \partial s) \end{aligned}$$

Two particular cases of note are $\partial \lambda / \partial a = \phi$ and $\partial \phi / \partial a = \phi$.

The (app) rule uses the notation $\mathcal{D}(f, \vec{e})$ to express the result of substituting each of the arguments in $\vec{e}$ into the body of the function f. The naive application of this rule to any function with a recursive call will loop forever. To combat this, if a function is already in the process of being evaluated with the same constraint, its result is given as true, and the recursive arguments are put into a special pile to be examined later on, see §2.4.4 for details.

The (cas) rule generates a conjunct for each alternative. The function $C(C)$ returns the set of all other constructors with the same result type as C, i.e.

$C([]) = \{:\}$. The generated condition says either the subject of the case analysis has a different constructor (so this particular alternative is not executed in this circumstance), or the right hand side of the alternative is safe given the conditions for this expression.

2.4.4 Obtaining a Fixed Point

We have noted that if a function is in the process of being evaluated, and its value is asked for again with the same constraints, then the call is deferred. After backwards analysis has been performed on the result of a function, there will be a constraint in terms of the arguments, along with a set of recursive calls. If these recursive calls had been analyzed further, then the checking computation would not have terminated.

Example 2.6

```
mapHead xs = case xs of
                 []      -> []
                 (x:xs) -> head x : mapHead xs
```

The function `mapHead` is exactly equivalent to `map head`. Running backward analysis over this function, the constraint generated is $\langle \mathrm{xs}_{\mathrm{mapHead}}, \mathrm{hd}, \{:\} \rangle$, and the only recursive call noted is `mapHead (xs·tl)`. The recursive call is written as $\mathrm{xs} \hookleftarrow \mathrm{xs}\cdot\mathrm{tl}$, showing how the value of `xs` changes. Observe that the path in the constraint only reaches the first element in the list, while the desired constraint would reach them all. In effect `mapHead` has been analyzed without considering any recursive applications.

The fixed point for this function can be derived by repeatedly replacing `xs` with `xs·tl` in the subject of the constraint, and joining these constraints with conjunction.

$$\langle \mathrm{xs}, \mathrm{hd}, \{:\} \rangle \wedge \langle \mathrm{xs}\cdot\mathrm{tl}, \mathrm{hd}, \{:\} \rangle \wedge \langle \mathrm{xs}\cdot\mathrm{tl}\cdot\mathrm{tl}, \mathrm{hd}, \{:\} \rangle \wedge \ldots \quad (1)$$

$$\equiv \quad \langle \mathrm{xs}, \mathrm{hd}, \{:\} \rangle \wedge \langle \mathrm{xs}, \mathrm{tl}\cdot\mathrm{hd}, \{:\} \rangle \wedge \langle \mathrm{xs}, \mathrm{tl}\cdot\mathrm{tl}\cdot\mathrm{hd}, \{:\} \rangle \wedge \ldots \quad (2)$$

$$\equiv \quad \langle \mathrm{xs}, \mathrm{hd}+\mathrm{tl}\cdot\mathrm{hd}+\mathrm{tl}\cdot\mathrm{tl}\cdot\mathrm{hd}+\ldots, \{:\} \rangle \quad (3)$$

$$\equiv \quad \langle \mathrm{xs}, (\lambda+\mathrm{tl}+\mathrm{tl}\cdot\mathrm{tl}+\ldots)\cdot\mathrm{hd}, \{:\} \rangle \quad (4)$$

$$\equiv \quad \langle \mathrm{xs}, \mathrm{tl}^*\cdot\mathrm{hd}, \{:\} \rangle \quad (5)$$

The justification is as follows. First use the backwards analysis rule given in Figure 2.1 to transform between (1) and (2) – selectors move from the subject to the path. To obtain (3) the first algebraic condition given in §2.3.1 is used. The factorisation of the `hd` element of the regular expression is applied. Finally this can be rewritten using the regular expression *operator as the result. □

More generally, given any constraint of the form $\langle x, r, c \rangle$ and a recursive call of the form $x \hookleftarrow x.p$, the fixed point is $\langle x, p^* \cdot r, c \rangle$. A special case is where p is λ, in which case $p^* \cdot r = r$.

Example 2.7

Consider the function `reverse` written using an accumulator:

```
reverse x = reverse2 x []

reverse2 x a = case x of
                 []     -> a
                 (y:ys) -> reverse2 ys (y:a)
```

Argument xs follows the pattern $x \hookleftarrow x.\mathtt{tl}$, but we also have the recursive call $a \hookleftarrow (x \cdot \mathtt{hd}:a)$. If the program being analyzed contained an instance of `map head (reverse x)`, the part of the condition that applies to a before the fixed pointing of a is $\langle a, \mathtt{tl}^* \cdot \mathtt{hd}, \{:\} \rangle$.

In this case a second rule for obtaining a fixed point can be used. For recursive calls of the form $a \hookleftarrow C\ x_1\ \cdots\ x_n\ a$, where s is the selector corresponding to the position of a, the rule is:

$$\bigwedge_{r' \in r^\#} \left(\left(\lambda \in L(r') \Rightarrow C \in c \right) \wedge \langle a, r', c \rangle \wedge \bigwedge_{i=1}^{n} \langle x_i, \frac{\partial r'}{\partial \mathcal{S}(C,i)}, c \rangle \right)$$

Where:

$$r^\# = \{r^0, r^1, \ldots, r^\infty\} \qquad r^0 = r \qquad r^{(n+1)} = \frac{\partial r^n}{\partial s}$$

It can be shown that $r^\#$ is always a finite set [Law04]. This expression is derived from the (con) rule §2.4.3, applied until it reaches a fixed point.

In the `reverse` example, $r^\#$ is $\{\mathtt{tl}^* \cdot \mathtt{hd}\}$, since $\partial \mathtt{tl}^* \cdot \mathtt{hd} / \partial \mathtt{tl} = \mathtt{tl}^* \cdot \mathtt{hd}$. Also $\lambda \notin L(\mathtt{tl}^* \cdot \mathtt{hd})$, so the result is:

$$\langle a, \mathtt{tl}^* \cdot \mathtt{hd}, \{:\} \rangle \wedge \langle x \cdot \mathtt{hd}, \frac{\partial \mathtt{tl}^* \cdot \mathtt{hd}}{\partial \mathtt{hd}}, \{:\} \rangle$$
$$\equiv\ \langle a, \mathtt{tl}^* \cdot \mathtt{hd}, \{:\} \rangle \wedge \langle x \cdot \mathtt{hd}, \lambda, \{:\} \rangle$$
$$\equiv\ \langle a, \mathtt{tl}^* \cdot \mathtt{hd}, \{:\} \rangle \wedge \langle x, \mathtt{hd}, \{:\} \rangle$$

Next applying the fixed pointing due to x, gives a final condition, as expected: $\langle a, \mathtt{tl}^* \cdot \mathtt{hd}, \{:\} \rangle \wedge \langle x, \mathtt{tl}^* \cdot \mathtt{hd}, \{:\} \rangle$ □

While the two rules given do cover a wide range of examples, they are not complete. Additional rules exist for other forms of recursion but not all recursive functions can be handled using the current scheme.

Example 2.8

```
interleave x y = case x of
                   []    -> y
                   (a:b) -> a : interleave y b
```

Here the recursive call is y ↩ x·tl, which does not have a rule defined for it. In such cases the checker conservatively outputs `False`, and also gives a warning message to the user. The checker always terminates.

The fixed point rules classify exactly which forms of recursion can be accepted by the checker. Defining more fixed point rules which can capture an increasingly large number of patterns is a matter for future work.

2.5   A WORKED EXAMPLE

Recall the `risers` example in §2.1. The first step of the checker is to transform this into reduced Haskell.

```
risers xs =
    case xs of
            []          -> []
            [x]         -> [[x]]
            (x:y:etc) -> risers2 (x <= y) x (risers (y:etc))

risers2 b x y = case y of
                    (s:ss) -> case b of
                                True  -> (x:s) : ss
                                False -> [x] : (s:ss)
```

The auxiliary `risers2` is necessary because reduced Haskell has no `where` clause. The checker proceeds as follows:

Step 1, Find all incomplete case statements.   The checker finds one, in the body of `risers2`, the argument y must be a non-empty list. The constraint is $\langle y_{risers2}, \lambda, \{:\} \rangle$.

Step 2, Propagate.   The auxiliary `risers2` is applied by `risers` with `risers (y:etc)` as the argument s. This gives $\langle (\text{risers } (\text{y:etc})), \lambda, \{:\} \rangle$. When rewritten in terms of arguments and paths of selectors, this gives the constraint $\langle (\text{risers } (\text{xs}_{risers}\text{·tl·hd} : \text{xs}_{risers}\text{·tl·tl})), \lambda, \{:\} \rangle$.

Step 3, Backward analysis.   The constraint is transformed using the backward analysis rules. The first rule invoked is (app), which says that the body of `risers` must evaluate to a non-empty list, in effect an inline version of the constraint. Backward analysis is then performed over the case statement, the constructors, and finally `risers2`. The conclusion is that provided xs_{risers} is a :, the result will be. The constraint is $\langle (\text{xs}_{risers}\text{·tl·hd} : \text{xs}_{risers}\text{·tl·tl}), \lambda, \{:\} \rangle$, which is true.

In this example, there is no need to perform any fixed pointing.

2.6 SOME SMALL EXAMPLES AND A CASE STUDY

In the following examples, each line represents one propagation step in the checker. The final constraint is given on the last line.

```
head x = case x of
                  (y:ys) -> y
main x = head x
> ⟨x_head, λ, {:}⟩
> ⟨x_main, λ, {:}⟩
```

This example requires only initial constraint generation, and a simple propagation. □

Example 2.9

```
main x = map head x
> ⟨x_head, λ, {:}⟩
> ⟨x_map_head, tl*·hd, {:}⟩
> ⟨x_main, tl*·hd, {:}⟩
```

This example shows specialization generating a new function map_head, fixed pointing being applied to map, and the constraints being propagated through the system. □

Example 2.10

```
main x = map head (reverse x)
> ⟨x_head, λ, {:}⟩
> ⟨x_map_head, tl*·hd, {:}⟩
> ⟨x_main, tl*, {:}⟩ ∨ ⟨x_main, tl*·hd, {:}⟩
```

This result may at first seem surprising. The first disjunct of the constraint says that applying tl any number of times to x_{main} the result must always be a :, in other words x must be infinite. This guarantees case safety because reverse is tail strict, so if its argument is an infinite list, no result will ever be produced, and a case error will not occur. The second disjunct says, less surprisingly, that every item in x must be a non-empty list. □

Example 2.11

```
main xs ys = case null xs || null ys of
                  True -> 0
                  False -> head xs + head ys
> ⟨x_head, λ, {:}⟩
> ⟨(null xs_main || null ys_main), λ, {True}⟩ ∨
  (⟨xs_main, λ, {:}⟩ ∧ ⟨ys_main, λ, {:}⟩)
> ⟨xs_main, λ, {[]}⟩ ∨ ⟨ys_main, λ, {[]}⟩ ∨ (⟨xs_main, λ, {:}⟩ ∧ ⟨ys_main, λ, {:}⟩)
> True
```

This example shows the use of a more complex condition to guard a potentially unsafe application of `head`. The backward analysis applied to `null` and `||` gives precise requirements, which when expanded results in a tautology, showing that no pattern match error can occur. □

Example 2.12

```
main x = tails x
tails x = foldr tails2 [[]] x
tails2 x y = (x:head y) : y
> ⟨x_head, λ, {:}⟩
> ⟨y_tails2, λ, {:}⟩
> ⟨n1_foldr_tails2, λ, {:}⟩ ∨ ⟨n2_foldr_tails2, tl*·tl, {:}⟩
> True
```

This final example uses a fold to calculate the `tails` function. As the auxiliary `tails2` makes use of `head` the program is not obviously free from pattern-match errors. The first two lines of the output are simply moving the constraint around. The third line is the interesting one. In this line the checker gives two alternative conditions for the case safety of `foldr tails2` – either its first argument is a `:`, or its second argument is empty or infinite. The way the requirement for empty or infinite length is encoded is by the path `tl*·tl`. If the list is `[]`, then there are no tails to match the path. If however, there is one tail, then that tail, and all successive tails must be `:`. So either `foldr` does not call its function argument because it immediately takes the `[]` case, or `foldr` recurses infinitely, and therefore the function is never called. Either way, because `foldr`'s second argument is a `:`, and because `tails2` always returns a `:`, the first part of the condition can be satisfied. □

2.6.1 The Clausify Program

Our goal is to check standard Haskell programs, and to provide useful feedback to the user. To test the checker against these objectives we have used several Haskell programs, all written some time ago for other purposes. The analysis of one program is discussed below.

The Clausify program has been around for a very long time, since at least 1990. It has made its way into the `nofib` benchmark suite [Par92], and was the focus of several papers on heap profiling [RW93]. It parses logical propositions and puts them in clausal form. We ignore the parser and jump straight to the transformation of propositions. The data structure for a formula is:

```
data F = Sym {char :: Char} | Not {n :: F}
       | Dis {d1, d2 :: F} | Con {c1, c2 :: F}
       | Imp {i1, i2 :: F} | Eqv {e1, e2 :: F}
```

and the main pipeline is:

```
unicl . split . disin . negin . elim
```

Each of these stages takes a proposition and returns an equivalent version – for example the `elim` stage replaces implications with disjunctions and negation. Each stage eliminates certain forms of proposition, so that future stages do not have to consider them. Despite most of the stages being designed to deal with a restricted class of propositions, the only function which contains a non-exhaustive pattern match is in the definition of `clause` (a helper function for `unicl`).

```
clause p = clause' p ([] , [])
    where
    clause' (Dis p q)       x   = clause' p (clause' q x)
    clause' (Sym s)        (c,a) = (insert s c , a)
    clause' (Not (Sym s))  (c,a) = (c , insert s a)
```

After encountering the non-exhaustive pattern match, the checker generates the following constraints:

> $\langle p_{clause'}, (\text{d1+d2})^*, \{\text{Dis},\text{Sym},\text{Not}\}\rangle \wedge \langle p_{clause'}, (\text{d1+d2})^*\cdot n, \{\text{Sym}\}\rangle$

> $\langle p_{clause'}, (\text{d1+d2})^*, \{\text{Dis},\text{Sym},\text{Not}\}\rangle \wedge \langle p_{clause}, (\text{d1+d2})^*\cdot n, \{\text{Sym}\}\rangle$

> $\langle p_{unicl'}, (\text{d1+d2})^*, \{\text{Dis},\text{Sym},\text{Not}\}\rangle \wedge \langle p_{unicl'}, (\text{d1+d2})^*\cdot n, \{\text{Sym}\}\rangle$

> $\langle x_{foldr\_unicl}, \text{tl}^*\cdot\text{hd}\cdot(\text{d1+d2})^*, \{\text{Dis},\text{Sym},\text{Not}\}\rangle \wedge$
> $\langle x_{foldr\_unicl}, \text{tl}^*\cdot\text{hd}\cdot(\text{d1+d2})^*\cdot n, \{\text{Sym}\}\rangle$

> $\langle x_{unicl}, \text{tl}^*\cdot\text{hd}\cdot(\text{d1+d2})^*, \{\text{Dis},\text{Sym},\text{Not}\}\rangle \wedge$
> $\langle x_{unicl}, \text{tl}^*\cdot\text{hd}\cdot(\text{d1+d2})^*\cdot n, \{\text{Sym}\}\rangle$

These constraints give accurate and precise requirements for a case error not to occur at each stage. However, when the condition is propagated back over the `split` function, the result becomes less pleasing. None of our fixed pointing schemes handle the original recursive definition of `split`:

```
split p = split' p []
    where
    split' (Con p q) a = split' p (split' q a)
    split' p a = p : a
```

can be transformed manually by the removal of the accumulator:

```
split (Con p q) = split p ++ split q
split p = [p]
```

This second version is accepted by the checker, which generates the constraint:

> $\langle p_{split}, (\text{c1+c2})^*, \{\text{Con},\text{Dis},\text{Sym},\text{Not}\}\rangle \wedge$
> $\langle p_{split}, (\text{c1+c2})^*\cdot(\text{d1+d2})\cdot(\text{d1+d2})^*, \{\text{Dis},\text{Sym},\text{Not}\}\rangle \wedge$
> $\langle p_{split}, (\text{c1+c2})^*\cdot(\text{d1+d2})^*\cdot n, \{\text{Sym}\}\rangle$

This constraint can be read as follows: the outer structure of a propositional argument to `split` is any number of nested `Con` constructors; the next level is any number of nested `Dis` constructors; at the innermost level there must be either a `Sym`, or a `Not` containing a `Sym`. That is, propositions are in *conjunctive normal form*.

27

The one surprising part of this constraint is the $(d1+d2) \cdot (d1+d2)^*$ part of the path in the 2nd conjunct. We might rather expect something similar to $(c1+c2)^* \cdot (d1+d2)^* \{Dis,Sym,Not\}$, but consider what this means. Take as an example the value (Con (Sym 'x') (Sym 'y')). This value meets all 3 conjunctions generated by the tool, but does not meet this new constraint: the path has the empty word property, so the root of the value can no longer be a Con constructor.

The next function encountered is disin which shifts disjunction inside conjunction. The version in the nofib benchmark has the following equation in its definition:

```
disin (Dis p q) = if conjunct dp || conjunct dq
                  then disin (Dis dp dq)
                  else (Dis dp dq)
   where
   dp = disin p
   dq = disin q
```

Unfortunately, when expanded out this gives the call

```
disin (Dis (disin p) (disin q))
```

which does not have a fixed point under the present scheme. Refactoring is required to enable this stage to succeed. Fortunately, in [RW93] a new version of disin is given, which is vastly more efficient than this one, and (as a happy side effect) is also accepted by the checker.

At this point the story comes to an end. Although a constraint is calculated for the new disin, this constraint is approximately 15 printed pages long! Initial exploration suggests at least one reason for such a large constraint: there are missed opportunities to simplify paths. We are confident that with further work the Clausify example can be completed.

2.7 RELATED WORK

Viewed as a **proof tool** this work can be seen as following Turner's goal to define a Haskell-like language which is total [Tur04]. Turner disallows incomplete pattern matches, saying this will "force you to pay attention to exactly those corner cases which are likely to cause trouble". Our checker may allow this restriction to be lifted, yet still retain a total programming language.

Viewed as a basic **pattern match checker**, the work on compiling warnings about incomplete and overlapping patterns is quite relevant [JHH[+]93, Mar05]. As noted in the introduction, these checks are only local.

Viewed as a **mistake detector** this tool has a similar purpose to the classic C Lint tool [Joh78], or Dialyzer [LS04] – a static checker for Erlang. The aim is to have a static checker that works on unmodified code, with no additional annotations. However, a key difference is that in Dialyzer all warnings indicate a genuine problem that needs to be fixed. Because Erlang is a dynamically typed language, a large proportion of Dialyzer's warnings relate to mistakes a type checker would have detected.

Viewed as a **soft type system** the checker can be compared to the tree automata work done on XML and XSL [Toz01], which can be seen as an algebraic data type and a functional language. Another soft typing system with similarities is by Aiken [AM91], on the functional language FL. This system tries to assign a type to each function using a set of constructors, for example `head` is given just `Cons` and not `Nil`.

2.8 CONCLUSIONS AND FURTHER WORK

A static checker for potential pattern-match errors in Haskell has been specified and implemented. This checker is capable of determining preconditions under which a program with non-exhaustive patterns executes without failing due to a pattern-match error. A range of small examples has been investigated successfully. Where programs cannot be checked initially, refactoring can increase the checker's success rate. Work in progress includes:

- The checker currently relies on specialization to remove higher order functions.

- The checker is fully polymorphic but it does not currently handle Haskell's type classes; we hope these can be transformed away without vast complication [Jon94].

- Another challenge is to translate from full Haskell into the reduced language. This work has been started: we have a converter for a useful subset.

- The checker should offer fuller traces that can be manually verified. Currently the predicate at each stage is given, without any record of how it was obtained, or what effect fixed pointing had. Although a more detailed trace would not help an end user, it would help strengthen the understanding of the algorithms.

- The central algorithms of the checker can be refined. In particular a better fixed pointing scheme is being developed. A complete analysis of which programs can be verified would be useful.

- A correctness proof is needed to prove that the checker is sound. This will require a semantics for the reduced Haskell-like language.

With these improvements we hope to check larger Haskell programs, and to give useful feedback to the programmer.

ACKNOWLEDGEMENT

The first author is a PhD student supported by a studentship from the Engineering and Physical Sciences Research Council of the UK.

REFERENCES

[AM91]   Alex Aiken and Brian Murphy. Static Type Inference in a Dynamically Typed Language. In *POPL '91: Proceedings of the 18th ACM SIGPLAN-SIGACT symposium on Principles of programming languages*, pages 279–290. ACM Press, 1991.

[Con71]   John Horton Conway. *Regular Algebra and Finite Machines*. London Chapman and Hall, 1971.

[Hug96]   John Hughes. Type Specialisation for the Lambda-calculus; or, A New Paradigm for Partial Evaluation based on Type Inference. In Olivier Danvy, Robert Glück, and Peter Thiemann, editors, *Partial Evaluation*, pages 183–215. Springer LNCS 1110, February 1996.

[JHH+93]   Simon Peyton Jones, C V Hall, K Hammond, W Partain, and P Wadler. The Glasgow Haskell Compiler: A Technical Overview. In *Proc. UK Joint Framework for Information Technology (JFIT) Technical Conference*, 1993. http://www.haskell.org/ghc/.

[Joh78]   S. C. Johnson. Lint, a C program checker. Technical Report 65, Bell Laboratories, 1978.

[Jon94]   Mark P. Jones. Dictionary-free Overloading by Partial Evaluation. In *ACM SIGPLAN Workshop on Partial Evaluation and Semantics-Based Program Manipulation*. ACM Press, June 1994.

[Law04]   Mark V. Lawson. *Finite Automata*. CRC Press, first edition, 2004.

[LS04]   Tobias Lindahl and Konstantinos Sagonas. Detecting software defects in telecom applications through lightweight static analysis: A war story. In Chin Wei-Ngan, editor, *Programming Languages and Systems: Proceedings of the Second Asian Symposium (APLAS'04)*, volume 3302 of *LNCS*, pages 91–106. Springer, November 2004.

[Mar05]   Luc Maranget. Warnings for Pattern Matching. Under consideration for publication in *Journal Functional Programming*, March 2005.

[Par92]   Will Partain. The nofib Benchmark Suite of Haskell Programs. In J Launchbury and PM Sansom, editors, *Functional Programming, Glasgow 1992*, pages 195–202. Springer-Verlag Workshops in Computing, 1992.

[Rey72]   John C. Reynolds. Definitional interpreters for higher-order programming languages. In *ACM '72: Proceedings of the ACM annual conference*, pages 717–740, New York, NY, USA, 1972. ACM Press.

[RW93]   Colin Runciman and David Wakeling. Heap Profiling of Lazy Functional Programs. *Journal of Functional Programming*, 3(2):217–245, 1993.

[The05]   The GHC Team. The Glorious Glasgow Haskell Compilation System User's Guide, Version 6.4. http://www.haskell/org/ghc/docs/latest/html/users_guide, March 2005.

[Toz01]   Akihiko Tozawa. Towards Static Type Checking for XSLT. In *DocEng '01: Proceedings of the 2001 ACM Symposium on Document engineering*, pages 18–27, New York, NY, USA, 2001. ACM Press.

[Tur04]   David Turner. Total Functional Programming. *Journal of Universal Computer Science*, 10(7):751–768, July 2004.

Chapter 3

Software Metrics: Measuring Haskell

Chris Ryder[1], Simon Thompson[1]

Abstract: Software metrics have been used in software engineering as a mechanism for assessing code quality and for targeting software development activities, such as testing or refactoring, at areas of a program that will most benefit from them. Haskell [PJ03] has many tools for software engineering, such as testing, debugging and refactoring tools, but software metrics have been neglected.

This paper identifies a collection of software metrics for use with Haskell programs. These metrics are subjected to statistical analysis to assess the correlation between their values and the number of bug fixing changes occurring during the development of two case study programs. In addition, the relationships between the metrics are also explored, showing how combinations of metrics can be used to improve their accuracy.

3.1 INTRODUCTION

Currently, most software engineering research for functional programs is focused on tracing and observation techniques, although recent work by Li and others [LRT03] has also looked at refactoring for functional programs. Such work is a valuable addition to the field, but can be hard to effectively apply to large programs because of the difficulty of choosing appropriate application points.

In order to make effective use of such techniques it is typically necessary to concentrate their application into areas of a program most likely to contain bugs. However, the task of selecting such areas is often left to human intuition. Imperative and object oriented languages have used *software measurement* (also known as *software metrics*) to aid this task [GKMS00, Hal77, FP98], and so this work examines the applicability of metrics to functional programs written in Haskell.

[1]Computing Laboratory, University Of Kent, Canterbury, Kent, CT2 7NF, UK;
Email: C.Ryder@kent.ac.uk, S.J.Thompson@kent.ac.uk

31

3.1.1 Prior Work

Software metrics have been an active area of research since the early 70's so there is a large body of prior work for OO and imperative languages, such as that by Fenton, Pfleeger and Melton [FP98, Mel96]. Some of the early work attracted criticism for its lack of validation, but in recent years this has been addressed, for instance by Briand and his co-workers [BEEM95]. Barnes and Hopkins [BH00] addressed the issue of validation by examining the correlation between metric values and the number of bug fixes over a programs development lifetime.

Surprisingly, there is little work exploring metrics for functional languages. One of the few pieces is a thesis by Van Den Berg [VdB95] which examines the use of metrics to compare the quality of software written in Miranda[2] with that written in Pascal. However, little consensus was found among programmers on how to rate the quality of Miranda programs, so it is not discussed further here.

3.1.2 Motivation

The motivation for investigating software metrics for functional programming languages comes from three common software engineering tasks, software testing, code reviews and refactoring.

Currently, these tasks rely on either human intuition, e.g. to decide which refactoring to apply to a function, or brute force, e.g. by reviewing every function. Each of these tasks can be helped by using software metrics to concentrate programmer's effort on areas of the program where most benefit is likely to be gained. For instance, functions which exhibit high metric values might be tested more rigorously, may be subject to an in-depth code review, or may be refactored to reduce their complexity. Conversely, functions which exhibit low metric values may not require as much testing, reviewing or refactoring. Targeting programmer effort using metrics in this manner can improve the quality of software by making more efficient use of programmer's time and skills.

In many ways metrics are analogous to compiler warnings. They indicate unusual features in the code, but there may be legitimate reasons for those features. Like warnings, metrics give a hint that part of the code may need to be inspected.

3.1.3 Overview of this paper

The remainder of this paper is divided into the following sections: Section 3.2 introduces a selection of metrics that can be used with Haskell. Section 3.3 describes the way in which we attempt to validate the metrics. Section 3.4 presents the results from the validation of the metrics. Section 3.5 presents the conclusions we draw from this work.

---

[2]Miranda is a trademark of Research Software Ltd.

3.2 WHAT CAN BE MEASURED

There is a large body of work describing metrics for imperative languages. Some of those metrics, such as *pathcount* which counts the number of execution paths through a function, may directly translate to Haskell. Other features of Haskell, such as pattern matching, may not be considered by imperative metrics so it is necessary to devise metrics for such features.

At the time this project was started we were unable to implement type-based metrics, such as measuring the complexity of a function's type, because we were unable to find a stand-alone implementation of the Haskell type system. Therefore the metrics presented here are a first step in assessing metrics for Haskell. Recently, the Glasgow Haskell Compiler (GHC) [MPJ04] has begun to provide a programming interface to its internal components, such as its type checker. This allows type-based metrics to be implemented, which we hope to pursue in future.

In the remainder of this section we present a selection of the Haskell metrics we analysed and discuss their relationship to imperative or OO metrics.

3.2.1 Patterns

Because patterns are widely used in Haskell programs it is interesting to investigate how they affect the complexity of a program. To do this it is necessary to consider which attributes of patterns might be measured, and how these attributes might affect the complexity. We discuss these case by case now:-

- *Pattern size* (*PSIZ*). There are many ways one might choose to measure the size of a pattern, but the simplest is to count the number of components in the abstract syntax tree of the pattern. The assumption is that as patterns increase in size they become more complex.

- *Number of pattern variables* (*NPVS*). Patterns often introduce variables into scope. One way in which this might affect complexity is by increasing the number of identifiers a programmer must know about in order to comprehend the code. Studies [Boe81, McC92, FH79] have shown that at least 50% of the effort of modifying a program is in comprehending the code being changed.

- *Number of overridden pattern variables* or *Number of overriding pattern variables*. Variables introduced in patterns may override existing identifiers, or be overridden by those in a `where` clause for instance. Overriding identifiers can be confusing and can lead to unintended program behaviour, particularly if the compiler is unable to indicate the conflict because the identifiers have the same type. Therefore one hypothesis is that high numbers of variables involved in overriding may indicate potential points of error.

- *Number of constructors* (*PATC*). Patterns are often used when manipulating algebraic data types by using the constructors of the data type in the pattern. Like NPVS, the hypothesis is that the higher the number of constructors in a pattern the more information a programmer needs to consider to understand it.

33

```
foo :: Int -> Int
foo a = a*a

bar :: [Int] -> [Int] -> [Int]
bar a b = map fn c
  where
    c = zip a b
    fn = \(x,y) -> foo (x+y)
```

foo, bar
a, b
c, fn
x, y

Number of items
in these scopes

FIGURE 3.1. Measuring distance by the number of declarations brought into scope for the function `foo`.

- *Number of wildcards* (*WILD*). When initially considering patterns it was suggested that wildcards should be ignored because they state that the item they are matching is of no interest. However, wildcards convey information about the structure of items in the pattern, e.g. the position of constructor arguments. Therefore it was decided that we should measure WILD to clarify their effect.

- *Depth of nesting*. Patterns are frequently nested, which can lead to complicated patterns. When measuring the depth of nesting one must consider how to measure the depth in patterns such as `[(a,b),(c,d)]`, which contain more than one nested pattern. This study uses two ways, *Sum of the depth of nesting* (*SPDP*) and *Maximum depth of nesting*, however the sum method may also be measuring the size of the pattern.

3.2.2 Distance

In all but the most trivial program there will be several declarations which will interact. The interactions between declarations are often described by *def-use* pairs [RW85]. For instance, the def-use pair (a,b) indicates that b uses the declaration a. Metrics that use def-use pairs are most often concerned with the testability of programs, because def-use pairs indicate interactions that might require testing.

When one considers a def-use pair, there will inevitably be a distance between the location of the use and the declaration in the source code. One hypothesis is that the larger the distance, the greater the probability that an error will occur in the way that declaration is used. Distance may be measured in a number of ways:

- *Number of new scopes*. One way to measure the distance between the use and declaration of an identifier is by how many new scopes have been introduced between the two points. This gives a "conceptual" distance which may indicate how complex the name-space is at that use. This leads to a hypothesis that a more complex name-space may make it harder to avoid introducing errors.

- *Number of declarations brought into scope*. An extension to the previous distance metric is to count how many declarations have been introduced into the name-space by any new scopes. This technique, illustrated in Figure 3.1, may give an idea of how "busy" the nested scopes are.

34

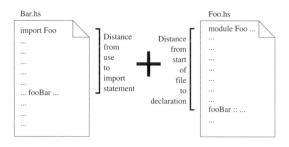

FIGURE 3.2.   Measuring distance across module boundaries.

- *Number of source lines*. The distance metrics described previously have measured the "conceptual" distance, however it is also important to consider the "spatial" distance in the source code. The hypothesis is that the further away items are in the source code, the harder it is to recall how they should be used. The simplest way to measure spatial distance is by the number of source lines.

- *Number of parse tree nodes*. A problem with counting source lines as a measure of distance is that source lines contain varying amounts of program code. One way to overcome this problem is to count the number of parse tree nodes on the path between two points of the parse tree instead. This may give a more consistent measure of the amount of code between the use and the declaration.

Measuring distance between modules using scope-based measures is straightforward, because imported identifiers will be in a top level scope of their own.

When measuring distance using source lines it is less clear how distance between modules should be calculated. For this work we have chosen to measure the cross-module distance by measuring the distance between the use of an identifier and the import statement that brings it into scope, plus the distance between the declaration and the start of the module in which it is defined. This is illustrated in Figure 3.2. This method reflects the number of lines a programmer may have to look through, first finding the module the identifier is imported from, then finding the identifier in the imported module. A variation of this method might be to measure only the distance in the imported module, for instance.

Because a function is likely to call several functions there will be several distance measures, one for each called function, which must be aggregated in some way to produce a single value for the calling function. This work examines three methods: summing, taking the maximum and taking the mean.

3.2.3   Callgraph Attributes

Because function calls form a crucial part of Haskell it appears that some interesting properties may be measured from the callgraph of a Haskell program. Some of these are described below.

- *Strongly connected component size (SCCS)*. Because parts of a callgraph may be cyclic it is possible to find the strongly connected components. A strongly connected component (SCC) is a subgraph in which all the nodes (functions) are connected (call) directly or indirectly to all the other nodes. Because all functions that are part of a SCC depend directly or indirectly upon each other, one might expect that as the size of the SCC increases, the number of changes is likely to increase as well, because a change to a single function may cause changes to other functions in the SCC. This is often known as the *ripple effect*.

  SCCS is a measure of coupling, similar to imperative and OO coupling metrics such as the *Coupling between object classes* (CBO) metric used by Chidamber and Kemerer [CK94]. The main difference is that CBO measures only direct coupling between objects, e.g. A calls B, while SCCS also measures indirect coupling between functions, e.g. A calls X which calls B.

- *Indegree (IDEG)*. The indegree of a function in the callgraph is the number of functions which call it, and thus IDEG is a measure of reuse. Functions with high IDEG values may be more important, because they are heavily reused in the program and therefore changes to them may affect much of the program. This metric is inspired by the *Fan-In* metric of Constantine and Yourdon [YC79], which measures how many times a module is used by other modules. Thus IDEG is Fan-In used on individual functions, rather than whole modules.

- *Outdegree (OUTD)*. The outdegree of a function in the callgraph is the number of functions it calls. One might assume that the larger the OUTD, the greater the chance of the function needing to change, since changes in any of the called functions may cause changes in the behaviour of the calling function. Like the IDEG metric, the OUTD is inspired by the work of Constantine and Yourdon, in this case by their *Fan-Out* metric which measures the number of modules used by a module. As with IDEG, the OUTD metric is used on individual functions, rather than on whole modules.

It is possible to isolate the subgraph that represents the callgraph rooted at a single function. One hypothesis is that the greater the complexity of the subgraph, the more likely the function is to change, because it is harder to comprehend the subgraph. Therefore one might measure several attributes from these subgraphs:

- *Arc-to-node ratio (ATNR)*. The arc-to-node ratio is a useful indicator of how "busy" a graph is. If a callgraph has a high ATNR, there is greater complexity in the interaction of the functions, and therefore one might hypothesise, a greater chance of errors occurring. This is similar to the FIFO metric suggested by Constantine and Yourdon, but FIFO looks only at the direct dependents and dependencies of the module being measured, while ATNR looks at the complexity of all the interdependencies of the entire subgraph.

- *Callgraph Depth (CGDP)* and *Callgraph Width (CGWD)*. The subgraph of a function may be cyclic but can be transformed into a tree by breaking its cycles, as is illustrated in Figure 3.3. Such a tree represents all the direct or

36

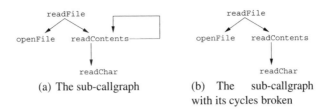

(a) The sub-callgraph

(b) The sub-callgraph with its cycles broken

FIGURE 3.3. **An example of a sub-callgraph for a function** `readFile`.

indirect dependencies of the function, and as such it is interesting to measure the size of this tree. Two common measures of size are the depth and the width. The deeper or wider the tree grows, the more complex it is likely to be.

The depth and width metrics described here are inspired by the *Depth of Inheritance Tree* (DIT) and *Number of Children* (NOC) metrics suggested by Chidamber and Kemerer for OO programs.

The DIT metric measures how deep a class is in the inheritance hierarchy of an OO program. The deeper a class is, the greater the number of methods it is likely to inherit, and hence the harder it is to predict its behaviour. In Haskell we model this by measuring the depth of the subgraph, because a deep subgraph is likely to be hard to comprehend than a shallow subgraph.

The NOC metric is the number of immediate children in the inheritance hierarchy of the class being analysed. The number of children indicates how much the class is reused, and thus how important the class is to the design of the program. Our width measure looks superficially similar to the NOC metric, but in fact measures dependencies, much like our depth metric. The Haskell metric most closely resembling NOC is the IDEG metric, which also measures reuse.

3.2.4 Function Attributes

As well as the specific attributes highlighted in previous sections, one may also measure some more general attributes such as the following.

- *Pathcount (PATH)*. Pathcount is a measure of the number of logical paths through a function. Barnes and Hopkins showed pathcount to be a good predictor of faults in Fortran programs, so it is interesting to investigate pathcount metrics for Haskell programs. Implementing pathcount for Haskell is mostly straightforward, although there are some places where the pathcount value is not obvious. For instance, consider Example 3.1.

  In this example there are three obvious execution paths, one for each pattern expression, but there is also a fourth, less obvious execution path. If the second pattern (`x:xs`) matches, the guard `x > 0` will be tested. If this guard fails execution will drop through to the third pattern expression, creating a fourth execution path. Although this is a contrived example, this kind of "hidden path" can occur quite easily, for instance by omitting an `otherwise` guard.

Example 3.1 (Hidden execution paths when using patterns and guards).

```
func :: [Int] -> Int
func []      = 0
func (x:xs)  | x > 0 = func xs
func (x:y:xs) = func xs
```

- *Operators (OPRT)* and *Operands (OPRD)*. Having discussed various metrics previously it is important not to ignore less sophisticated measures such as function size. A large function is more likely to be complex than a small one.

  There are many ways to measure program size. Van Den Berg used a variation of Halstead's [Hal77] operator and operand metrics in his work with Miranda. This work updates Van Den Berg's metrics for Haskell by defining all literals and identifiers that are not operators as operands. Operators are the standard operators and language keywords, such as `:`, `++`, `where`, etc. Delimiters such as `()` and `[]`, etc, are also included as operators. Although OPRT and OPRD were implemented as separate metrics, they are really a connected pair.

In this section we have presented a selection of metrics which cover a wide range of attributes of the Haskell language. With the exception of the WILD metric, these metrics are expected to increase in value as the complexity increases.

The metrics introduced here are all measuring distinct attributes, and it may be that some of these can be combined to produce more sophisticated and accurate measures. However it is important to validate these "atomic" metrics before attempting to combine them.

3.3 VALIDATION METHODOLOGY

To validate the metrics described in Section 3.2 a number of case studies were undertaken. For this work we followed the methodology described by Barnes and Hopkins and took a series of measurements from a program over its development lifetime, and then correlated those measures with the number of bug fixing or refactoring changes occurring during that time. Metrics that correlate well with the bug fix counts may be good indicators of targets for testing or refactoring.

A limitation of this method of validation is that all bug fixing changes are considered to be of equal importance. In reality it is likely that some bug fixes might be considered "trivial" because they were easy to implement or had only minimal impact on the operation of the program, while others may be considered to be much more serious because they were hard to implement or had a significant impact on the operation of the program. It is not clear how the relative seriousness of a bug fix should be incorporated into this analysis, for example, should serious bug fixes be counted as multiple trivial bug fixes? or should trivial bug fixes be discarded? Furthermore, it would be difficult to objectively assess the seriousness of the changes. Therefore, we do not include "bug seriousness" in our analysis.

We experienced some difficulty in finding suitable case study programs. Candidate programs needed to have source code stored in a CVS repository with a change history that contained enough changes to allow for meaningful analysis.

Most of the programs investigated had no clear separation between bug fixes, refactorings and feature additions, with different types of changes often being committed to CVS in the same commit. Unfortunately it is not possible to automatically classify these changes, e.g. by assuming small changes are bug fixes and large changes are feature additions, with any degree of accuracy because the sizes of the changes are not uniform. For instance, a feature addition may involve lots of small changes to lots of functions, and thus be indistinguishable from a collection of small bug fix changes, while conversely a bug fixing change may require a large change to a function and thus look like a feature addition.

Because it was not possible to automatically classify changes it was necessary to manually inspect each change in the CVS history of the programs to determine the type of change, a very time-consuming process. However, this issue only affects the validation process, not the use of the metrics.

The need to manually inspect changes necessitated choosing programs that were small enough to be able to inspect manually within a reasonable amount of time, but choosing smaller programs causes problems if there are too few changes for statistically significant results to be obtained. The first of our case study programs, a Peg Solitaire program described later, suffers from this to some extent.

The use of a revision control system that uses fine grained commits, such as `darcs`, may encourage programmers to clearly and individually record bug fixes.

The two programs chosen for the case study are both products of another research project at the University of Kent. The programs were both maintained in a CVS repository, giving easy access to the change histories. The programs were developed separately from our work and we had no influence in their development, other than to request that changes be committed to the CVS repository individually, making it significantly easier to classify the types of the changes.

3.3.1 Peg Solitaire Case Study

The first case study program was a Peg Solitaire game [TR03] with both textual and graphical interfaces, consisting of a number of modules which did not necessarily all exist simultaneously. The module sizes are shown in Table 3.1.

3.3.2 Refactoring Case Study

The second case study program was a tool for refactoring Haskell programs [LRT03]. The program used a parser library which was not examined in this study, therefore only the code that manipulated parse trees was analysed. Table 3.1 shows this program was approximately twice the size of the Peg Solitaire program.

	Module	Min Size (LOC)	Max Size (LOC)	Num. Changes
Peg Solitaire	Board	86	220	9
	Main	25	27	38
	Solve	39	101	7
	Stack	26	31	0
	GPegSolitaire	228	350	78
	TPegSolitaire	98	177	16
	Total Number of Changes			148
Refactoring	EditorCommands	198	213	4
	PFE0	332	337	2
	PfeRefactoringCmds	18	24	5
	PrettySymbols	23	23	0
	RefacAddRmParam	142	434	56
	RefacDupDef	62	157	19
	RefacLocUtils	201	848	88
	RefacMoveDef	322	796	56
	RefacNewDef	77	478	58
	RefacRenaming	67	236	23
	RefacTypeSyn	20	21	0
	RefacUtils	764	1088	126
	ScopeModule	222	222	0
	TiModule	140	140	0
	Main	36	103	7
	Total Number of Changes			444

TABLE 3.1.   Summary of the Peg Solitaire and Refactoring case study programs.

3.3.3   Analysing change histories and metrics

The change histories of the two programs were manually examined to determine the nature of the changes, such as feature additions, bug fixes, etc, and the number of bug fixing changes occurring for every function during the development lifetime was recorded. It is important to note that the programs did compile after every change, therefore the change counts do not include errors that would have been caught by the compiler, except where they are part of a larger change.

The metrics described in Section 3.2 were then run on each version of each program, and the maximum value of each metric was taken for every function. The measurements were then correlated with the number of bug fixing changes for each function using the statistical macros of Excel. Although it is possible that taking the maximum value may introduce artifacts, the metric values for a given function tend not to change very often so we do not believe this to be a problem.

3.4   RESULTS

This section presents some of the results of correlating the measurements taken from the case study programs with their change histories. Metrics whose values increase with increased complexity would be expected to show a positive correlation with the number of changes, while metrics whose values decrease with

	Metric	Correlation (r)	r^2
PS	OUTD	0.4783	0.229
	SCCS	0.3446	0.119
RE	Distance by the sum of number of scopes	0.632	0.399
	Distance by the maximum number of scopes	0.6006	0.361
	NPVS	0.5927	0.351
	OPRD	0.5795	0.336
	OUTD	0.5723	0.328

TABLE 3.2.   Highest correlations for Peg Solitaire (PS) and Refactoring (RE).

increased complexity are likely to have negative correlations.

We also investigated the correlation between different metrics to see if any metrics were related. The full and detailed results for this work are not presented here due to space constraints, but are analysed in detail in the thesis by Ryder [Ryd04]. Instead, the following main observations are discussed:

- The OUTD metric is correlated with the number of changes.

- All the distance metrics show similar levels of correlation.

- Callgraphs tend to grow uniformly in both width and depth.

- Most of the pattern metrics are measuring the size of a pattern.

3.4.1   Correlation of individual metrics

The first results we analysed were those taken by correlating metric values against the number of changes. Table 3.2 summarises the highest statistically significant correlation values obtained from the two case studies, as well as their r^2 values. The r^2 values show the proportion of the variance in common between the metric and the number of bug fixes. This gives an indication of the influence of the correlation on the number of bug fixes. For instance, consider the OUTD metric in Table 3.2. It has an r^2 value of 0.229, which states that there is 22.9% of the variance in common between OUTD and the number of bug fixes. In the rest of this section correlation values will be followed by their r^2 values in parenthesis, e.g. the correlation and r^2 values of OUTD will be shown as 0.4783 (0.229).

These results show that, for most of the metrics, there was no statistically significant correlation in the data taken from the Peg Solitaire program. Only the SCCS and OUTD metrics show correlation that was statistically significant at the 5% level, with values of 0.3446 (0.119) and 0.4783 (0.229) respectively.

Conversely, the Refactoring program shows statistically significant correlations for all the metrics except for the SCCS and IDEG metrics.

IDEG, which measures reuse, is not statistically significant for either program, so one can assume that the reuse of a function has little effect on its complexity.

None of the distance measures were significant at the 5% level for the Peg Solitaire program, however they were all significant for the Refactoring program.

Most of the measures resulted in correlations between 0.4 (0.16) and 0.55 (0.303), but the greatest correlation was provided by the *Distance by the sum of the number of scopes* metric, with a correlation of 0.632 (0.399). These results seem to confirm that the greater the distance between where something is used and where it is declared, the greater the probability of an error occurring in how it is used. The results also seem to suggest that it does not matter too much how the distance is measured, with the "semantic" measures having slightly stronger correlation with the number of bug fixes than the "spatial" measures on average.

However, we do not know what text editor was used in the development of these case study programs. It may be that a "smart" editor that allows the programmer to jump directly to definitions may reduce the effect of distance.

From the callgraph measures, OUTD provided the greatest correlation for both programs, with a correlation value of 0.4783 (0.229) for the Peg Solitaire program and 0.5723 (0.328) for the Refactoring program. This provides some evidence that functions that call lots of other functions are likely to change more often than functions that do not call many functions. This is also known to occur for the related *Fan-Out* OO metric described previously in Section 3.2.3.

Of the other callgraph measures, SCCS has significant correlation for the Peg Solitaire program, but not for the Refactoring program, as was discussed earlier. Although none of the other callgraph measures have significant correlation for the Peg Solitaire program, they do have significant values for the Refactoring program, ranging from 0.3285 (0.108) for CGWD, to 0.4932 (0.243) for CGDP.

The results for the function attributes showed that although none of the metrics were significant at the 5% level for the Peg Solitaire program, the OPRD and OPRT measures were significant at the 10% level. For each program the OPRD and OPRT measurements showed very similar correlation values. The PATH measure showed a small correlation of 0.286 (0.082) for the Refactoring program.

3.4.2 Cross-correlation of metrics

Having looked at the correlation of metric values with the number of changes, it is interesting to look at the correlation between metric values, which might indicate relationships between the attributes being measured.

Initially, the cross-correlation between metrics of the same class is examined, but later we examine correlation across metrics of different classes. Table 3.3 shows the clusters of metrics which appear to be strongly correlated.

The cluster formed by the pattern metrics, C3 in Table 3.3, implies that the pattern metrics are measuring a similar attribute, most likely the size of a pattern.

The distance measures form two clusters, C1 and C4 in Table 3.3. Cluster C1 suggests there is little difference between measuring distance by the number of source lines or by the number of parse tree nodes, and shows that measuring the sum of the number of scopes or declarations in scopes does not give much more information than measuring the number of source lines. This might be because declarations that are further away in scope tend to be further away in the source code. Likewise, as the number of declarations increases, so the distances between

C1	Sum of the number of scopes Sum of the number of declarations Sum of the number of source lines Maximum number of source lines	C3	NPVS SPDP PSIZ PATC (*in Refactoring program only*)
	Average number of source lines Sum of the number of parse tree nodes Maximum number of parse tree nodes Average number of parse tree nodes	C4	Average number of scopes Maximum number of declarations Maximum number of scopes Average number of declarations
C2	CGDP CGWD	C5	OPRD OPRT

TABLE 3.3.   Strongly correlated metrics for the case study programs.

declarations and where they are used tend to increase.

Cluster C4 shows that distance measured by the maximum or average number of scopes or declarations in scope is not strongly correlated with distance by the sum of the number of scopes or declarations in scope. One reason for this might be that the identifiers used in a function are generally a similar distance from their declarations, e.g. all the uses of a pattern variable in a function might have a similar distance measure. This would cause the average and maximum values to be similar between functions, while the sum measure would vary much more.

Examining the cross-correlation of the callgraph metrics, cluster C2 in Table 3.3, shows that apart from the CGDP and CGWD metrics, there is very little correlation between this class of metrics. This seems to confirm that they are measuring distinct attributes of callgraphs. The correlation between the CGWD and CGDP metrics is interesting because it seems to suggest that callgraphs for individual functions tend to grow uniformly in both depth and width.

The cluster C5 is unsurprising since these metrics are really part of a pair of interconnected metrics. However, the PATH metric does not appear to be part of the cluster, showing that it is unlikely to be measuring the size of a function.

3.4.3   Cross-correlation of all the metrics

If the clusters of strongly correlated metrics are replaced with a representative of each cluster, it is possible to analyse the correlation between the various classes of metrics. For this work, each cluster was represented by the metric with the highest correlation value in the cluster. The measurements from the Peg Solitaire case study showed no correlation between the various classes of metrics, while the cross-correlation for the Refactoring case study is shown in Table 3.4.

The correlation between NPVS and OPRD seen in cluster C1 of Table 3.4 is probably because variables are counted as operands, so an increase in the number of pattern variables will necessarily entail an increase in the number of operands. The correlation with the *Sum of number of scopes* measure is less clear. It suggests that as the number of pattern variables increases, the distance to any called functions, measured by the sum of the number of scopes, also increases. This may be because pattern variables are often introduced where new scopes are constructed.

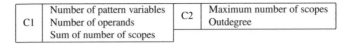

C1	Number of pattern variables Number of operands Sum of number of scopes	C2	Maximum number of scopes Outdegree

TABLE 3.4.   Cross-correlated metrics for the Refactoring program.

Cluster C2 of Table 3.4 suggests that the largest distance to any function called from any single function will increase as the number of called functions increases. This may be because as more functions are called, they will tend to be further away, since the called functions can not all be located in the same place.

3.4.4   Regression analysis of metrics

In order to obtain a greater correlation with the number of changes it may be possible to combine a number of metrics. Determining the best combination of metrics can be done using a regression analysis. The regression analysis of the results from both case studies showed that statistically significant correlation can be achieved for both programs, with correlation values of 0.583 (0.34) for the Peg Solitaire program and 0.6973 (0.487) for the Refactoring program, which are higher than any of the individual metrics correlation values.

The coefficients of the regression analysis for the Peg Solitaire program show that the largest contribution, with a coefficient of 0.4731, comes from OUTD, suggesting that the most important attribute is the number of direct dependencies.

The coefficient for the *Sum of number of source lines* distance metric, -0.2673, is negative which suggests that if the functions used are a long way away in the source code it is *less* likely to introduce errors. This may be caused by cross-module function calls, which imply that the calling function is using some well defined and stable interface, and hence is less likely to have to be changed as a result of the called function being changed. This suggests that cross-module calls may need to be measured differently to intra-module calls.

The coefficients from the Refactoring program regression analysis shows that the largest contribution by some margin comes from the *Sum of number of scopes* metric with a coefficient of 0.315. This suggests that, for the Refactoring program, it is important to know how complicated the name-space is for each function.

3.5   CONCLUSIONS AND FURTHER WORK

In this paper we have described a number of software metrics that can be used on Haskell programs. Using two case study programs we have shown that it may be possible to use some of these metrics to indicate functions that may have an increased risk of containing errors, and which may therefore benefit from more rigorous testing.

Unfortunately, because we were only able to assess two case study programs there remain questions about the general applicability of these metrics to Haskell programs. The authors would therefore welcome contributions of Haskell programs that would make suitable case studies in order to further expand this analysis. Nevertheless, we were still able to show interesting results.

By analysing the cross-correlation of the metrics we have shown that some of the metrics measure similar or closely related attributes. The regression analysis of the metrics has shown that combining the measurements does increase the correlation, and therefore the accuracy, of the metrics. From this we can see that there is no single attribute that makes a Haskell program complex, but rather a combination of features. However, good estimates can be obtained using only the OUTD metric, which measures the dependencies of a function. This suggests that, in common with OO and imperative programs, most of the complexity in a Haskell program lies not within individual functions, but rather in their interaction. We note also that the OUTD metric does not appear to be cross-correlated with the measures of function size, OPRD and OPRT, therefore this result is unlikely to be caused simply by larger functions being more likely to contain bugs.

Overall, this preliminary study using mostly translations of imperative or OO metrics has shown that metrics *can* be used on Haskell programs to indicate areas with increased probability of containing bugs. The success of this preliminary work encourages further exploration, in particular, by designing metrics to analyse Haskell specific features which may provide better predictors of bug locations.

As part of the thesis by Ryder, the results of this preliminary study of metrics have been used to experiment with visualisation tools. These tools aim to exploit the metrics to aid programmers in exploring the source code of their programs, demonstrating one area where metrics can be of use.

3.5.1 Further Work

It is important to be realistic with the findings in this paper. They are based upon two Haskell programs, which may not be representative of Haskell programs in general. To clarify these results further it would be necessary to repeat these studies on a larger range of programs, although the time and effort involved in manually inspecting the change histories of the programs may be prohibitive.

What can be achieved much more easily is to further analyse the relationships between the metrics. This further analysis has been performed as part of the thesis by Ryder, but is not included here due to space constraints.

The metrics described in this paper are mostly translations of imperative or OO metrics, but Haskell programs contain features not analysed by such metrics, e.g. a powerful type system, higher-order and polymorphic functions, etc. Although we were unable to implement metrics for these features during this project, recent developments in the Haskell community, such as the GHC API [MPJ04, RT05] and Strafunski[LV03], have now made it possible. Therefore, one area to expand this work is the design and evaluation of metrics for these advanced Haskell features.

We would also like to integrate the ideas of software metrics into the HaRe [LRT03] refactoring tool. The aim of such a project would be to use metrics to target refactorings, in line with Fowlers' [FBB+99] work on "bad smells".

REFERENCES

[BEEM95]   L. Briand, K. El Emam, and S. Morasca. Theoretical and empirical validation of software product measures. Technical Report ISERN-95-03, Fraunhofer Inst., Germany, 1995.

[BH00]   D.J. Barnes and T.R. Hopkins. The evolution and testing of a medium sized numerical package. *Advances in Software Tools for Scientific Computing*, volume 10 of *Lecture Notes in Computational Science and Engineering*. Springer-Verlag, January 2000.

[Boe81]   B. W. Boehm. *Software Engineering Economics*. Prentice-Hall, 1981.

[CK94]   S. R. Chidamber and C. F. Kemerer. A metrics suite for object oriented design. *IEEE Transactions on Software Engineering*, 20(6), 1994.

[FBB+99]   M. Fowler, K. Beck, J. Brant, W. Opdyke, and D. Roberts. *Refactoring: Improving the Design of Existing Code*. Addison-Wesley, 1999.

[FH79]   R. K. Fjeldstad and W. T. Hamlen. Application program maintenance study: report to our respondents. *Proc. of GUIDE 48*, 1979. The Guide Corporation.

[FP98]   N. E. Fenton and S. L. Pfleeger. *Software Metrics: A Rigorous and Practical Approach*. PWS Publishing Co., 1998.

[GKMS00]   T. L. Graves, A. F. Karr, J. S. Marron, and H. P. Siy. Predicting fault incidence using software change history. *IEEE Transactions on Soft. Eng.*, 26(7), 2000.

[Hal77]   M. H. Halstead. *Elements of Software Science*. Elsevier, 1977.

[LRT03]   H. Li, C. Reinke, and S. Thompson. Tool support for refactoring functional programs. *Proceedings of the 2003 Haskell Workshop*, 2003. ACM Press.

[LV03]   R. Lämmel and J. Visser. A Strafunski Application Letter. *Proc. of PADL'03*, vol. 2562 of *LNCS*, 2003. Springer-Verlag.

[McC92]   C. McClure. *The Three Rs of Software Automation*. Prentice-Hall, 1992.

[Mel96]   A. Melton, *Software Measurement*. Thompson Computer Press, 1996.

[MPJ04]   S. Marlow and S. Peyton Jones. The Glasgow Haskell Compiler. Microsoft Research, Cambridge, UK. http://www.haskell.org/ghc/.

[PJ03]   S. Peyton Jones. *Haskell 98 Language and Libraries*. Cambridge University Press, Cambridge, UK, 2003. http://www.haskell.org/definition/.

[RT05]   C. Ryder and S. Thompson. Porting HaRe to the GHC API. Technical Report 8-05, Computing Laboratory, University of Kent, UK, October 2005.

[RW85]   S. Rapps and E. J. Weyuker. Selecting software test data using data flow information. *IEEE Transactions on Software Engineering*, 11(4), 1985.

[Ryd04]   C. Ryder. *Software Measurement for Functional Programming*. PhD thesis, Computing Lab, University of Kent, UK, 2004.

[TR03]   S. Thompson and C. Reinke. A case study in refactoring functional programs. *Proceedings of 7th Brazilian Symposium on Programming Languages*, May 2003. Journal of Universal Computer Science, Springer-Verlag.

[VdB95]   K. Van den Berg. *Software Measurement and Functional Programming*. PhD thesis, Uni. of Twente, Department of Computer Science, Netherlands, 1995.

[YC79]   E. Yourdon and L. L. Constantine. *Structured Design: Fundamentals of a Discipline of Computer Program and Systems Design*. Prentice-Hall, 1979.

Chapter 4

Type-Specialized Serialization with Sharing

Martin Elsman[1]

Abstract: We present an ML combinator library for serialization, which supports serialization of mutable and cyclic data structures and at the same time preserves sharing. The technique generates compact serialized values, both due to sharing, but also due to type specialization. The library is type safe in the sense that a type specialized serializer can be applied only to values of the specialized type.

The combinator library, which is written entirely in ML, may relieve language designers and compiler writers from the technical details of built-in serializers and, evenly important, support programmers with a portable solution to serialization.

The combinator library is used in practice for serializing symbol table information in a separate compilation system for the MLKit compiler, a compiler for the programming language Standard ML. The technique is shown to scale well and allows the MLKit to be compiled with any Standard ML compliant compiler.

4.1   INTRODUCTION

Built-in serialization support in modern languages is arguably controversial. It complicates language specifications and limits the possibilities for compiler writers to choose efficient object representations. However, most practical programming language systems provide means for serialization. For Java and C#, for instance, serialization is part of the language specification, yet for other languages, programmers have relied on implementation support for serialization. The importance of efficient serialization techniques is partly due to its relation to remote method invocation (RMI) and distributed computing (marshalling). Other uses of

[1]IT University of Copenhagen, Rued Langgaards Vej 7, DK-2300 Copenhagen S, Denmark; Email: mael@itu.dk.

serialization include storing of program state on disk for future program invocations.

Built-in serializers have many good properties. They are easy to use by application programmers, are often efficient, and support serialization of all types of objects, including function objects. However, the generality and efficiency come with a price. Built-in serializers are often tightly integrated with an implementation's runtime system, which may complicate and even limit modifications to the runtime system (e.g., its copying garbage collector or runtime type tagging scheme).

In this paper, we expand on Kennedy's type indexed approach to serialization [Ken04], which provides the programmer with a combinator library for constructing pairs of a serializer and a deserializer for a given datatype. The approach has the following key advantages:

- Compactness due to type specialization. No type information (tagging) is written to the byte stream by the serializer, which leads to compact serialized data. Necessary type information for deserializing the serialized value is present in the type specialized deserializer.

- No need for runtime tags. The combinator library imposes no restrictions on the representation of values. In particular, the technique supports a tag-free representation of values, as the library is written entirely in the language itself.

- Type safety. A type specialized serializer may be applied only to values of the specialized type. A subset of the library is truly type safe in the sense that with this subset it is not possible to construct serializers that do not behave as expected. Moreover, the technique can be extended so that, before a value is deserialized, a type checksum in the serialized data is checked against the type checksum of the specialized deserializer.

We make three main contributions:

1. Support for automatic compactness due to sharing. With the serialization library, serialization of two equivalent values leads to sharing in the serialized data. Moreover, when the values are deserialized, their representation in program memory is shared, which may lead to drastic memory savings during program execution.

2. Support for serialization of mutable and cyclic data structures. The serialization library preserves sharing of mutable data (e.g., ML references) and distinguishes between non-shared mutable data. This feature broadens the applicability of a serialization combinator library to allow for serialization of anything but functional values, which is a significant improvement over Kennedy's solution.

3. Justification of the approach through practice. We demonstrate that the approach works for serializing large symbol tables (which contains cyclic mutable data) in the MLKit, a cross-module optimizing compiler for the programming language Standard ML.

48

Although a combinator library approach to serialization may appear more troublesome to use from an application programmer's point of view, it may easily be augmented with a tool for applying the serialization combinators, given a datatype description. Moreover, in languages with richer type systems than in ML, generic programming [JJ97] may be used to relieve the application programmer from writing excessive boiler-plate code.

For efficiency our approach make extensive use of hashing for recognising sharing and cycles in objects. In comparison with built-in serializers, the combinator for serializing ML references cannot make use of the actual pointer to the ML reference (indeed, a garbage collection could change the pointer during serialization). Thus, the best possible solution for the library to compute a hash for an ML reference is to compute the hash value of the content of the reference. Unfortunately, this solution does not give distinct hash values to two distinct ML references containing identical values, which leads to serialization algorithms with a worst case quadratic time complexity. We identify a partial solution to this problem, which requires the programmer to identify if an ML reference appears linearly (i.e., only once) in the serialized data, in which case, the programmer may use an efficient refLin combinator.

In Section 4.2, we present the serialization library interface and show some example uses of the library combinators. In Section 4.3, we describe the implementation of the combinator library. In particular, we describe the use of hashing and an implementation of type dynamic in ML to support sharing and cycles in deserialized values, efficiently. In Section 4.4, we describe the performance benefits of using the linear-reference combinator when serializing symbol table information in the MLKit. Related work is described in Section 4.5. Finally, in Section 4.6, we conclude and describe possible future work.

4.2 THE SERIALIZATION LIBRARY

The interface to the serialization library is given in Standard ML as a structure P with the signature PICKLE presented in Figure 4.1.

The serialization interface is based on an abstract type 'a pu. Given a value of type τ pu, for some type τ, it is possible to serialize values of type τ into a stream of characters, using the function pickle. Similarly, the function unpickle allows for deserializing a serialized value.

The interface provides a series of *base combinators*, for serializing values such as integers, words, and strings. The interface also provides a series of *constructive combinators*, for constructing serializers for pairs, triples, lists, and general datatypes. For example, it is possible to construct a serializer for lists of integer pairs:

```
val pu_ips:(int*int)list P.pu = P.list(P.pair(P.int,P.int))
val s:string = P.pickle pu_ips [(2,3),(1,2),(2,3)]
```

Although the pair (2,3) appears twice in the serialized list, sharing is introduced by the serializer, which means that when the list is deserialized, the pairs (2,3)

49

```
signature PICKLE = sig

(* abstract pickle/unpickle type *)
type 'a pu
val pickle   : 'a pu -> 'a -> string
val unpickle : 'a pu -> string -> 'a

(* type safe combinators *)
val word   : word pu
val int    : int pu
val string : string pu
val pair   : 'a pu * 'b pu -> ('a*'b) pu
val triple : 'a pu * 'b pu * 'c pu -> ('a*'b*'c) pu
val list   : 'a pu -> 'a list pu
val refCyc : 'a -> 'a pu -> 'a ref pu

(* unsafe combinators *)
val ref0   : 'a pu -> 'a ref pu
val refLin : 'a pu -> 'a ref pu
val data   : ('a->int) * ('a pu->'a pu) list -> 'a pu
val data2  : ('a->int) * ('a pu*'b pu->'a pu) list
           * ('b->int) * ('a pu*'b pu->'b pu) list
           -> 'a pu * 'b pu
val con0   : 'a -> 'b -> 'a pu
val con1   : ('a->'b) -> ('b->'a) -> 'a pu -> 'b pu
val conv   : ('a->'b) * ('b->'a) -> 'a pu -> 'b pu
end
```

FIGURE 4.1.   The PICKLE signature.

in the list share the same representation.

The first part of the serialization combinators are truly type safe in the sense that, with this subset, deserialization results in a value equivalent to the value being serialized. The combinator conv makes it possible to construct serializers for Standard ML records, quadruples, and other datatypes that are easily converted into an already serializable type.

4.2.1 Datatypes

For constructing serializers for datatypes, the combinator data may be used, but only for datatypes that are not mutually recursive with other datatypes. The combinator data2 makes it possible to construct serializers for two mutually recursive datatypes.

Given a datatype t with value constructors $C_0 \cdots C_{n-1}$, a serializer (of type t pu) may be constructed by passing to the data combinator, (1) a function mapping a value constructed using C_i to the integer i and (2) a list of functions $[f_0, \cdots, f_{n-1}]$, where each function f_i is a serializer for the datatype for the constructor C_i, parametrized over a serializer to use for recursive instances of t. As an example, consider the following datatype:

```
datatype T = L | N of T * int * T
```

To construct a serializer for the datatype T, the data combinator can be applied, together with the utility functions con0 and con1:

```
val pu_T : T P.pu = P.data (fn L => 0 | N _ => 1,
  [fn pu=>P.con0 L pu,
   fn pu=>P.con1 N (fn N a=>a) (P.triple(pu,P.int,pu))])
```

Consider the value declaration

```
val t = N(N(L,2,L),1,N(N(L,2,L),3,L))
```

The value bound to t is commonly represented in memory as shown in Figure 4.2(a). Serializing the value and deserializing it again results in a value that shares the common value N(L,2,L), as pictured in Figure 4.2(b):

```
val t' = (P.unpickle pu_T o P.pickle pu_T) t
```

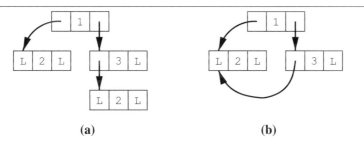

(a)   (b)

FIGURE 4.2. Representation of a tree value (a) without sharing and (b) with sharing.

4.2.2 References

In Standard ML, cyclic data can be constructed, only by use of references (not considering recursive closures). The combinator ref0 assumes that the reference—when serialized—does not contribute to a cycle in the value. On the other hand, the combinator RefCyc takes as its first argument a dummy value for the type of the reference content, which allows the deserializer to reintroduce cycles appearing in the original value. The final combinator for constructing serializers for references is the refLin combinator, which assumes that for each of the reference values, there is only ever one pointer to the reference. As we shall see in Section 4.4, this combinator is important for efficiently serializing large values containing distinct references pointing at identical data (i.e., boolean references).

51

4.3 IMPLEMENTATION

Before we present the implementation of the serialization library, we first present a module `Dyn` for embedding values of arbitrary type into a type `dyn` (type dynamic) and a stream module for implementing input and output streams. The signature DYN for the structure `Dyn` is as follows:

```
signature DYN = sig
  type dyn
  val new  : ('a*'a->bool) -> ('a->word)
           -> ('a->dyn) * (dyn->'a)
  val eq   : dyn * dyn -> bool
  val hash : dyn -> word
end
```

Here is an implementation of this module, based on Filinski's implementation of type dynamic [Fil96, page 106], but extended to provide a hash function and an equality function on values of type `dyn`:

```
structure Dyn :> DYN = struct
  datatype method = RESET | EQ | SET | HASH
  type dyn = method -> word
  fun new eq h =
   let val r = ref NONE
   in ( fn x => fn HASH => h x
                 | RESET => (r := NONE; 0w0)
                 | SET => (r := SOME x; 0w0)
                 | EQ => (case !r of NONE => 0w0
                                   | SOME y =>
                         if eq(x,y) then 0w1
                         else 0w0)
        , fn f => ( r:=NONE ; f SET ; valOf(!r) )
        )
   end
  fun eq (f1,f2) = ( f2 RESET ; f1 SET ; f2 EQ = 0w1 )
  fun hash f = f HASH
end
```

The stream module S has the following signature:

```
signature STREAM = sig
  type 'kind stream
  type IN and OUT   (* kinds *)
  type loc = word
  val getLoc   : 'k stream -> loc
  val outw     : word * OUT stream -> OUT stream
  val getw     : IN stream -> word * IN stream
  val toString : OUT stream -> string
  val openOut  : unit -> OUT stream
  val openIn   : string -> IN stream
end
```

A stream is either an input stream of kind IN or an output stream of kind OUT. The function getLoc makes it possible to extract the location of a stream as a word. For output streams there is a function for writing words, outw, which compresses word values by assuming that smaller word values are written more often than larger ones. Dually, there is a function getw for reading compressed word values.

The final non-standard library used by the implementation is a hash table library. In the following, we assume a structure H matching a simplified version of the signature POLYHASH from the SML/NJ Library:

```
signature POLYHASH = sig
  type ('key, 'data) ht
  val mkTable : ('k->int) * ('k*'k->bool) -> int*exn
                -> ('k,'d) ht
  val insert : ('k,'d) ht -> 'k*'d -> unit
  val peek : ('k,'d) ht -> 'k -> 'd option
end
```

4.3.1 Representing Serializers

The abstract type 'a pu is defined by the following type declarations:

```
type pe = (Dyn.dyn, S.loc) H.ht
type upe = (S.loc, Dyn.dyn) H.ht
type instream = S.IN S.stream * upe
type outstream = S.OUT S.stream * pe
type 'a pu = {pickler   : 'a -> outstream -> outstream,
              unpickler : instream -> 'a*instream,
              hasher    : 'a -> word*int -> word*int,
              eq        : 'a*'a -> bool}
```

A *pickler environment* (of type pe) is a hash table mapping values of type Dyn.dyn to stream locations. Moreover, an *unpickler environment* (of type upe) is a hash table mapping stream locations to values of type Dyn.dyn. A value of type outstream is a pair of an output stream and a pickler environment. Similarly, a value of type instream is a pair of an input stream and an unpickler environment.

Given a type τ, a value of type τ pu is a record containing a pickler for values of type τ, an unpickler for values of type τ, a hash function for values of type τ, and an equality function for values of type τ.

From a value pu of type τ pu, for some type τ, it is straightforward to implement the functions pickle and unpickle as specified in the PICKLE signature, by composing functionality in the stream structure S with the pickler and unpickler fields in the value pu.

4.3.2 Serializers for Base Types

For constructing serializers, we shall make use of a small module Hash for constructing hash functions for serializable values:

```
structure Hash = struct
  val maxDepth = 50
  fun add w (a,d) = (w + a * 0w19, d - 1)
  fun maybeStop f (a,d) = if d <= 0 then (a,d) else f (a,d)
end
```

To ensure termination of hash functions in case of cycles and to avoid that values are traversed fully, the combinators count the number of hash operations performed by the hash functions.

We can now show how serializers are constructed for base types, exemplified by a serializer for word values:

```
val word : word pu =
  {pickler = fn w => fn (s,pe) => (S.outw(w,s),pe),
   unpickler = fn(s,upe) => let val (w,s) = S.getw s
                            in (w,(s,upe))
                            end,
   hasher = Hash.add,
   eq = op =}
```

4.3.3 Product Types

For constructing a pair serializer, the pair combinator takes as argument a serializer for each of the components of the pair:

```
fun pair (pu1 : 'a pu, pu2 : 'b pu) : ('a * 'b) pu =
  {pickler = fn (v1,v2) =>
                 #pickler pu2 v2 o #pickler pu1 v1,
   unpickler = fn s => let val (v1,s) = #unpickler pu1 s
                           val (v2,s) = #unpickler pu2 s
                       in ((v1,v2),s)
                       end,
   hasher = fn (v1,v2) => Hash.maybeStop
     (#hasher pu2 v2 o #hasher pu1 v1),
   eq = fn ((a1,a2),(b1,b2)) =>
     #eq pu1 (a1,b1) andalso #eq pu2 (a2,b2)}
```

Notice the use of the Hash.maybeStop combinator, which returns the hash result when the hash counter has reached zero.

Combinators for serializing triples and quadruples are easily constructed using the conv and pair combinators.

4.3.4 A Sharing Combinator

We shall now see how it is possible to make explicit use of stream locations and environment information to construct a combinator share that leads to sharing of serialized and deserialized data.

The share combinator, which is listed in Figure 4.3, takes any serializer as argument and generates a serializer of the same type as the argument.

54

```
fun share (pu:'a pu) : 'a pu =
  let val REF = 0w0 and DEF = 0w1
      val (toDyn,fromDyn) = Dyn.new (#eq pu)
        (fn v => #1 (#hasher pu v (0w0,Hash.maxDepth)))
  in {pickler = fn v => fn (s,pe) =>
      let val d = toDyn v
      in case H.peek pe d of
          SOME loc => (S.outw(loc,S.outw(REF,s)),pe)
        | NONE => let val s = S.outw(DEF,s)
                      val loc = S.getLoc s
                      val res = #pickler pu v (s,pe)
                  in case H.peek pe d of SOME _ => res
                      | NONE => (H.insert pe (d,loc); res)
                  end
      end,
      unpickler = fn (s,upe) =>
      let val (tag,s) = S.getw s
      in if tag = REF then
          let val (loc,s) = S.getw s
          in case H.peek upe loc of
              SOME d => (fromDyn d, (s,upe))
            | NONE => raise Fail "impossible:share"
          end
        else (* tag = DEF *)
          let val loc = S.getLoc s
              val (v,(s,upe)) = #unpickler pu (s,upe)
          in H.insert upe (loc,toDyn v); (v,(s,upe))
          end
      end,
      hasher = fn v => Hash.maybeStop (#hasher pu v),
      eq = #eq pu}
  end
```

FIGURE 4.3.   The share combinator.

For serializing a value, it is first checked if some identical value is associated
with a location l in the pickle environment. In this case, a REF-tag is written to
the outstream together with a reference to the location l. If there is no value in the
pickle environment identical to the value to be serialized, a DEF-tag is written to
the output stream, the current location l of the output stream is recorded, the value
is serialized, and an entry is added to the pickle environment mapping the value
into the location l. In this way, future serialized values identical to the serialized
value can share representation with the serialized value in the outstream.

Dually, for deserializing a value, first the tag (i.e., REF or DEF) is read from
the input stream. If the tag is a REF-tag, a location l is read and used for looking
up the resulting value in the unpickler environment. If, on the other hand, the tag is
a DEF-tag, the location l of the input stream is recorded, a value v is deserialized
with the argument deserializer, and finally, an entry is added to the unpickler

environment mapping the location l into the value v, which is also the result of the deserialization.

One important point to notice here is that efficient inhomogeneous environments, mapping values of different types into locations, are possible only through the use of the `Dyn` library, which supports a hash function on values of type `dyn` and an equality function on values of type `dyn`.[2]

4.3.5 References and Cycles

To construct a serialization combinator for references, a number of challenges must be overcome. First, for any two reference values contained in some value, it can be observed (either by equality or by trivial assignment) whether or not the two reference values denote the same reference value. It is crucial that such reference invariants are not violated by serialization and deserialization. Second, for data structures that do not contain recursive closures, all cycles go through a `ref` constructor. Thus in general, to ensure termination of constructed serializers, it is necessary (and sufficient) to recognize cycles that go through `ref` constructors. The pickle environment introduced earlier is used for this purpose. Third, once a cyclic value has been serialized, it is crucial that when the value is deserialized again, the cycle in the new constructed value is reestablished.

The general serialization combinator for references is shown in Figure 4.4. The dummy value given as argument to the `refCyc` combinator is used for the purpose of "tying the knot" when a serialized value is deserialized. The first time a reference value is serialized, a DEF-tag is written to the current location l of the outstream. Thereafter, the pickle environment is extended to associate the reference value with the location l. Then the argument to the reference constructor is serialized. On the other hand, if it is recognized that the reference value has been serialized earlier by finding an entry in the pickle environment mapping the reference value to a stream location l, a REF-tag is written to the outstream, followed by the location l.

For deserializing a reference value, first the location l of the input stream is obtained. Second, a reference value r is created with the argument being the dummy value that was given as argument to the `refCyc` combinator. Then the unpickle environment is extended to map the location l to the reference value r. Thereafter, a value is deserialized, which is then assigned to the reference value r. This assignment establishes the cycle and the dummy value no longer appears in the deserialized value.

As mentioned in the introduction, it is difficult to find a better hash function for references than that of using the hash function for the reference argument.

---

[2]The straightforward implementation in Standard ML of type dynamic using exceptions can also be extended with a hash function and an equality function, which is done by defining the type `dyn` to have type `{v:exn, eq:exn*exn->bool, h:exn->word}`, where `v` is the actual value packed in a locally generated exception, `eq` is an equality function returning `true` only for identical values applied to the same exception constructor, and `h` is a hash function for the packed value.

```
fun refCyc (dummy:'a) (pu:'a pu) : 'a ref pu =
  let val REF = 0w0 and DEF = 0w1
      val (toDyn,fromDyn) = Dyn.new (op =)
        (fn ref v => #1 (#hasher pu v (0w0,Hash.maxDepth)))
  in {pickler =
      fn r as ref v => fn (s,pe) =>
        let val d = toDyn r
        in case H.peek pe d of
             SOME loc => (S.outw(loc,S.outw(REF,s)),pe)
           | NONE => let val s = S.outw(DEF,s)
                         val loc = S.getLoc s
                     in H.insert pe (d,loc)
                      ; #pickler pu v (s, pe)
                     end
        end,
     unpickler =
      fn (s,upe) =>
        let val (tag,s) = S.getw s
        in if tag = REF then
             let val (loc,s) = S.getw s
             in case H.peek upe loc of
                  SOME d => (fromDyn d, (s, upe))
                | NONE => raise Fail "impossible:ref"
             end
           else (* tag = DEF *)
             let val loc = S.getLoc s
                 val r = ref dummy
                 val _ = H.insert upe (loc,toDyn r)
                 val (v,(s,upe)) = #unpickler pu (s,upe)
             in r := v ; (r, (s,upe))
             end
        end,
     hasher = fn ref v => #hasher pu v,
     eq = op =}
  end
```

FIGURE 4.4.   Cycle supporting serializer for references.

Equality on references reduces to pointer equality.

The two other serialization combinators for references (i.e., ref0 and refLin) are implemented as special cases of the general reference combinator refCyc. The ref0 combinator assumes that no cycles appear through reference values serialized using this combinator. The refLin combinator assumes that the entire value being serialized contains only one pointer to each value being serialized using this combinator (which also does not allow cycles) and that the share combinator is used at a higher level in the type structure, but lower than a point where there can be multiple pointers to the value. With these assumptions, the refLin combinator avoids the problem mentioned earlier of filling up hash table buckets in the pickle environment with distinct values having the same hash value. In general, however, it is an unpleasant task for a programmer to establish the requirements of the `refLin` combinator.

4.3.6 Datatypes

It turns out to be difficult in Standard ML to construct a general serialization combinator that works for any number of mutually recursive datatypes. In this section, we describe the implementation of the serialization combinator `data` from Section 4.2.1, which can be used for constructing a serializer and a deserializer for a single recursive datatype. It is straightforward to extend this implementation to any particular number of mutually recursive datatypes. The implementation of the `data` serialization combinator is shown in Figure 4.5.

To allow for arbitrary sharing between parts of a data structure (of some datatype) and perhaps parts of another data structure (of the same datatype), the combinator makes use of the `share` combinator from Section 4.3.4. It is essential that the `share` combinator is not only applied to the resulting serialization combinator for the datatype, but that this sharing version of the combinator is the one that is used for recursive occurrences of the type being defined. Otherwise, it would not, for instance, be possible to obtain sharing between the tail of a list and some other list appearing in the value being serialized. Also, it would not be possible to support the sharing obtained with the tree value in Figure 4.2(b).

Thus, in the implementation, the four functions (the pickler, unpickler, equality function, and hash function) that make up the serializer are mutually recursive and a caching mechanism (the function `getPUP`) makes sure that the `share` combinator is applied only once.

4.4 EXPERIMENTS WITH THE MLKIT

We now present experiments with serializing symbol table information in the MLKit [TBE+01], a Standard ML compiler that allows arbitrary symbol table information to migrate across module boundaries at compile time [Els99].

Many of the compilation phases in the MLKit make use of the possibility of passing compilation information across compilation boundaries, thus symbol tables tend to be large. For instance, the region inference analysis in the MLKit [TT97] is a type-based analysis, which associates function identifiers with so called region type schemes, which provide information about in which regions function arguments and results are stored.

Table 4.4 presents measurements for serializing symbol tables for the Standard ML Basis Library. The table shows serialization times, deserialization times, and file sizes for three different serialization configurations. The measurements were run on a 2.80 GHz Intel Pentium 4 Linux box with 512Mb of RAM. The first configuration implements full sharing of values (i.e., with consistent use of the `share` combinator from Section 4.3.4.) The second configuration disables the special treatment of programmer specified linear references by using the more

```
fun data (toInt:'a->int, fs:('a pu->'a pu)list) : 'a pu =
  let val res : 'a pu option ref = ref NONE
      val ps : 'a pu vector option ref = ref NONE
      fun p v (s,pe) =
       let val i = toInt v
           val s = S.outw (Word.fromInt i, s)
       in #pickler(getPUPI i) v (s,pe)
       end
      and up (s,upe) =
       case S.getw s of (w,s) =>
         #unpickler(getPUPI (Word.toInt w)) (s,upe)
      and eq(a1:'a,a2:'a) : bool =
       let val n = toInt a1
       in n = toInt a2 andalso #eq (getPUPI n) (a1,a2)
       end
      and getPUP() =
       case !res of
         NONE => let val pup = share {pickler=p,hasher=h,
                                      unpickler=up,eq=eq}
                 in res := SOME pup
                  ; pup
                 end
       | SOME pup => pup
      and getPUPI (i:int) =
       case !ps of
         NONE => let val ps0 = map (fn f => f (getPUP())) fs
                     val psv = Vector.fromList ps0
                 in ps := SOME psv
                  ; Vector.sub(psv,i)
                 end
       | SOME psv => Vector.sub(psv,i)
      and h v =
       Hash.maybeStop (fn p =>
         let val i = toInt v
         in Hash.add (Word.fromInt i)
                     (#hasher (getPUPI i) v p)
         end)
  in getPUP()
  end
```

FIGURE 4.5.   Single datatype serialization combinator.

general `ref0` combinator instead of the `refLin` combinator. Finally, the third
configuration supports sharing only for references (which also avoids problems
with cycles). The third configuration entails unsoundness of the special treatment
of programmer specified linear references, which is therefore also disabled in this
configuration.

TABLE 4.1. Serialization time (S-time in seconds), deserialization time (D-time in seconds), and file sizes for serializing the compiler basis for the Standard ML Basis Library. Different rows in the table show measurements for different configurations of the serializer.

	S-time (s)	D-time (s)	Size (Mb)
Full sharing	14.2	4.0	1.88
No use of `refLin`	302	3.7	1.96
No sharing	297	3.4	4.10

4.5 RELATED WORK

There is a series of related work concerned with dynamic typing issues for distributed programming where values of dynamic type are transmitted over a network [ACPP91, Dug98, Dug99, LM93]. Recently, Leifer et al. have worked on ensuring that invariants on distributed abstract data types are not violated by checking the identity of operations on abstract datatypes [LPSW03].

The Zephyr Abstract Syntax Description Language (ASDL) project [WAKS97] aims at providing a language independent data exchange format by generating serialization code from generic datatype specifications. Whereas generated ASDL serialization code does not maintain sharing, it does avoid storing of redundant type information by employing a type specialized prefix encoding of tree values. The approach is in this respect similar to ours and to the Packed Encoding Rules (PER) of ASN.1 [Uni02].

Independently of the present work, Kennedy has developed a similar combinator library for serializing data structures [Ken04]. His combinator library is used in the SML.NET compiler [KRB03] for serializing type information to disk so as to support separate compilation. Contrary to our approach, Kennedy's `share` combinator requires the programmer to provide functionality for mapping values to integers, which in principle violates abstraction principles. Kennedy does not in his library make use of dynamic types, which are crucial for defining a proper sharing combinator. Also, Kennedy's `fix` combinators for constructing serializers for datatypes do not support sharing of subparts of datatypes, as our datatype combinators. Whereas our serialization technique supports proper serialization of all non-functional data, Kennedy's combinator library does not support serialization of mutable or cyclic data.

Also related to this work is work on garbage collection algorithms for introducing sharing to save space by the use of hash-consing [AG93].

4.6 CONCLUSION AND FUTURE WORK

We have presented an ML combinator library for serialization, which may introduce sharing in deserialized values even in cases where sharing was not present in the value that was serialized. The approach works with mutable and cyclic data, and is implemented entirely in ML itself through use of higher-order functions, references, and an implementation of dynamic types. The approach may relieve language designers and compiler writers from the technical details of built-in serializers and support programmers with a portable solution to serialization.

A possibility for future work is to investigate if it is possible to use a variant of multiset discrimination [Hen03] for eliminating the need for the linear reference combinator of Section 4.3.5. Other possibilities for future work includes an implementation of a tool for generating serializers for a given datatype, using the combinator library, or to make use of generic programming [JJ97] to avoid excessive boiler-plate code for serializing large datatypes.

ACKNOWLEDGMENTS

I would like to thank Henning Niss and Ken Friis Larsen for many interesting discussions about this work and the anonymous reviewers for their detailed comments and suggestions.

REFERENCES

[ACPP91] Martín Abadi, Luca Cardelli, Benjamin Pierce, and Gordon Plotkin. Dynamic typing in a statically typed language. *ACM Transactions on Programming Languages and Systems*, 13(2):237–268, April 1991.

[AG93] Andrew W. Appel and Marcelo J. R. Gonçalves. Hash-consing garbage collection. Technical Report CS-TR-412-93, Princeton University, February 1993.

[Dug98] Dominic Duggan. A type-based semantics for user-defined marshalling in polymorphic languages. In *Second International Workshop on Types in Compilation (TIC'98)*, March 1998.

[Dug99] Dominic Duggan. Dynamic typing for distributed programming in polymorphic languages. *Transactions on Programming Languages and Systems*, 21(1):11–45, January 1999.

[Els99] Martin Elsman. *Program Modules, Separate Compilation, and Intermodule Optimisation*. PhD thesis, Department of Computer Science, University of Copenhagen, January 1999.

[Fil96] Andrzej Filinski. *Controlling Effects*. PhD thesis, School of Computer Science, Carnegie Mellon University, Pittsburgh, Pennsylvania, USA, May 1996.

[Hen03] Fritz Henglein. Multiset discrimination. In preparation, September 2003. Available from http://www.plan-x.org/msd/.

[JJ97] P. Jansson and J. Jeuring. PolyP—a polytypic programming language extension. In *Symposium on Principles of Programming Languages (POPL'97)*, pages 470–482. ACM Press, 1997.

[Ken04] Andrew J. Kennedy. Pickler combinators. *Journal of Functional Programming*, 14(6):727–739, November 2004. Functional Pearl.

[KRB03]   Andrew Kennedy, Claudio Russo, and Nick Benton. *SML.NET 1.1 User Guide*, November 2003. Microsoft Research Ltd. Cambridge, UK.

[LM93]   Xavier Leroy and Michel Mauny. Dynamics in ML. *Journal of Functional Programming*, 3(4), 1993.

[LPSW03]   James Leifer, Gilles Peskine, Peter Sewell, and Keith Wansbrough. Global abstraction-safe marshalling with hash types. In *International Conference on Functional Programming (ICFP'03)*, August 2003.

[TBE⁺01]   Mads Tofte, Lars Birkedal, Martin Elsman, Niels Hallenberg, Tommy Højfeld Olesen, and Peter Sestoft. Programming with regions in the ML Kit (for version 4). Technical Report TR-2001-07, IT University of Copenhagen, October 2001.

[TT97]   Mads Tofte and Jean-Pierre Talpin. Region-based memory management. *Information and Computation*, 132(2):109–176, 1997.

[Uni02]   International Telecommunication Union. ASN.1 encoding rules: Specification of Packed Encoding Rules (PER). Information Technology. SERIES-X: Data Networks and Open Systems Communications. X.691, July 2002.

[WAKS97]   Daniel C. Wang, Andrew W. Appel, Jeff L. Korn, and Christopher S. Serra. The Zephyr abstract syntax description language. In *USENIX Conference on Domain-Specific Languages*, October 1997.

Chapter 5

Logical Relations for Call-by-value Delimited Continuations

Kenichi Asai[1]

Abstract: Logical relations, defined inductively on the structure of types, provide a powerful tool to characterize higher-order functions. They often enable us to prove correctness of a program transformer written with higher-order functions concisely. This paper demonstrates that the technique of logical relations can be used to characterize call-by-value functions as well as delimited continuations. Based on the traditional logical relations for call-by-name functions, logical relations for call-by-value functions are first defined, whose CPS variant is used to prove the correctness of an offline specializer for the call-by-value λ-calculus. They are then modified to cope with delimited continuations and are used to establish the correctness of an offline specializer for the call-by-value λ-calculus with delimited continuation constructs, shift and reset. This is the first correctness proof for such a specializer. Along the development, correctness of the continuation-based and shift/reset-based let-insertion and A-normalization is established.

5.1 INTRODUCTION

Whenever we build a program transformer, be it a compiler, an optimizer, or a specializer, we need to establish its correctness. We have to show that the semantics of a program does not change before and after the transformation. As a program transformer gets sophisticated, however, it becomes harder to prove its correctness. In particular, the non-trivial use of higher-order functions in the transformer makes the correctness proof particularly difficult. A simple structural

[1]Ochanomizu University, 2-1-1 Otsuka, Bunkyo-ku, Tokyo 112-8610, Japan; Email: asai@is.ocha.ac.jp

induction on the input program does not usually work, because we can not easily characterize their behavior.

The technique of logical relations [16] is one of the proof methods that is often used in such a case. With the help of types, it enables us to define a set of relations that captures necessary properties of higher-order functions. Notably, Wand [20] used this technique to prove correctness of an offline specializer [14] in which higher-order functions rather than closures were used for the representation of abstractions. However, the logical relations used by Wand were for call-by-name functions. They were used to prove the correctness of a specializer for the call-by-name λ-calculus, but are not directly applicable to the call-by-value languages.

In this paper, we demonstrate that the technique of logical relations can be used to characterize call-by-value functions as well as delimited continuations. We first modify Wand's logical relations so that we can use them for call-by-value functions. We then prove the correctness of an offline specializer for the call-by-value λ-calculus. It is written in continuation-passing style (CPS) and uses the continuation-based let-insertion to avoid computation elimination/duplication.

It is well-known that by using delimited continuation constructs, *shift* and *reset*, introduced by Danvy and Filinski [7], it is possible to implement the let-insertion in direct style [18]. We demonstrate that the correctness of this direct-style specializer with the shift/reset-based let-insertion can be also established by properly characterizing delimited continuations in logical relations.

Then, the specializer is extended to cope with shift and reset in the source language. To this end, the specialization-time delimited continuations are used to implement the delimited continuations in the source language. To characterize such delimited continuations, we define logical relations based on Danvy and Filinski's type system [6]. Thanks to the explicit reference to the types of continuations and the final result, we can establish the correctness of the specializer. This is the first correctness proof for the offline specializer for the call-by-value λ-calculus with shift and reset. The present author previously showed the correctness of a similar offline specializer [3], but it produced the result of specialization in CPS.

The contributions of this paper are summarized as follows:

- We show that the technique of logical relations can be used to characterize call-by-value functions as well as delimited continuations.

- We show for the first time the correctness of the offline specializer for the call-by-value λ-calculus with shift and reset.

- Along the development, we establish the correctness of the continuation-based let-insertion, the shift/reset-based let-insertion, the continuation-based A-normalization [13], and the shift/reset-based A-normalization.

The paper is organized as follows. After showing preliminaries in Section 5.2, the call-by-name specializer and its correctness proof by Wand are reviewed in Section 5.3. We then show the logical relations for call-by-value functions in

64

Section 5.4, and use (a CPS variant of) them to prove the correctness of a specializer for the call-by-value λ-calculus in Section 5.5. In Section 5.6, we transform the specializer into direct style and prove its correctness. Then, we further extend the specializer to cope with shift and reset. We show an interpreter and an A-normalizer in Section 5.7, a specializer in Section 5.8, a type system in Section 5.9, and logical relations with which the correctness is established in Section 5.10. Related work is in Section 5.11 and the paper concludes in Section 5.12. A complete proof of correctness of the offline specializer for shift and reset is found in the technical report [4].

ACKNOWLEDGMENTS

Most of the work has been done while the author was visiting Northeastern University. Special thanks to Mitch Wand for hosting my stay as well as support and encouragements. The use of de Bruijn levels to avoid the name generation problem was suggested by Olivier Danvy.

5.2 PRELIMINARIES

The metalanguage we use is a left-to-right λ-calculus extended with shift and reset as well as datatype constructors. The syntax is given as follows:

$$
\begin{aligned}
M, K \quad = \quad & x \mid \lambda x.M \mid MM \mid \xi k.M \mid \langle M \rangle \mid n \mid M+1 \mid \\
& \mathrm{Var}(n) \mid \mathrm{Lam}(n,M) \mid \mathrm{App}(M,M) \mid \mathrm{Shift}(n,M) \mid \mathrm{Reset}(M) \mid \\
& \overline{\mathrm{Lam}}(n,M) \mid \overline{\mathrm{App}}(M,M) \mid \overline{\mathrm{Shift}}(n,M) \mid \overline{\mathrm{Reset}}(M) \mid \\
& \underline{\mathrm{Lam}}(n,M) \mid \underline{\mathrm{App}}(M,M) \mid \underline{\mathrm{Shift}}(n,M) \mid \underline{\mathrm{Reset}}(M)
\end{aligned}
$$

$\xi k.M$ and $\langle M \rangle$ represent shift and reset, respectively, and appear only later in the paper. Datatype constructors are for representing the input and output terms to our specializer. In this baselanguage, an integer n is used to represent a variable. For this purpose, the language contains an integer and an add-one operation. As usual, we use overline and underline to indicate static and dynamic terms, respectively. We assume that all the datatype constructors are strict. Among the metalanguage, a value (ranged over by a metavariable V) is either a variable, an abstraction, an integer, or one of constructors whose arguments are values.

When a specializer produces its output, it needs to generate fresh variables. To make the presentation simple, we use so-called the de Bruijn levels [9] (not indices). Define the following five strict operators:

$$
\begin{aligned}
\mathrm{var}(m) \quad &= \quad \lambda n.\mathrm{Var}(m) \\
\mathrm{lam}(f) \quad &= \quad \lambda n.\mathrm{Lam}(n, f(n+1)) \\
\mathrm{app}(f_1, f_2) \quad &= \quad \lambda n.\mathrm{App}(f_1\, n, f_2\, n) \\
\mathrm{shift}(f) \quad &= \quad \lambda n.\mathrm{Shift}(n, f(n+1)) \\
\mathrm{reset}(f) \quad &= \quad \lambda n.\mathrm{Reset}(f\, n)
\end{aligned}
$$

They are used to represent a term parameterized with a variable name. Given a term M in the de Bruijn level notation, we define the operation $\downarrow_n M$ of obtaining a concrete term as: $\downarrow_n M = M\,n$. Thus, we have:

$$\downarrow_3 (\mathrm{app}(\mathrm{lam}(\lambda x.\,\mathrm{lam}(\lambda y.\,\mathrm{var}(x))),\mathrm{lam}(\lambda y.\,\mathrm{var}(y))))$$
$$= \ \mathrm{App}(\mathrm{Lam}(3,\mathrm{Lam}(4,\mathrm{Var}(3))),\mathrm{Lam}(3,\mathrm{Var}(3)))\ .$$

Since we can freely transform a term with de Bruijn levels into the one without, we will use the former as the output of specializers.

Throughout this paper, we use three kinds of equalities between terms in the metalanguage: $=$ for definition or α-equality, $\sim_n$ for β-equality under call-by-name semantics, and $\sim_v$ for β-equality under call-by-value semantics. The call-by-value β-equality in the presence of shift and reset is defined by Kameyama and Hasegawa [15, Fig. 2].

5.3 SPECIALIZER FOR CALL-BY-NAME λ-CALCULUS

In this section, we review the specializer for the call-by-name λ-calculus and its correctness proof using the technique of logical relations presented by Wand [20].

A specializer reduces expressions that are known (or *static*) at specialization time and leaves unknown (or *dynamic*) expressions intact. Thus, it consists of two parts: an interpreter for static expressions and a residualizer for dynamic expressions. An interpreter for the input language is defined as follows:

$$
\begin{aligned}
I_1\,[\![\mathrm{Var}(n)]\!]\,\rho &= \ \rho\,(n) \\
I_1\,[\![\mathrm{Lam}(n,M)]\!]\,\rho &= \ \lambda x.\,I_1\,[\![M]\!]\,\rho[x/n] \\
I_1\,[\![\mathrm{App}(M_1,M_2)]\!]\,\rho &= \ (I_1\,[\![M_1]\!]\,\rho)\,(I_1\,[\![M_2]\!]\,\rho)
\end{aligned}
$$

where $\rho[x/n]$ is the same environment as ρ except that $\rho\,(n) = x$.

The residualizer is almost the identity function except for the use of de Bruijn levels to avoid name clashes:

$$
\begin{aligned}
\mathcal{D}_1\,[\![\mathrm{Var}(n)]\!]\,\rho &= \ \rho\,(n) \\
\mathcal{D}_1\,[\![\mathrm{Lam}(n,M)]\!]\,\rho &= \ \mathrm{lam}(\lambda x.\,\mathcal{D}_1\,[\![M]\!]\,\rho[\mathrm{var}(x)/n]) \\
\mathcal{D}_1\,[\![\mathrm{App}(M_1,M_2)]\!]\,\rho &= \ \mathrm{app}(\mathcal{D}_1\,[\![M_1]\!]\,\rho, \mathcal{D}_1\,[\![M_2]\!]\,\rho)
\end{aligned}
$$

An offline specializer is given by putting the interpreter and the residualizer together:

$$
\begin{aligned}
\mathcal{P}_1\,[\![\mathrm{Var}(n)]\!]\,\rho &= \ \rho\,(n) \\
\mathcal{P}_1\,[\![\overline{\mathrm{Lam}}(n,W)]\!]\,\rho &= \ \lambda x.\,\mathcal{P}_1\,[\![W]\!]\,\rho[x/n] \\
\mathcal{P}_1\,[\![\underline{\mathrm{Lam}}(n,W)]\!]\,\rho &= \ \mathrm{lam}(\lambda x.\,\mathcal{P}_1\,[\![W]\!]\,\rho[\mathrm{var}(x)/n]) \\
\mathcal{P}_1\,[\![\overline{\mathrm{App}}(W_1,W_2)]\!]\,\rho &= \ (\mathcal{P}_1\,[\![W_1]\!]\,\rho)\,(\mathcal{P}_1\,[\![W_2]\!]\,\rho) \\
\mathcal{P}_1\,[\![\underline{\mathrm{App}}(W_1,W_2)]\!]\,\rho &= \ \mathrm{app}(\mathcal{P}_1\,[\![W_1]\!]\,\rho, \mathcal{P}_1\,[\![W_2]\!]\,\rho)
\end{aligned}
$$

The specializer goes wrong if the input term is not well-annotated. Well-annotatedness of a term is specified as a binding-time analysis that, given an unannotated term, produces a well-annotated term. Here, we show a type-based binding-time analysis. Define binding-time types of expressions as follows:

$$\tau \ = \ d\mid\tau\to\tau$$

An expression of type d denotes that the expression is dynamic, while an expression of type $\tau \to \tau$ shows that it is a static function. We use a judgment of the form $A \vdash M : \tau$ $[W]$, which reads: under a type environment A, a term M has a binding-time type τ and is annotated as W. The binding-time analysis is defined by the following typing rules:

$$A[n : \tau] \vdash \mathrm{Var}(n) : \tau \; [\mathrm{Var}(n)]$$

$$\frac{A[n : \sigma] \vdash M : \tau \; [W]}{A \vdash \mathrm{Lam}(n, M) : \sigma \to \tau \; [\overline{\mathrm{Lam}}(n, W)]} \qquad \frac{A \vdash M_1 : \sigma \to \tau \; [W_1] \quad A \vdash M_2 : \sigma \; [W_2]}{A \vdash \mathrm{App}(M_1, M_2) : \tau \; [\overline{\mathrm{App}}(W_1, W_2)]}$$

$$\frac{A[n : d] \vdash M : d \; [W]}{A \vdash \mathrm{Lam}(n, M) : d \; [\underline{\mathrm{Lam}}(n, W)]} \qquad \frac{A \vdash M_1 : d \; [W_1] \quad A \vdash M_2 : d \; [W_2]}{A \vdash \mathrm{App}(M_1, M_2) : d \; [\underline{\mathrm{App}}(W_1, W_2)]}$$

To show the correctness of the specializer, Wand [20] uses the technique of logical relations. Define logical relations between terms in the metalanguage by induction on the structure of binding-time types as follows:

$$(M, M') \in R_d \iff I_1 \llbracket \downarrow_n M \rrbracket \rho_{id} \sim_n M' \text{ for any large } n \text{ (defined below)}$$
$$(M, M') \in R_{\sigma \to \tau} \iff \forall (N, N') \in R_\sigma. \, (MN, M'N') \in R_\tau$$

where $\rho_{id}(n) = z_n$ for all n. It relates free variables in the base- and metalanguage. Since the logical relations are defined on open terms, we need to relate free variables in the base- and metalanguage in some way. We choose here to relate a baselanguage variable $\mathrm{Var}(n)$ to a metalanguage variable z_n.

In the definition of R_d, M is a metalanguage term in the de Bruijn level notation that is either a value representing a baselanguage term or a term that is equal to (or evaluates to) a value representing a baselanguage term in the underlying semantics of the metalanguage (in this section, call-by-name).

The choice of n in R_d needs a special attention. Since M is possibly an open term, n has to be chosen so that it does not capture free variables in M. We ensure this property by the side condition "for any large n." n is defined to be large if n is greater than any free variables in the baselanguage term M.

For environments ρ and ρ', we say $(\rho, \rho') \models A$ iff $(\rho(n), \rho'(n)) \in R_{A(n)}$ for all $n \in dom(A)$, where $dom(A)$ is the domain of A. Then, we can show the following theorem by structural induction over types:

Theorem 5.1 (Wand [20]). *If $A \vdash M : \tau$ $[W]$ and $(\rho, \rho') \models A$, then $(\mathcal{P}_1 \llbracket W \rrbracket \rho, I_1 \llbracket M \rrbracket \rho') \in R_\tau$.*

By instantiating it to an empty environment ρ_ϕ, we obtain the following corollary, which establishes the correctness of specialization.

Corollary 5.2 (Wand [20]). *If $\vdash M : d$ $[W]$, then $I_1 \llbracket \downarrow_0 (\mathcal{P}_1 \llbracket W \rrbracket \rho_\phi) \rrbracket \rho_{id} \sim_n I_1 \llbracket M \rrbracket \rho_\phi$.*

5.4 LOGICAL RELATIONS FOR CALL-BY-VALUE λ-CALCULUS

Define logical relations for the call-by-value λ-calculus as follows:

$$(M, M') \in R_d \iff I_1 \left[\!\left[\downarrow_n M\right]\!\right] \rho_{id} \sim_v M' \text{ for any large } n$$
$$(M, M') \in R_{\sigma \to \tau} \iff \forall (V, V') \in R_\sigma. (MV, M'V') \in R_\tau$$

There are two differences from the logical relations in the previous section. First, call-by-value equality $\sim_v$ is used instead of call-by-name equality $\sim_n$ in the definition of R_d. Secondly, M and M' are allowed to be in $R_{\sigma \to \tau}$ if they transform only related *values* (rather than arbitrary terms) into related terms.

If we could prove Theorem 5.1 with this definition of R_τ, we would have obtained as a corollary the correctness of the specializer in the call-by-value semantics. However, the proof fails for static applications. In fact, the specializer is not correct under the call-by-value semantics.

5.5 SPECIALIZER IN CPS

The correctness under the call-by-value semantics does not hold for the specializer in Section 5.3 because it may discard a non-terminating computation. The standard method to recover the correctness is to perform *let-insertion* [5]. Since let-insertion requires explicit manipulation of continuations, we first rewrite our specializer into CPS as follows:

$$
\begin{aligned}
\mathcal{P}_2 \left[\!\left[\mathrm{Var}(n)\right]\!\right] \rho \kappa &= \kappa(\rho(n)) \\
\mathcal{P}_2 \left[\!\left[\overline{\mathrm{Lam}}(n, W)\right]\!\right] \rho \kappa &= \kappa(\lambda x. \lambda k. \mathcal{P}_2 \left[\!\left[W\right]\!\right] \rho[x/n] k) \\
\mathcal{P}_2 \left[\!\left[\underline{\mathrm{Lam}}(n, W)\right]\!\right] \rho \kappa &= \kappa(\mathrm{lam}(\lambda x. \mathcal{P}_2 \left[\!\left[W\right]\!\right] \rho[\mathrm{var}(x)/n] \lambda x. x)) \\
\mathcal{P}_2 \left[\!\left[\overline{\mathrm{App}}(W_1, W_2)\right]\!\right] \rho \kappa &= \mathcal{P}_2 \left[\!\left[W_1\right]\!\right] \rho \lambda m. \mathcal{P}_2 \left[\!\left[W_2\right]\!\right] \rho \lambda n. m n \kappa \\
\mathcal{P}_2 \left[\!\left[\underline{\mathrm{App}}(W_1, W_2)\right]\!\right] \rho \kappa &= \mathcal{P}_2 \left[\!\left[W_1\right]\!\right] \rho \lambda m. \mathcal{P}_2 \left[\!\left[W_2\right]\!\right] \rho \lambda n. \kappa(\mathrm{app}(m, n))
\end{aligned}
$$

We then replace the last rule with the following:

$$
\mathcal{P}_2 \left[\!\left[\underline{\mathrm{App}}(W_1, W_2)\right]\!\right] \rho \kappa = \mathcal{P}_2 \left[\!\left[W_1\right]\!\right] \rho \lambda m. \mathcal{P}_2 \left[\!\left[W_2\right]\!\right] \rho \lambda n. \\
\mathrm{let}(\mathrm{app}(m, n), \mathrm{lam}(\lambda t. \kappa(\mathrm{var}(t))))
$$

where $\mathrm{let}(M_1, \mathrm{lam}(\lambda t. M_2))$ is an abbreviation for $\mathrm{app}(\mathrm{lam}(\lambda t. M_2), M_1)$. Whenever an application is residualized, we insert a let-expression to residualize it exactly once with a unique name t, and continue the rest of the specialization with this name. Since the residualized application is not passed to the continuation κ, it will never be discarded even if κ discards its argument.

The let-insertion technique can be regarded as performing A-normalization [13] on the fly during specialization. If we extract the rules for variables, dynamic abstractions, and dynamic applications from $\mathcal{P}_2$, we obtain the following one-pass A-normalizer written in CPS [13]:

$$
\begin{aligned}
\mathcal{A}_1 \left[\!\left[\mathrm{Var}(n)\right]\!\right] \rho \kappa &= \kappa(\rho(n)) \\
\mathcal{A}_1 \left[\!\left[\mathrm{Lam}(n, M)\right]\!\right] \rho \kappa &= \kappa(\mathrm{lam}(\lambda x. \mathcal{A}_1 \left[\!\left[M\right]\!\right] \rho[\mathrm{var}(x)/n] \lambda x. x)) \\
\mathcal{A}_1 \left[\!\left[\mathrm{App}(M_1, M_2)\right]\!\right] \rho \kappa &= \mathcal{A}_1 \left[\!\left[M_1\right]\!\right] \rho \lambda m. \mathcal{A}_1 \left[\!\left[M_2\right]\!\right] \rho \lambda n. \\
& \qquad \mathrm{let}(\mathrm{app}(m, n), \mathrm{lam}(\lambda t. \kappa(\mathrm{var}(t))))
\end{aligned}
$$

We now want to show the correctness of the specializer $\mathcal{P}_2$ under the call-by-value semantics. Namely, we want to show $I_1 \llbracket \downarrow_0 (\mathcal{P}_2 \llbracket W \rrbracket \rho_\phi \lambda x.x) \rrbracket \rho_{id} \sim_v I_1 \llbracket M \rrbracket \rho_\phi$ along the similar story as we did in Section 5.3. Let us define the base case R_d as follows:

$$(M, M') \in R_d \quad \Longleftrightarrow \quad I_1 \llbracket \downarrow_n M \rrbracket \rho_{id} \sim_v M' \text{ for any large } n \ .$$

Then, we want to show $(\mathcal{P}_2 \llbracket W \rrbracket \rho_\phi \lambda x.x, I_1 \llbracket M \rrbracket \rho_\phi) \in R_d$ with a suitable definition of $R_{\sigma \to \tau}$. To prove it, we first generalize the statement to make induction work. Rather than proving only the case where environments and continuations are the empty ones, we prove something like:

$$(\mathcal{P}_2 \llbracket W \rrbracket \rho \lambda v.K, (\lambda v'.K')(I_1 \llbracket M \rrbracket \rho')) \in R_\tau$$

for some suitable ρ, ρ', $\lambda v.K$, and $\lambda v'.K'$. Since I_1 is written in direct style, we introduce its continuation as a form of a direct application.

Now, how can we define $R_{\sigma \to \tau}$? Unlike Section 5.3, it is not immediately clear how to define $R_{\sigma \to \tau}$ because the specializer is written in CPS. We need to relate $\mathcal{P}_2 \llbracket W \rrbracket \rho \lambda v.K$ and $(\lambda v'.K')(I_1 \llbracket M \rrbracket \rho')$ properly. To do so, we need to characterize precisely the two continuations, $\lambda v.K$ and $\lambda v'.K'$, and the final results. Going back to the definition of $\mathcal{P}_2$, we notice two things:

- $\mathcal{P}_2 \llbracket W \rrbracket \rho \lambda v.K$ as a whole returns a dynamic expression.

- $\lambda v.K$ returns a dynamic expression, given some value v.

In ordinary CPS programs, the return type of continuations is polymorphic. It can be of any type, usually referred to as a type *Answer*. Here, we used continuations in a non-standard way, however. We instantiated the *Answer* type into a type of dynamic expressions and used it to construct dynamic expressions.

Taking into account that the type of dynamic expressions is d, the above observation leads us to the following definition of logical relations:

$$\begin{aligned}
(M, M') \in R_d &\quad \Longleftrightarrow \quad I_1 \llbracket \downarrow_n M \rrbracket \rho_{id} \sim_v M' \text{ for any large } n \\
(M, M') \in R_{\sigma \to \tau} &\quad \Longleftrightarrow \quad \forall (V, V') \in R_\sigma. \ \forall (\lambda v.K, \lambda v'.K') \models \tau \rightsquigarrow d. \\
&\qquad (MV \lambda v.K, (\lambda v'.K')(M'V')) \in R_d
\end{aligned}$$

where $(\lambda v.K, \lambda v'.K') \models \tau \rightsquigarrow d$ is simultaneously defined as follows:

$$(\lambda v.K, \lambda v'.K') \models \tau \rightsquigarrow d \quad \Longleftrightarrow \quad \forall (V, V') \in R_\tau. \ ((\lambda v.K)V, (\lambda v'.K')V') \in R_d$$

Intuitively, $(\lambda v.K, \lambda v'.K') \models \tau \rightsquigarrow d$ means that $\lambda v.K$ and $\lambda v'.K'$ are related continuations that, given related values of type τ, produce related results of type d. Using this definition, $(M, M') \in R_{\sigma \to \tau}$ states that M and M' are related if they produce related results of type d, given related values of type σ and related continuations of type $\tau \rightsquigarrow d$. In the following, we use $\rightsquigarrow$ for the type of continuations.

With this definition of logical relations, we can prove the correctness of $\mathcal{P}_2$ under the call-by-value semantics.

Theorem 5.3. *If $A \vdash M : \tau\ [W]$, $(\rho, \rho') \models A$, and $(\lambda v. K, \lambda v'. K') \models \tau \rightsquigarrow d$, then $(\mathcal{P}_2\ [\![W]\!]\ \rho\ \lambda v. K, (\lambda v'. K')\ (I_1\ [\![M]\!]\ \rho')) \in R_d$.*

The proof of this theorem is by induction on the structure of the proof of $A \vdash M : \tau\ [W]$. Even though $\mathcal{P}_2$ is written in CPS, the induction does work thanks to the explicit reference to the types of continuations and the final result. The proof proceeds in a CPS manner. In particular, the cases for (both static and dynamic) applications go from left to right. We use the induction hypotheses for the function part and the argument part in this order.

By instantiating the theorem to the case where both the environment and the continuation are empty, we obtain the following corollary that establishes the correctness of a specializer using the continuation-based let-insertion:

Corollary 5.4. *If $\vdash M : d\ [W]$, then $I_1\ [\![\downarrow_0 (\mathcal{P}_2\ [\![W]\!]\ \rho_\phi\ \lambda x. x)]\!]\ \rho_{id} \sim_v I_1\ [\![M]\!]\ \rho_\phi$.*

If we annotate the input to the specializer completely dynamic, the specializer behaves exactly the same as the A-normalizer. Thus, the theorem can be instantiated to the following corollary, which proves the correctness of the continuation-based A-normalization.

Corollary 5.5. $I_1\ [\![\downarrow_0 (\mathcal{A}_1\ [\![M]\!]\ \rho_\phi\ \lambda x. x)]\!]\ \rho_{id} \sim_v I_1\ [\![M]\!]\ \rho_\phi$ *for any closed M.*

5.6 SPECIALIZER IN DIRECT STYLE

In this section, we present a specializer written in direct style and show its correctness under the call-by-value semantics. Since we have already established the correctness of a specializer written in CPS in the previous section, the development in this section is easy. Roughly speaking, we transform the results in the previous section *back to direct style* [8]. During this process, we use the first-class delimited continuation constructs, *shift* and *reset*, to cope with non-standard use of continuations. Intuitively, shift captures the current continuation up to its enclosing reset [7]. Here is the definition of the specializer written in direct style:

$$
\begin{aligned}
\mathcal{P}_3\ [\![\mathrm{Var}(n)]\!]\ \rho &= \rho\,(n) \\
\mathcal{P}_3\ [\![\underline{\mathrm{Lam}(n, W)}]\!]\ \rho &= \lambda x.\ \mathcal{P}_3\ [\![W]\!]\ \rho[x/n] \\
\mathcal{P}_3\ [\![\underline{\mathrm{Lam}(n, W)}]\!]\ \rho &= \mathrm{lam}(\lambda x.\ \langle \mathcal{P}_3\ [\![W]\!]\ \rho[\mathrm{var}(x)/n]\rangle) \\
\mathcal{P}_3\ [\![\mathrm{App}(W_1, W_2)]\!]\ \rho &= (\mathcal{P}_3\ [\![W_1]\!]\ \rho)\,(\mathcal{P}_3\ [\![W_2]\!]\ \rho) \\
\mathcal{P}_3\ [\![\underline{\mathrm{App}(W_1, W_2)}]\!]\ \rho &= \xi\kappa.\,\mathrm{let}(\mathrm{app}(\mathcal{P}_3\ [\![W_1]\!]\ \rho, \mathcal{P}_3\ [\![W_2]\!]\ \rho), \mathrm{lam}(\lambda t.\,\kappa\,(\mathrm{var}(t))))
\end{aligned}
$$

As in the previous section, we obtain the one-pass A-normalizer written in direct style with shift and reset [3] by extracting dynamic rules from $\mathcal{P}_3$:

$$
\begin{aligned}
\mathcal{A}_2\ [\![\mathrm{Var}(n)]\!]\ \rho &= \rho\,(n) \\
\mathcal{A}_2\ [\![\mathrm{Lam}(x, M)]\!]\ \rho &= \mathrm{lam}(\lambda x.\ \langle \mathcal{A}_2\ [\![M]\!]\ \rho[\mathrm{var}(x)/n]\rangle) \\
\mathcal{A}_2\ [\![\mathrm{App}(M_1, M_2)]\!]\ \rho &= \xi\kappa.\,\mathrm{let}(\mathrm{app}(\mathcal{A}_2\ [\![M_1]\!]\ \rho, \mathcal{A}_2\ [\![M_2]\!]\ \rho), \mathrm{lam}(\lambda t.\,\kappa\,(\mathrm{var}(t))))
\end{aligned}
$$

To define suitable logical relations for the specializer written in direct style (with shift and reset), we need to correctly handle delimited continuations. This is done by observing the exact correspondence between continuations in the previous section and delimited continuations in this section. In particular, we type the result of the delimited continuations as d.

Logical relations for the direct-style specializer with delimited continuations are defined as follows:

$$
\begin{aligned}
(M, M') \in R_d &\iff I_1 \, [\![\,\downarrow_n M]\!] \, \rho_{id} \sim_v M' \text{ for any large } n \\
(M, M') \in R_{\sigma \to \tau} &\iff \forall (V, V') \in R_\sigma. \forall (\lambda v. K, \lambda v'. K') \models \tau \rightsquigarrow d. \\
&\quad (\langle ((\lambda v. K) \, (M V) \rangle, (\lambda v'. K') \, (M' V')) \in R_d
\end{aligned}
$$

where $(\lambda v. K, \lambda v'. K') \models \tau \rightsquigarrow d$ is simultaneously defined as follows:

$$
(\lambda v. K, \lambda v'. K') \models \tau \rightsquigarrow d \iff \forall (V, V') \in R_\tau. \, (\langle (\lambda v. K) \, V \rangle, (\lambda v'. K') \, V') \in R_d
$$

Then, the correctness of the specializer is stated as follows:

Theorem 5.6. *If* $A \vdash M : \tau \, [W]$, $(\rho, \rho') \models A$, *and* $(\lambda v. K, \lambda v'. K') \models \tau \rightsquigarrow d$, *then* $(\langle (\lambda v. K) \, (\mathcal{P}_3 \, [\![W]\!] \, \rho) \rangle, (\lambda v'. K') \, (I_1 \, [\![M]\!] \, \rho')) \in R_d$.

Although both the specializer and the interpreter are written in direct style, the proof proceeds in a CPS manner. In particular, the cases for applications go from left to right, naturally reflecting the call-by-value semantics.

By instantiating the theorem to the case where both the environment and the continuation are empty, we obtain the following corollary that establishes the correctness of a specializer using the shift/reset-based let-insertion:

Corollary 5.7. *If* $\vdash M : d \, [W]$, *then* $I_1 \, [\![\,\downarrow_0 \, \langle \mathcal{P}_3 \, [\![W]\!] \, \rho_\phi \rangle]\!] \, \rho_{id} \sim_v I_1 \, [\![M]\!] \, \rho_\phi$.

As before, if we annotate the input to the specializer completely dynamic, the specializer behaves exactly the same as the A-normalizer. Thus, the theorem can be instantiated to the following corollary, which proves the correctness of the direct-style A-normalization.

Corollary 5.8. $I_1 \, [\![\,\downarrow_0 \, \langle \mathcal{A}_2 \, [\![M]\!] \, \rho_\phi \rangle]\!] \, \rho_{id} \sim_v I_1 \, [\![M]\!] \, \rho_\phi$ *for any closed* M.

5.7 INTERPRETER AND A-NORMALIZER FOR SHIFT AND RESET

So far, shift and reset appeared only in the metalanguage. In the following sections, we develop a specializer written in direct style that can handle shift and reset in the baselanguage. We first define an interpreter, a residualizer, and an A-normalizer for the call-by-value λ-calculus with shift and reset. We then try to combine the interpreter and the A-normalizer to obtain a specializer in the next section. Here is the interpreter written in direct style:

$$
\begin{aligned}
I_2 \, [\![\text{Var}(n)]\!] \, \rho &= \rho \, (n) \\
I_2 \, [\![\text{Lam}(n, M)]\!] \, \rho &= \lambda x. \, I_2 \, [\![M]\!] \, \rho[x/n] \\
I_2 \, [\![\text{App}(M_1, M_2)]\!] \, \rho &= (I_2 \, [\![M_1]\!] \, \rho) \, (I_2 \, [\![M_2]\!] \, \rho) \\
I_2 \, [\![\text{Shift}(n, M)]\!] \, \rho &= \xi k. \, I_2 \, [\![M]\!] \, \rho[k/n] \\
I_2 \, [\![\text{Reset}(M)]\!] \, \rho &= \langle I_2 \, [\![M]\!] \, \rho \rangle
\end{aligned}
$$

We used shift and reset operations themselves to interpret shift and reset expressions. A residualizer is defined as follows:

$$
\begin{aligned}
\mathcal{D}_2\,[\![\mathrm{Var}(n)]\!]\,\rho &= \rho(n) \\
\mathcal{D}_2\,[\![\mathrm{Lam}(n,M)]\!]\,\rho &= \mathrm{lam}(\lambda x.\,\mathcal{D}_2\,[\![M]\!]\,\rho[\mathrm{var}(x)/n]) \\
\mathcal{D}_2\,[\![\mathrm{App}(M_1,M_2)]\!]\,\rho &= \mathrm{app}(\mathcal{D}_2\,[\![M_1]\!]\,\rho,\mathcal{D}_2\,[\![M_2]\!]\,\rho) \\
\mathcal{D}_2\,[\![\mathrm{Shift}(n,M)]\!]\,\rho &= \mathrm{shift}(\lambda k.\,\mathcal{D}_2\,[\![M]\!]\,\rho[\mathrm{var}(k)/n]) \\
\mathcal{D}_2\,[\![\mathrm{Reset}(M)]\!]\,\rho &= \mathrm{reset}(\mathcal{D}_2\,[\![M]\!]\,\rho)
\end{aligned}
$$

It simply renames bound variables and keeps other expressions unchanged. As before, this residualizer is not suitable for specializers. We instead use the following A-normalizer:

$$
\begin{aligned}
\mathcal{A}_3\,[\![\mathrm{Var}(n)]\!]\,\rho &= \rho(n) \\
\mathcal{A}_3\,[\![\mathrm{Lam}(n,M)]\!]\,\rho &= \mathrm{lam}(\lambda x.\,\langle\mathcal{A}_3\,[\![M]\!]\,\rho[\mathrm{var}(x)/n]\rangle) \\
\mathcal{A}_3\,[\![\mathrm{App}(M_1,M_2)]\!]\,\rho &= \xi k.\,\mathrm{let}(\mathrm{app}(\mathcal{A}_3\,[\![M_1]\!]\,\rho,\mathcal{A}_3\,[\![M_2]\!]\,\rho),\mathrm{lam}(\lambda t.\,k\,(\mathrm{var}(t)))) \\
\mathcal{A}_3\,[\![\mathrm{Shift}(n,M)]\!]\,\rho &= \mathrm{shift}(\lambda k.\,\langle\mathcal{A}_3\,[\![M]\!]\,\rho[\mathrm{var}(k)/n]\rangle) \\
\mathcal{A}_3\,[\![\mathrm{Reset}(M)]\!]\,\rho &= \mathrm{reset}(\langle\mathcal{A}_3\,[\![M]\!]\,\rho\rangle)
\end{aligned}
$$

It replaces all the application expressions in the body of abstractions, shift expressions, and reset operations with a sequence of let-expressions.

5.8 SPECIALIZER FOR SHIFT AND RESET

In this section, we show a specializer for the call-by-value λ-calculus with shift and reset. Our first attempt is to combine the interpreter and the A-normalizer as we did before for the calculi without shift and reset:

$$
\begin{aligned}
\mathcal{P}_4\,[\![\mathrm{Var}(n)]\!]\,\rho &= \rho(n) \\
\mathcal{P}_4\,[\![\underline{\mathrm{Lam}}(n,W)]\!]\,\rho &= \lambda x.\,\mathcal{P}_4\,[\![W]\!]\,\rho[x/n] \\
\mathcal{P}_4\,[\![\overline{\mathrm{Lam}}(n,W)]\!]\,\rho &= \mathrm{lam}(\lambda x.\,\langle\mathcal{P}_4\,[\![W]\!]\,\rho[\mathrm{var}(x)/n]\rangle) \\
\mathcal{P}_4\,[\![\underline{\mathrm{App}}(W_1,W_2)]\!]\,\rho &= (\mathcal{P}_4\,[\![W_1]\!]\,\rho)\,(\mathcal{P}_4\,[\![W_2]\!]\,\rho) \\
\mathcal{P}_4\,[\![\overline{\mathrm{App}}(W_1,W_2)]\!]\,\rho &= \xi k.\,\mathrm{let}(\mathrm{app}(\mathcal{P}_4\,[\![W_1]\!]\,\rho,\mathcal{P}_4\,[\![W_2]\!]\,\rho),\mathrm{lam}(\lambda t.\,k\,(\mathrm{var}(t)))) \\
\mathcal{P}_4\,[\![\underline{\mathrm{Shift}}(n,W)]\!]\,\rho &= \xi k.\,\mathcal{P}_4\,[\![W]\!]\,\rho[k/n] \\
\mathcal{P}_4\,[\![\overline{\mathrm{Shift}}(n,W)]\!]\,\rho &= \mathrm{shift}(\lambda k.\,\langle\mathcal{P}_4\,[\![W]\!]\,\rho[\mathrm{var}(k)/n]\rangle) \\
\mathcal{P}_4\,[\![\underline{\mathrm{Reset}}(W)]\!]\,\rho &= \langle\mathcal{P}_4\,[\![W]\!]\,\rho\rangle \\
\mathcal{P}_4\,[\![\overline{\mathrm{Reset}}(W)]\!]\,\rho &= \mathrm{reset}(\langle\mathcal{P}_4\,[\![W]\!]\,\rho\rangle)
\end{aligned}
$$

Although this specializer does seem to work for carefully annotated inputs, it is hard to specify the well-annotated term as a simple binding-time analysis. The difficulty comes from the inconsistency between the specialization-time continuation and the runtime continuation.

In the rule for the static shift, a continuation is grabbed at specialization time, which means that we implicitly assume the grabbed continuation coincides with the actual continuation at runtime. This was actually true for the interpreter: we implemented shift in the baselanguage using shift in the metalanguage. In the specializer, however, the specialization-time continuation does not always coincide with the actual continuation. To be more specific, in the rule for dynamic abstractions, we specialize the body W in a static reset (*i.e.*, in the empty continuation) to perform A-normalization, but the actual continuation at the time when W is executed is not necessarily the empty one. Rather, it is the one when the abstraction is applied at runtime.

Given that the specialization-time continuation is not always consistent with the actual one, we have to make sure that the continuation is captured statically only when it represents the actual one. Furthermore, we have to make sure that whenever shift is residualized, its enclosing reset is also residualized. One way to express this information in the type system would be to split all the typing rules into two, one for the case when the specialization-time continuation and the actual continuation coincide (or, the continuation is known, static) and the other for the case when they do not (the continuation is unknown, dynamic). We could then statically grab the continuation only when it represents the actual one.

However, this solution leads to an extremely weak specialization. Unless an enclosing reset is known at specialization time, we cannot grab continuations statically. Thus, under dynamic abstractions, no shift operation is possible at specialization time. Furthermore, because we use a type-based binding-time analysis, it becomes impossible to perform *any* specialization under dynamic abstractions. Remember that a type system does not tell us what subexpressions appear in a given expression, but only the type of the given expression. From a type system, we cannot distinguish the expression that does not contain any shift expressions from the one that does. Thus, even if W_1 turns out to have a static function type in $\mathrm{App}(W_1, W_2)$ (and thus it appears that this application can be performed statically), we cannot actually perform this application, because the toplevel operator of W_1 might be a shift operation that passes a function to the grabbed continuation. In other words, we cannot determine the binding-time of $\mathrm{App}(W_1, W_2)$ from the binding-time of W_1, which makes it difficult to construct a simple type-based binding-time analysis.

The solution we employ takes a different approach. We maintain the consistency between specialization-time continuations and actual ones *all the time*. In other words, we make the continuation always static. The modified specializer is presented as follows:

$$
\begin{aligned}
\mathcal{P}_5 \, [\![\mathrm{Var}(n)]\!] \, \rho &= \rho\,(n) \\
\mathcal{P}_5 \, [\![\underline{\mathrm{Lam}}(n, W)]\!] \, \rho &= \lambda x.\, \mathcal{P}_5 \, [\![W]\!] \, \rho[x/n] \\
\mathcal{P}_5 \, [\![\underline{\mathrm{Lam}}(n, W)]\!] \, \rho &= \mathrm{lam}(\lambda x.\, \mathrm{shift}(\lambda k.\, \langle \mathrm{reset}(\mathrm{app}(\mathrm{var}(k), \mathcal{P}_5 \, [\![W]\!] \, \rho[\mathrm{var}(x)/n])) \rangle)) \\
\mathcal{P}_5 \, [\![\overline{\mathrm{App}}(W_1, W_2)]\!] \, \rho &= (\mathcal{P}_5 \, [\![W_1]\!] \, \rho)\,(\mathcal{P}_5 \, [\![W_2]\!] \, \rho) \\
\mathcal{P}_5 \, [\![\underline{\mathrm{App}}(W_1, W_2)]\!] \, \rho &= \xi k.\, \mathrm{reset}(\mathrm{let}(\mathrm{app}(\mathcal{P}_5 \, [\![W_1]\!] \, \rho, \mathcal{P}_5 \, [\![W_2]\!] \, \rho), \mathrm{lam}(\lambda t.\, k\,(\mathrm{var}(t))))) \\
\mathcal{P}_5 \, [\![\overline{\mathrm{Shift}}(n, W)]\!] \, \rho &= \xi k.\, \mathcal{P}_5 \, [\![W]\!] \, \rho[k/n] \\
\mathcal{P}_5 \, [\![\underline{\mathrm{Shift}}(n, W)]\!] \, \rho &= \xi k.\, \mathcal{P}_5 \, [\![W]\!] \, \rho[\mathrm{lam}(\lambda v.\, \langle k\,(\mathrm{var}(v)) \rangle)/n] \\
\mathcal{P}_5 \, [\![\overline{\mathrm{Reset}}(W)]\!] \, \rho &= \langle \mathcal{P}_5 \, [\![W]\!] \, \rho \rangle
\end{aligned}
$$

There are four changes from $\mathcal{P}_4$. The first and the most important change is in the rule for dynamic abstractions. Rather than specializing the body W of a dynamic abstraction in the empty context, we specialize it in the context $\mathrm{reset}(\mathrm{app}(\mathrm{var}(k),\cdot))$. This specialization-time continuation $\mathrm{reset}(\mathrm{app}(\mathrm{var}(k),\cdot))$ turns out to be consistent with the runtime continuation, because the variable k is bound in the dynamic shift placed directly under the dynamic abstraction and represents the continuation when the abstraction is applied at runtime.

The second change is in the rule for dynamic applications where dynamic reset is inserted around the residualized let-expression. The third change is in the rule for dynamic shift. Rather than residualizing a dynamic shift, which requires residualization of the corresponding reset, the current continuation is grabbed and it is turned into a dynamic expression via η-expansion. Finally, the rule for dynamic reset is removed since all the shift operations are taken care of during specialization time, and there is no need to residualize reset. (This does not necessarily mean that the result of specialization does not contain any reset expressions. Reset is residualized in the rule for dynamic abstractions and applications.)

These changes not only define a correct specializer but result in a quite powerful one. It can now handle *partially static continuations*. Consider the term $\mathrm{Lam}(f,\underline{\mathrm{Lam}}(x,\underline{\mathrm{App}}(\mathrm{Var}(f),\overline{\mathrm{Shift}}(k,\overline{\mathrm{App}}(\mathrm{Var}(k),\overline{\mathrm{App}}(\mathrm{Var}(k),\mathrm{Var}(x)))))))$. (This term is well-annotated in the type system shown in the next section.) When we specialize this term, the continuation k grabbed by $\overline{\mathrm{Shift}}(k,\cdots)$ is partially static: we know that the first thing to do when k is applied is to pass its argument to f, but the computation that should be performed after that is unknown. It is the continuation when $\underline{\mathrm{Lam}}(x,\cdots)$ is applied to an argument. Even in this case, $\mathcal{P}_5$ can expand this partial continuation into the result of specialization. By naming the unknown continuation h, $\mathcal{P}_5$ produces the following output (after removing unnecessary dynamic shift and inlining the residualized let-expressions):

$$\mathrm{lam}(\lambda f.\,\mathrm{lam}(\lambda x.\,\mathrm{shift}(\lambda h.$$
$$\mathrm{reset}(\mathrm{app}(\mathrm{var}(h),\mathrm{app}(\mathrm{var}(f),\mathrm{reset}(\mathrm{app}(\mathrm{var}(h),\mathrm{app}(\mathrm{var}(f),\mathrm{var}(x)))))))))))\ .$$

Observe that the partial continuation $\mathrm{reset}(\mathrm{app}(\mathrm{var}(h),\mathrm{app}(\mathrm{var}(f),\cdot)))$ is expanded twice in the result. If f were static, we could have been able to perform further specialization, exploiting the partially static information of the continuation.

On the other hand, the above changes cause an interesting side-effect to the result of specialization: all the residualized lambda abstractions now have a 'standardized' form $\mathrm{lam}(\lambda x.\,\mathrm{shift}(\lambda k.\,\cdots))$ (and this is the only place where shift is residualized). In particular, even when we specialize $\underline{\mathrm{Lam}}(x,W)$ where shift is not used during the evaluation of W, the residualized abstraction has typically the form $\mathrm{lam}(\lambda x.\,\mathrm{shift}(\lambda k.\,\mathrm{reset}(\mathrm{app}(\mathrm{var}(k),M))))$ where k does not occur free in M. (If let-expressions are inserted, the result becomes somewhat more complicated.) If we used $\mathcal{P}_3$ instead, we would have obtained the equivalent but simpler result: $\mathrm{lam}(\lambda x.\,M)$. In other words, $\mathcal{P}_5$ is not a conservative extension of $\mathcal{P}_3$.

A question then is whether it is possible to obtain the latter result on the fly using $\mathcal{P}_5$ with some extra work. We expect that it is not likely. As long as a simple type-based binding-time analysis is employed, it is impossible to tell if the execution of the body of a dynamic abstraction includes any shift operations. So, unless we introduce some extra mechanisms to keep track of this information, there is no way to avoid the insertion of a dynamic shift in the rule for dynamic abstractions. Then, rather than making the specializer complicated, we would employ a simple post-processing to remove unnecessary shift expressions.

5.9   TYPE SYSTEM FOR SHIFT AND RESET

Since our proof technique relies on the logical relations, we need to define a type system for the call-by-value λ-calculus with shift and reset to prove the correctness of $\mathcal{P}_5$. In this section, we briefly review Danvy and Filinski's type system [6]. More thorough explanation is found in [3, 6].

In the presence of first-class (delimited) continuations, we need to explicitly specify the types of continuations and the final result. For this purpose, Danvy and Filinski use a judgment of the form $A, \alpha \vdash M : \tau, \beta$ $[W]$. It reads: under the type assumption A, an expression M has a type τ in a continuation of type $\tau \rightsquigarrow \alpha$ and the final result is of type β. Since we use this type system as the static part of our binding-time analysis, we decorate it with $[W]$ to indicate that M is annotated as W. If M does not contain any shift operations, the types α and β are always the same, namely, the *Answer* type. In the presence of shift and reset, however, they can be different and of any type.

The type of functions also needs to include the types of continuations and the final result. It has the form: $\sigma/\alpha \rightarrow \tau/\beta$. It is a type of functions that receive an argument of type σ and returns a value of type τ to a continuation of type $\tau \rightsquigarrow \alpha$ and the final result is of type β. As a result, types are specified as follows:

$$\tau \quad = \quad d \mid \tau/\tau \rightarrow \tau/\tau \ .$$

Here goes the type system:

$$A[n : \tau], \alpha \vdash \mathrm{Var}(n) : \tau, \alpha \ [\mathrm{Var}(n)]$$

$$\frac{A[n : \sigma], \alpha \vdash M : \tau, \beta \ [W]}{A, \delta \vdash \mathrm{Lam}(n, M) : \sigma/\alpha \rightarrow \tau/\beta, \delta \ [\overline{\mathrm{Lam}}(n, W)]} \qquad \frac{A, \sigma \vdash M : \sigma, \tau \ [W]}{A, \alpha \vdash \mathrm{Reset}(M) : \tau, \alpha \ [\overline{\mathrm{Reset}}(W)]}$$

$$\frac{\begin{array}{c} A, \delta \vdash M_1 : \sigma/\alpha \rightarrow \tau/\varepsilon, \beta \ [W_1] \\ A, \varepsilon \vdash M_2 : \sigma, \delta \ [W_2] \end{array}}{A, \alpha \vdash \mathrm{App}(M_1, M_2) : \tau, \beta \ [\overline{\mathrm{App}}(W_1, W_2)]} \qquad \frac{A[n : \tau/\delta \rightarrow \alpha/\delta], \sigma \vdash M : \sigma, \beta \ [W]}{A, \alpha \vdash \mathrm{Shift}(n, M) : \tau, \beta \ [\overline{\mathrm{Shift}}(n, W)]}$$

The above type system is a generalization of the standard type system where types of continuations are made explicit. In Section 5.6, the result type of continuations and the type of final results were always d. In the above type system, it means that a judgment had always the form $A, d \vdash M : \tau, d$ $[W]$ and the function type had always the form $\sigma/d \rightarrow \tau/d$. So if we write them as $A \vdash M : \tau$ $[W]$ and $\sigma \rightarrow \tau$, respectively, we obtain exactly the same type system as the one for the ordinary λ-calculus (the three static rules shown in Section 5.3).

The dynamic rules can be obtained by simply replacing all the static function types with d (and types that occur within the function type). The dynamic rules

75

are as follows:

$$\frac{A[n:d],d \vdash M:d,d\ [W]}{A,\delta \vdash \mathrm{Lam}(n,M):d,\delta\ [\underline{\mathrm{Lam}}(n,W)]} \qquad \frac{A[n:d],\sigma \vdash M:\sigma,\beta\ [W]}{A,d \vdash \mathrm{Shift}(n,M):d,\beta\ [\underline{\mathrm{Shift}}(n,W)]}$$

$$\frac{A,\delta \vdash M_1:d,\beta\ [W_1] \quad A,d \vdash M_2:d,\delta\ [W_2]}{A,d \vdash \mathrm{App}(M_1,M_2):d,\beta\ [\underline{\mathrm{App}}(W_1,W_2)]}$$

5.10 LOGICAL RELATIONS FOR SHIFT AND RESET

In this section, we define the logical relations for the call-by-value λ-calculus with shift and reset, which are used to prove the correctness of the specializer $\mathcal{P}_5$ presented in Section 5.8. They are the generalization of the logical relations in Section 5.6 in that the types of the final result and the result of continuations are not restricted to d.

$$
\begin{aligned}
(M,M') \in R_d &\iff I_1\,[\![\downarrow_n M]\!]\,\rho_{id} \sim_v M' \text{ for any large } n \\
(M,M') \in R_{\sigma/\alpha \to \tau/\beta} &\iff \forall (V,V') \in R_\sigma.\,\forall (\lambda v.K,\lambda v'.K') \models \tau \rightsquigarrow \alpha. \\
&\qquad (\langle (\lambda v.K)\,(M\,V)\rangle, \langle (\lambda v'.K')\,(M'\,V')\rangle) \in R_\beta
\end{aligned}
$$

where $(\lambda v.K,\lambda v'.K') \models \tau \rightsquigarrow \alpha$ is simultaneously defined as follows:

$$(\lambda v.K,\lambda v'.K') \models \tau \rightsquigarrow \alpha \iff \forall (V,V') \in R_\tau.\,(\langle (\lambda v.K)\,V\rangle, \langle (\lambda v'.K')\,V'\rangle) \in R_\alpha$$

Then, the correctness of the specializer is stated as follows:

Theorem 5.9. *If* $A,\alpha \vdash M:\tau,\beta\ [W]$, $(\rho,\rho') \models A$, *and* $(\lambda v.K,\lambda v'.K') \models \tau \rightsquigarrow \alpha$, *then* $(\langle (\lambda v.K)\,(\mathcal{P}_5\,[\![W]\!]\,\rho)\rangle, \langle (\lambda v'.K')\,(I_2\,[\![M]\!]\,\rho')\rangle) \in R_\beta$.

By instantiating the theorem to the case where both the environment and the continuation are empty, we obtain the following corollary that establishes the correctness of a direct-style specializer that can handle shift and reset:

Corollary 5.10. *If* $d \vdash M:d,d\ [W]$, *then* $I_2\,[\![\downarrow_0 \langle \mathcal{P}_5\,[\![W]\!]\,\rho_\phi\rangle]\!]\,\rho_{id} \sim_v \langle I_2\,[\![M]\!]\,\rho_\phi\rangle$.

The complete proof of the theorem is found in the technical report [4].

5.11 RELATED WORK

This work extends our earlier work [3] where we presented offline specializers for λ-calculus with shift and reset that produced the output in CPS. The present work is a direct-style account of the previous work, but it contains non-trivial definition of logical relations for shift and reset. We also presented the *online* specializers for the λ-calculus with shift and reset [2]. However, their correctness has not been formally proved.

Thiemann [17] presented an offline partial evaluator for Scheme including call/cc. In his partial evaluator, call/cc is reduced if the captured continuation and the body of call/cc are both static. This is close to our first attempt in Section 5.8.

76

Our solution is more liberal and reduces more continuation-capturing constructs, but with a side-effect that all the residualized abstractions include a toplevel shift, which could be removed by a simple post-processing. More recently, Thiemann [19] showed a sophisticated effect-based type system to show the equivalence of the continuation-based let-insertion and the state-based let-insertion. His type system captures the information on the let-residualized code as an effect. It might be possible to extend his framework to avoid unnecessary shift at the front of dynamic abstractions on the fly.

The correctness proof for offline specializers using the technique of logical relations appears in Jones et al. [14, Chapter 8]. Wand [20] used it to prove the correctness of an offline specializer for the call-by-name λ-calculus. The present work is a non-trivial extension of his work to cope with delimited continuations. Wand's formulation was based on substitution, but we used the environment-based formulation, which is essentially the same but is more close to the implementation.

Filinski presented normalization-by-evaluation algorithms for the call-by-value λ-calculus [10] and the computational λ-calculus [11]. He showed their correctness denotationally using logical relations. The same framework is extended to the untyped λ-calculus by Filinski and Rohde [12].

The type system used in this paper is due to Danvy and Filinski [6]. A similar type system is studied by Ariola, Herbelin, and Sabry [1], which explicitly mentions the type of continuations.

5.12 CONCLUSION

This paper demonstrated that logical relations can be defined to characterize not only call-by-name higher-order functions but also call-by-value functions as well as delimited continuations. They were used to show the correctness of various offline specializers, including the one for the call-by-value λ-calculus with shift and reset. Along the development, we established the correctness of the continuation-based let-insertion, the shift/reset-based let-insertion, the continuation-based A-normalization, and the shift/reset-based A-normalization.

REFERENCES

[1] Ariola, Z. M., H. Herbelin, and A Sabry "A Type-Theoretic Foundation of Continuations and Prompts," *Proceedings of the ninth ACM SIGPLAN International Conference on Functional Programming (ICFP'04)*, pp. 40–53 (September 2004).

[2] Asai, K. "Online Partial Evaluation for Shift and Reset," *ACM SIGPLAN Workshop on Partial Evaluation and Semantics-Based Program Manipulation (PEPM '02)*, pp. 19–30 (January 2002).

[3] Asai, K. "Offline Partial Evaluation for Shift and Reset," *ACM SIGPLAN Symposium on Partial Evaluation and Semantics-Based Program Manipulation (PEPM '04)*, pp. 3–14 (August 2004).

[4] Asai, K. "Logical Relations for Call-by-value Delimited Continuations," Technical Report OCHA-IS 06-1, Department of Information Sciences, Ochanomizu University (April 2006).

[5] Bondorf, A., and O. Danvy "Automatic autoprojection of recursive equations with global variables and abstract data types," *Science of Computer Programming*, Vol. 16, pp. 151–195, Elsevier (1991).

[6] Danvy, O., and A. Filinski "A Functional Abstraction of Typed Contexts," Technical Report 89/12, DIKU, University of Copenhagen (July 1989).

[7] Danvy, O., and A. Filinski "Abstracting Control," *Proceedings of the 1990 ACM Conference on Lisp and Functional Programming*, pp. 151–160 (June 1990).

[8] Danvy, O., and J. L. Lawall "Back to Direct Style II: First-Class Continuations," *Proceedings of the 1992 ACM Conference on Lisp and Functional Programming*, pp. 299–310 (June 1992).

[9] de Bruijn, N. G. "Lambda Calculus Notation with Nameless Dummies, a Tool for Automatic Formula Manipulation, with Application to the Church-Rosser Theorem," *Indagationes Mathematicae*, Vol. 34, pp. 381–392 (1972).

[10] Filinski, A. "A Semantic Account of Type-Directed Partial Evaluation," In G. Nadathur, editor, *Principles and Practice of Declarative Programming (LNCS 1702)*, pp. 378–395 (September 1999).

[11] Filinski, A. "Normalization by Evaluation for the Computational Lambda-Calculus," In S. Abramsky, editor, *Typed Lambda Calculi and Applications (LNCS 2044)*, pp. 151–165 (May 2001).

[12] Filinski, A., and H. K. Rohde "A Denotational Account of Untyped Normalization by Evaluation," In I. Walukiewicz, editor, *Foundations of Software Science and Computation Structures (LNCS 2987)*, pp. 167–181 (March 2004).

[13] Flanagan, C., A. Sabry, B. F. Duba, and M. Felleisen "The Essence of Compiling with Continuations," *Proceedings of the ACM SIGPLAN '93 Conference on Programming Language Design and Implementation (PLDI)*, pp. 237–247 (June 1993).

[14] Jones, N. D., C. K. Gomard, and P. Sestoft *Partial Evaluation and Automatic Program Generation*, New York: Prentice-Hall (1993).

[15] Kameyama, Y., and M. Hasegawa "A Sound and Complete Axiomatization of Delimited Continuations," *Proceedings of the eighth ACM SIGPLAN International Conference on Functional Programming (ICFP'03)*, pp. 177–188 (August 2003).

[16] Mitchell, J. C. *Foundations for Programming Languages*, Cambridge: MIT Press (1996).

[17] Thiemann, P. "Towards Partial Evaluation of Full Scheme," *Proceedings of Reflection'96*, pp. 105–115 (April 1996).

[18] Thiemann, P. J. "Cogen in Six Lines," *Proceedings of the ACM SIGPLAN International Conference on Functional Programming (ICFP'96)*, pp. 180–189 (May 1996).

[19] Thiemann, P. "Continuation-Based Partial Evaluation without Continuation," In R. Cousot, editor, *Static Analysis (LNCS 2694)*, pp. 366–382 (June 2003).

[20] Wand, M. "Specifying the Correctness of Binding-Time Analysis," *Journal of Functional Programming*, Vol. 3, No. 3, pp. 365–387, Cambridge University Press (July 1993).

Chapter 6

Epigram Reloaded:

A Standalone Typechecker for ETT

James Chapman[1], Thorsten Altenkirch[1], Conor McBride[1]

Abstract Epigram, a functional programming environment with dependent types, interacts with the programmer via an extensible high level language of programming constructs which *elaborates* incrementally into Epigram's Type Theory, ETT, a rather spartan λ-calculus with dependent types, playing the rôle of a 'core language'. We implement a standalone typechecker for ETT in Haskell, allowing us to reload existing libraries into the system safely without re-elaboration.

Rather than adopting a rewriting approach to computation, we use a *glued* representation of values, pairing first-order syntax with a functional representation of its semantics, computed *lazily*. This approach separates β-*reduction* from βη-*conversion*. We consequently can not only allow the η-laws for λ-abstractions and pairs, but also collapse each of the unit and empty types.

6.1 INTRODUCTION

Epigram[2] [22, 5] is at the same time a functional programming language with dependent types and a type-driven, interactive program development system. Its type system is strong enough to express a wide range of program properties, from basic structural invariants to full specifications. Types assist interactive programming and help to keep track of the constraints an evolving program has to satisfy.

Epigram interacts with the programmer in an extensible high level language of programming constructs which is *elaborated* incrementally into Epigram's Type Theory, ETT. ETT is a rather spartan λ-calculus with dependent types, based on Luo's UTT (Unified Type Theory) [16] and more broadly on Martin-Löf's Type Theory [18]. It plays the rôle of a 'core language': it can be evaluated symbolically; it can also be compiled into efficient executable code, exploiting a new

---

[1]University of Nottingham, {jmc,txa,ctm}@cs.nott.ac.uk
[2]The Epigram system and its documentation are available from www.e-pig.org.

potential for optimisations due to the presence of dependent types [7].

Elaboration is *supposed* to generate well typed terms in ETT, but here we implement a standalone typechecker for ETT in Haskell. Why do we need this? Firstly, elaboration is expensive. We want to reload existing libraries into the system without re-elaborating their high-level source. However, to preserve safety and consistency, we should make sure that the reloaded code does typecheck.

Secondly, consumers may want to check mobile Epigram code before running it. A secure run-time system need not contain the elaborator: an ETT checker is faster, smaller and more trustworthy. McKinna suggested such a type theory for trading in 'deliverables' [23], programs paired with proofs, precisely combining computation and logic, with a single compact checker. More recent work on proof-carrying code [24] further emphasizes minimality of the 'trusted code base'.

Thirdly, as Epigram evolves, the elaborator evolves with it; ETT is much more stable. The present work provides an implementation of ETT which should accept the output of any version of the elaborator and acts as a target language reference for anyone wishing to extend or interoperate with the system.

We hope this paper will serve as a useful resource for anyone curious about how dependent typechecking can be done, especially as the approach we take is necessarily quite novel. Our treatment of evaluation in ETT takes crucial advantage of Haskell's laziness to deliver considerable flexibility in how much or little computation is done. Rather than adopting a conventional rewriting approach to computation, we use a *glued* representation of values, pairing first-order syntax with a functional representation of its semantics, computed *as required*.

This semantic approach readily separates β-*reduction* from βη-*conversion*. We support more liberal notions of 'conversion up to observation' by allowing not only the η-laws for λ-abstractions and pairs, but also identifying all elements of the unit type, 1. We further identify all elements of the empty type, O, thus making all types representing negative propositions $P \rightarrow O$ *proof irrelevant*! These rules are new to Epigram—the definition [22] considers only β-equality. Adding them makes the theory more extensional, accepting more sensible programs and simplifying elaboration by allowing general solutions to more type constraints. It is also a stepping stone towards Observational Type Theory[4] based on [2]. The laws for 1 and O do not fit with Coquand and Abel's syntax-directed approach to conversion checking [1], but require a type-directed algorithm like ours.

Acknowledgments   We gratefully acknowledge the support of EPSRC grant EP/C512022/1 'Observational Equality for Dependently Typed Programming'. We also thank James McKinna, Edwin Brady and Peter Morris for many useful discussions, and the anonymous referees for their helpful advice.

6.2 DEPENDENT TYPES AND TYPECHECKING

The heart of dependent type theory is the typing rule for application:

$$\frac{\Gamma \vdash f : \Pi x{:}S.\,T \qquad \Gamma \vdash s : S}{\Gamma \vdash f\,s : [x \mapsto s{:}S]T}$$

$$\frac{\qquad}{\vdash} \quad \frac{\Gamma \vdash S : \star}{\Gamma; x : S \vdash} \quad \frac{\Gamma \vdash s : S}{\Gamma; x \mapsto s : S \vdash}$$

FIGURE 6.1. Context validity rules $\boxed{\Gamma \vdash}$

The usual notion of function type $S \to T$ is generalised to the dependent function type $\Pi x : S. T$, where T may mention, hence *depend* on x. We may still write $S \to T$ if x does not appear in T. Π-types can thus indicate some relationship between the input of a function and its output. The type of our application instantiates T with the value of the argument s, by means of local definition. An immediate consequence is that *terms* now appear in the language of *types*. Moreover, we take types to be a subset of terms, with type $\star$, so that Π can also express polymorphism.

Once we have terms in types, we can express many useful properties of data. For example, consider *vector* types given by Vec : Nat $\to \star \to \star$, where a natural number fixes the *length* of a vector. We can now give concatenation the type

vconc : $\Pi X : \star. \Pi m : \mathsf{Nat}. \Pi n : \mathsf{Nat}. \mathsf{Vec}\ m\ X \to \mathsf{Vec}\ n\ X \to \mathsf{Vec}\ (m+n)\ X$

When we concatenate two vectors of length 3, we acquire a vector of length $3+3$; it would be most inconvenient if such a vector could not be used in a situation calling for a vector of length 6. That is, the arrival of terms in types brings with it, the need for *computation* in types. The computation rules for ETT do not only explain how to run programs, they play a crucial rôle in determining which types are considered the same. A key typing rule is *conversion*, which identifies the types of terms up to ETT's judgemental equality, not just syntactic equality.

$$\frac{\Gamma \vdash s : S \quad \Gamma \vdash S \simeq T : \star}{\Gamma \vdash s : T}$$

Formally, ETT is a system of inference rules for judgements of three forms

context validity	typing	equality
$\Gamma \vdash$	$\Gamma \vdash t : T$	$\Gamma \vdash t_1 \simeq t_2 : T$

We work relative to a *context* of parameters and definitions, which must have valid types and values—this is enforced by the context validity rules (figure 6.1). The empty context is valid and we may only extend it according to the two rules, introducing a parameter with a valid type or a well typed definition. In the implementation, we check each extension to the context as it happens, so we only ever work in valid contexts. In the formal presentation, we follow tradition in making context validity a precondition for each atomic typing rule.

Figure 6.2 gives the typing rules for ETT. We supply a unit type, 1, an empty type O, dependent function types $\Pi x : S. T$ and dependent pair types $\Sigma x : S. T$, abbreviated by $S \wedge T$ in the non-dependent case. We annotate λ-terms with their domain types and pairs with their range types in order to ensure that types can be

Declared and defined variables   Universe

$$\frac{\Gamma \vdash}{\Gamma \vdash x : S} x{:}S \in \Gamma \qquad \frac{\Gamma \vdash}{\Gamma \vdash x : S} x \mapsto s{:}S \in \Gamma \qquad \frac{\Gamma \vdash}{\Gamma \vdash \star : \star}$$

Conversion   Local definition

$$\frac{\Gamma \vdash s : S \quad \Gamma \vdash S \simeq T : \star}{\Gamma \vdash s : T} \qquad \frac{\Gamma ; x \mapsto s{:}S \vdash t : T}{\Gamma \vdash [x \mapsto s{:}S] t : [x \mapsto s{:}S] T}$$

Type formation,   introduction,   and elimination

$$\frac{\Gamma \vdash}{\Gamma \vdash 1 : \star} \qquad \frac{\Gamma \vdash}{\Gamma \vdash \langle \rangle : 1}$$

$$\frac{\Gamma \vdash}{\Gamma \vdash \mathsf{O} : \star} \qquad \frac{\Gamma \vdash z : \mathsf{O}}{\Gamma \vdash z\,\text{Œ} : \Pi X{:}\star.\,X}$$

$$\frac{\Gamma ; x{:}S \vdash T : \star}{\Gamma \vdash \Pi x{:}S.\,T : \star} \qquad \frac{\Gamma ; x{:}S \vdash t : T}{\Gamma \vdash \lambda x{:}S.\,t : \Pi x{:}S.\,T} \qquad \frac{\Gamma \vdash f : \Pi x{:}S.\,T \quad \Gamma \vdash s : S}{\Gamma \vdash f\,s : [x \mapsto s{:}S]T}$$

$$\frac{\Gamma ; x{:}S \vdash T : \star}{\Gamma \vdash \Sigma x{:}S.\,T : \star} \qquad \frac{\Gamma \vdash s : S \quad \Gamma ; x{:}S \vdash T : \star \quad \Gamma \vdash t : [x \mapsto s{:}S]T}{\Gamma \vdash \langle s;t \rangle_T : \Sigma x{:}S.\,T} \qquad \frac{\Gamma \vdash p : \Sigma x{:}S.\,T}{\Gamma \vdash p\,\pi_0 : S \quad \Gamma \vdash p\,\pi_1 : [x \mapsto p\,\pi_0{:}S]T}$$

FIGURE 6.2. **Typing rules** $\boxed{\Gamma \vdash t : T}$

synthesised, not just checked. We write O's eliminator, Œ ('naught E'), and Σ-type projections, π_0 and π_1 postfix like application—the eliminator for Π-types.

The equality rules (figure 6.3)[3] include β-laws which allow computations and expand definitions, but we also add η-laws and proof-irrelevance for certain types, justified by the fact that some terms are indistinguishable by observation. A proof-irrelevant type has, *as far as we can tell*, at most one element; examples are the unit type 1 and the empty type O. These rules combine to identify all inhabitants of $(A \to 1) \wedge (B \to \mathsf{O})$, for example.

Equality (hence type-) checking is decidable if all computations terminate. A carefully designed language can achieve this by executing only trusted programs in types, but we do not address this issue here. Indeed, our current implementation uses $\star : \star$ and hence admits non-termination due to Girard's paradox [11]. Here, we deliver the core functionality of typechecking. Universe stratification and positivity of inductive definitions are well established[15, 16] and orthogonal to the subject of this article.

6.3 EPIGRAM AND ITS ELABORATION

Epigram's high-level source code is *elaborated* incrementally into ETT. The elaborator produces the detailed evidence which justifies high-level programming con-

---

[3]We have omitted a number of trivial rules here, e.g. the rules stating that $\simeq$ is an equivalence and a number of congruence rules.

```
┌─────────────────────────────────────────────────────────────────────┐
│ definition lookup and disposal                                        │
│                                                                       │
│        Γ ⊢                            Γ ⊢ s ≃ s′ : S   Γ;x↦s:S ⊢ t ≃ t′ : T │
│   ─────────── x↦s:S ∈ Γ        ──────────────────────────────────── │
│   Γ ⊢ x ≃ s : S                 Γ ⊢ [x↦s:S]t ≃ [x↦s′:S]t′ : [x↦s:S]T │
│                                                                       │
│ structural rules for eliminations                                     │
│                                                                       │
│       Γ ⊢ u ≃ u′ : O              Γ ⊢ f ≃ f′ : Πx:S.T   Γ ⊢ s ≃ s′ : S │
│   ──────────────────────        ──────────────────────────────────── │
│   Γ ⊢ u Œ ≃ u′ Œ : Πx:⋆.x         Γ ⊢ f s ≃ f′ s′ : [x ↦ s:S]T       │
│                                                                       │
│   Γ ⊢ p ≃ p′ : Σx:S.T               Γ ⊢ p ≃ p′ : Σx:S.T              │
│   ──────────────────────        ──────────────────────────────────── │
│   Γ ⊢ p π₀ ≃ p′ π₀ : S           Γ ⊢ p π₁ ≃ p′ π₁ : [x ↦ (p π₀):S]T  │
│                                                                       │
│ β-rules                                                               │
│                                                                       │
│       Γ ⊢ λx:S.t : Πx:S.T   Γ ⊢ s : S                                │
│   ──────────────────────────────────────────                        │
│   Γ ⊢ (λx:S.t) s ≃ [x ↦ s:S]t : [x ↦ s:S]T                          │
│                                                                       │
│   Γ ⊢ ⟨s;t⟩_T : Σx:S.T              Γ ⊢ ⟨s;t⟩_T : Σx:S.T            │
│   ──────────────────────        ──────────────────────────────────  │
│   Γ ⊢ ⟨s;t⟩_T π₀ ≃ s : S         Γ ⊢ ⟨s;t⟩_T π₁ ≃ t : [x ↦ s:S]T    │
│                                                                       │
│ observational rules                                                   │
│                                                                       │
│   Γ ⊢ u : 1   Γ ⊢ u′ : 1   Γ ⊢ z : O   Γ ⊢ z′ : O                   │
│   ──────────────────────   ──────────────────────                   │
│       Γ ⊢ u ≃ u′ : 1           Γ ⊢ z ≃ z′ : O                       │
│                                                                       │
│                              Γ ⊢ p π₀ ≃ p′ π₀ : S                    │
│   Γ;x:S ⊢ f x ≃ f′ x : T   Γ ⊢ p π₁ ≃ p′ π₁ : [x ↦ (p π₀):S]T        │
│   ──────────────────────   ──────────────────────────────────────   │
│   Γ ⊢ f ≃ f′ : Πx:S.T          Γ ⊢ p ≃ p′ : Σx:S.T                  │
└─────────────────────────────────────────────────────────────────────┘
```

FIGURE 6.3. Equality rules $\boxed{\Gamma \vdash t \simeq t' : T}$

veniences, such as the kind of 'filling in the blanks' we usually associate with type inference. For example, we may declare Nat and Vec as follows:

$$\underline{\text{data}} \quad \frac{}{\text{Nat} : \star} \quad \underline{\text{where}} \quad \frac{}{\text{zero} : \text{Nat}} \quad \frac{n : \text{Nat}}{\text{suc } n : \text{Nat}}$$

$$\underline{\text{data}} \quad \frac{n : \text{Nat} \,;\, X : \star}{\text{Vec } n \, X : \star} \quad \underline{\text{where}} \quad \frac{}{\text{vnil} : \text{Vec zero } X} \quad \frac{x : X \,;\, xs : \text{Vec } n \, X}{\text{vcons } x \, xs : \text{Vec (suc } n) \, X}$$

The elaborator fleshes out the implicit parts of programs. Elaboration makes hidden quantifiers and their instances explicit. The above yields:

Nat : ⋆	Vec : Πn:Nat. ΠX:⋆. ⋆
zero: Nat	vnil : ΠX:⋆. Vec zero X
suc : Nat → Nat	vcons: ΠX:⋆. Πn:Nat. X → Vec n X → Vec (suc n) X

For each datatype, the elaborator overloads the operator <u>elim</u> (postfix in ETT) with the standard induction principle. For n : Nat and xs : Vec $n\,X$, we acquire

$n\,\underline{\text{elim}}_{\text{Nat}}$:	$xs\,\underline{\text{elim}}_{\text{Vec}}$:
$\quad \Pi P : \text{Nat} \to \star.$	$\quad \Pi P : \Pi n:\text{Nat}. \Pi xs:\text{Vec } n\,X. \star .$
$\quad P\,\text{zero} \to$	$\quad P\,\text{zero}\,(\text{vnil\_}X) \to$
$\quad (\Pi n':\text{Nat}.$	$\quad (\Pi n':\text{Nat}. \Pi x:X. \Pi xs':\text{Vec } n'\,X.$
$\quad\quad P\,n' \to P\,(\text{suc } n')) \to$	$\quad\quad P\,n'\,xs' \to P\,(\text{suc } n')\,(\text{vcons } X\,n'\,x\,xs')) \to$
$\quad P\,n$	$\quad P\,n\,xs$

These types are read as schemes for constructing structurally recursive programs. Epigram has no hard-wired notion of pattern matching—rather, if you invoke an eliminator via the 'by' construct $\Leftarrow$, the elaborator reads off the appropriate patterns from its type. If we have an appropriate definition of $+$, we can define concatenation for vectors using $\underline{\text{elim}}$ (prefix in Epigram source) as follows:

$$\underline{\text{let}} \; \frac{x, y \,:\, \mathsf{Nat}}{x+y \,:\, \mathsf{Nat}} \qquad \begin{aligned} &x+y \;\Leftarrow\; \underline{\text{elim}}\,x \\ &\mathsf{zero}\,+y \;\Rightarrow y \\ &\mathsf{suc}\,x'+y \;\Rightarrow \mathsf{suc}\,(x'+y) \end{aligned}$$

$$\underline{\text{let}} \; \frac{xs \,:\, \mathsf{Vec}\,m\,X \;;\; ys \,:\, \mathsf{Vec}\,n\,X}{\mathbf{vconc}\,xs\,ys \,:\, \mathsf{Vec}\,(m+n)\,X} \quad \begin{aligned} &\mathbf{vconc}\,xs\,ys \;\Leftarrow\; \underline{\text{elim}}\,xs \\ &\mathbf{vconc}\,\mathsf{vnil} \qquad\qquad ys \;\Rightarrow ys \\ &\mathbf{vconc}\,(\mathsf{vcons}\,x\,xs')\,ys \;\Rightarrow \mathsf{vcons}\,x\,(\mathbf{vconc}\,xs'\,ys) \end{aligned}$$

The elaborator then generates this lump of ETT, inferring the 'P' argument to $xs\,\underline{\text{elim}}_{\mathsf{Vec}}$ and constructing the other two from the branches of the program.

$$\begin{aligned}
\mathbf{vconc} \mapsto\; &\lambda X \!:\! \star.\, \lambda m \!:\! \mathsf{Nat}.\, \lambda n \!:\! \mathsf{Nat}.\, \lambda xs \!:\! \mathsf{Vec}\,m\,X.\, \lambda ys \!:\! \mathsf{Vec}\,n\,X. \\
&xs\,\underline{\text{elim}}_{\mathsf{Vec}}\,(\lambda m \!:\! \mathsf{Nat}.\, \lambda xs \!:\! \mathsf{Vec}\,m\,X.\, \Pi n \!:\! \mathsf{Nat}.\; \mathsf{Vec}\,n\,X \to \mathsf{Vec}\,(m+n)\,X) \\
&(\lambda n \!:\! \mathsf{Nat}.\, \lambda ys \!:\! \mathsf{Vec}\,n\,X.\, ys) \\
&(\lambda m' \!:\! \mathsf{Nat}.\, \lambda x \!:\! X.\, \lambda xs' \!:\! \mathsf{Vec}\,m'\,X.\, \lambda h \!:\! \Pi n \!:\! \mathsf{Nat}.\; \mathsf{Vec}\,n\,X \to \mathsf{Vec}\,(m'+n)\,X. \\
&\lambda n \!:\! \mathsf{Nat}.\, \lambda ys \!:\! \mathsf{Vec}\,n\,X.\, \mathsf{vcons}\,X\,(m'+n)\,x\,(h\,n\,ys)) \\
&n\,ys
\end{aligned}$$

The elaborator works even harder in more complex situations, like this:

$$\underline{\text{let}} \; \frac{xs \,:\, \mathsf{Vec}\,(\mathsf{suc}\,n)\,X}{\mathbf{vtail}\,xs \,:\, \mathsf{Vec}\,n\,X} \qquad \begin{aligned} &\mathbf{vtail}\,xs \;\Leftarrow\; \underline{\text{elim}}\,xs \\ &\mathbf{vtail}\,(\mathsf{vcons}\,x\,xs') \;\Rightarrow xs' \end{aligned}$$

Here, the unification on lengths which eliminates the vnil case and specialises the vcons case rests on a $\underline{\text{noConfusion}}$ theorem—constructors disjoint and injective—proven by the elaborator for each datatype, and on the $\underline{\text{subst}}$ operator—replacing equal with equal. These techniques are detailed in [19, 20], but their effect is to deliver a large dull term which justifies the dependent case analysis.

$$\begin{aligned}
\mathbf{vtail} \mapsto\; &\lambda n \!:\! \mathsf{Nat}.\, \lambda X \!:\! \star.\, \lambda xs \!:\! \mathsf{Vec}\,(\mathsf{suc}\,n)\,X.\, xs\,\underline{\text{elim}}_{\mathsf{Vec}} \\
&(\lambda m \!:\! \mathsf{Nat}.\, \lambda ys \!:\! \mathsf{Vec}\,m\,X.\, \Pi n \!:\! \mathsf{Nat}.\, \Pi xs \!:\! \mathsf{Vec}\,(\mathsf{suc}\,n)\,X.\, \Pi q \!:\! m = \mathsf{suc}\,n.\, \Pi q' \!:\! ys = xs.\, \mathsf{Vec}\,n\,X) \\
&(\lambda n \!:\! \mathsf{Nat}.\, \lambda xs \!:\! \mathsf{Vec}\,(\mathsf{suc}\,n)\,X.\, \lambda q \!:\! \mathsf{zero} = \mathsf{suc}\,n.\, \lambda q' \!:\! \mathsf{vnil} = xs.\, q\,\underline{\text{noConfusion}}_{\mathsf{Nat}}\,(\mathsf{Vec}\,n\,X)) \\
&(\lambda n' \!:\! \mathsf{Nat}.\, \lambda x \!:\! X.\, \lambda xs' \!:\! \mathsf{Vec}\,n'. \\
&\lambda h \!:\! \Pi n \!:\! \mathsf{Nat}.\, \Pi xs \!:\! \mathsf{Vec}\,(\mathsf{suc}\,n)\,X.\, \Pi q \!:\! n' = \mathsf{suc}\,n.\, \Pi q' \!:\! xs' = xs.\, \mathsf{Vec}\,n\,X. \\
&\lambda n \!:\! \mathsf{Nat}.\, \lambda xs \!:\! \mathsf{Vec}\,(\mathsf{suc}\,n)\,X.\, \lambda q \!:\! \mathsf{suc}\,n' = \mathsf{suc}\,n.\, \lambda q' \!:\! \mathsf{vcons}\,X\,n'\,x\,xs' = xs. \\
&q\,\underline{\text{noConfusion}}_{\mathsf{Nat}}\,(\mathsf{Vec}\,n\,X) \\
&\quad(\lambda q \!:\! n' = n.\, q\,\underline{\text{subst}} \\
&\qquad(\lambda n \!:\! \mathsf{Nat}.\, \Pi xs' \!:\! \mathsf{Vec}\,n'\,X.\, \Pi h \!:\! \Pi n \!:\! \mathsf{Nat}.\, \Pi xs \!:\! \mathsf{Vec}\,(\mathsf{suc}\,n)\,X.\, \Pi q \!:\! n' = \mathsf{suc}\,n.\, \Pi q' \!:\! xs' = xs.\, \mathsf{Vec}\,n\,X. \\
&\qquad \Pi xs \!:\! \mathsf{Vec}\,(\mathsf{suc}\,n)\,X.\, \Pi q' \!:\! \mathsf{vcons}\,X\,n'\,x\,xs' = xs.\, \mathsf{Vec}\,n\,X) \\
&\qquad(\lambda xs' \!:\! \mathsf{Vec}\,n'\,X.\, \lambda h \!:\! \Pi n \!:\! \mathsf{Nat}.\, \Pi xs \!:\! \mathsf{Vec}\,(\mathsf{suc}\,n)\,X.\, \Pi q \!:\! n' = \mathsf{suc}\,n.\, \Pi q' \!:\! xs' = xs.\, \mathsf{Vec}\,n\,X. \\
&\qquad \lambda xs \!:\! \mathsf{Vec}\,(\mathsf{suc}\,n')\,X.\, \lambda q' \!:\! \mathsf{vcons}\,X\,n'\,x\,xs' = xs.\, q'\,\underline{\text{subst}}\,(\lambda xs \!:\! \mathsf{Vec}\,(\mathsf{suc}\,n')\,X.\, \mathsf{Vec}\,n'\,X)\,xs') \\
&\qquad xs'\,h\,xs\,q')) \\
&(\mathsf{suc}\,n)\,xs\,(\mathsf{refl}\,\mathsf{Nat}\,(\mathsf{suc}\,n))\,(\mathsf{refl}\,(\mathsf{Vec}\,(\mathsf{suc}\,n)\,X)\,xs)
\end{aligned}$$

Merely *checking* all these details is much simpler than inferring them in the first place. Reloading ETT involves none of the complexity of implicit syntax handling or dependent pattern matching. Meanwhile, our observational equality rules help the elaborator by allowing more type constraints to have general solutions.

6.4 ETT SYNTAX IN HASKELL

We now implement ETT in Haskell. We first represent its syntax.

```
data Term  = R Reference              -- free variable (carries definition)
           | V Int                    -- bound variable (de Bruijn index)
           | Pi Type Scope            -- Πx : S. T
           | Si Type Scope            -- Σx : S. T
           | L Type Scope             -- λx : S. t
           | P Term (Term, Scope)     -- ⟨s;t⟩_T
           | Term :$ Elim Term        -- elimination form
           | C Const                  -- constant
           | Let (Term, Type) Scope   -- [x ↦ s : S]t
type Type  = Term    -- types are just a subset of terms
data Scope = (:.){ adv :: String, bdy :: Term }
data Elim t = A t | P0 | P1 | OE      -- − t, − π₀, − π₁, − Œ
data Const = Star | One | Void | Zero -- ⋆, 1, ⟨⟩, O
```

As in [21], we explicitly separate free variables from bound, using a de Bruijn index [13] representation for the latter. Each time we bind a variable, the indices shift by one; we wrap up the term in scope of the new bound variable in the datatype Scope. This distinction helps to avoid silly mistakes, supports useful overloading and allows us to cache a string used only for display-name generation.

Correspondingly a λ-term carries a Type for its domain and a Scope for its body. Σ and Π types are represented similarly. Pairs P Term (Term, Scope) carry the range of their Σ-type—you cannot guess this from the type of the second projection, which gives only its instance for the value of the first projection.

We gather the constants in Const. We also collect the elimination forms Term :$ Elim Term, so that we can define their computational behaviour in one place. Elim is an instance of Functor in the obvious way. By way of example, the 'twice' function, $\lambda X : \star. \lambda f : X \to X. \lambda x : X. f \ (f \ x)$ becomes the following:

$$twice = \mathsf{L} \ (\mathsf{C} \ \mathsf{Star}) \ (\texttt{"X"} :. \ \ \mathsf{L} \ (\mathsf{Pi} \ (\mathsf{V} \ 0) \ (\texttt{"x"} :. \mathsf{V} \ 1)) \ (\texttt{"f"} :.$$
$$\mathsf{L} \ (\mathsf{V} \ 1) \ (\texttt{"x"} :. \ \ \mathsf{V} \ 1 :\$ \ \mathsf{A} \ (\mathsf{V} \ 1 :\$ \ \mathsf{A} \ (\mathsf{V} \ 0)) \ )))$$

In section 6.6, we shall equip this syntax with a semantics, introducing the type Value which pairs these first-order terms with a functional representation of Scopes. We exploit this semantics in the free variables R Reference, which include both parameters and global definitions. A Reference carries its Name but also caches its type, and in the case of a definition, its value.

```
type Reference = Name := Typed Object
data Typed x   = (:∈){ trm :: x, typ :: Value }
data Object    = Para | Defn Value
```

It is easy to extend Object with tagged constructor objects and Elim with datatype eliminators which switch on the tags—constructing their types is explained in [21].

6.4.1 Navigation under binders

The operations $/\!/$ and $\backslash\!\backslash$ provide a means to navigate into and out of binders.

$(/\!/) :: \mathsf{Scope} \to \mathsf{Value} \to \mathsf{Term}$
         -- instantiates the bound variable of a Scope with a Value
$(\backslash\!\backslash) :: (\mathsf{Name}, \mathsf{String}) \to \mathsf{Term} \to \mathsf{Scope}$
         -- binds a variable free in a Term to make a Scope

Namespace management uses the techniques of [21]. Names are backward lists of Strings, resembling long names in module systems.

type $\mathsf{Name} = \mathsf{BList}\ \mathsf{String}$
data $\mathsf{BList}\ x = \mathsf{B0}\ |\ \mathsf{BList}\ x \vartriangleleft x$ **deriving** Eq

Our work is always relative to a root name: we define a Checking monad which combines the threading of this root and the handling of errors. For this presentation we limit ourselves to Maybe for errors.

newtype $\mathsf{Checking}\ x = \mathsf{MkChecking}\{\mathsf{runChecking} :: \mathsf{Name} \to \mathsf{Maybe}\ x\}$
instance $\mathsf{Monad}\ \mathsf{Checking}$ **where**
    $\mathsf{return}\ x = \mathsf{MkChecking}\ \$\ \lambda\_ \to \mathsf{return}\ x$
    $\mathsf{MkChecking}\ f \ggg g = \mathsf{MkChecking}\ \$\ \lambda name \to$ **do**
      $a \leftarrow f\ name$
      $\mathsf{runChecking}\ (g\ a)\ name$

User name choices never interfere with machine Name choices. Moreover, we ensure that different tasks never choose clashing names by locally extending the root name of each subtask with a different suffix.

$(\odot) :: \mathsf{String} \to \mathsf{Checking}\ x \to \mathsf{Checking}\ x$
$name \odot (\mathsf{MkChecking}\ f) = \mathsf{MkChecking}\ \$\ \lambda root \to f\ (root \vartriangleleft name)$
$\mathsf{root} :: \mathsf{Checking}\ \mathsf{Name}$
$\mathsf{root} = \mathsf{MkChecking}\ \mathsf{return}$

Whether we really need to or not, we uniformly give every subcomputation a distinct local name, trivially guaranteeing the absence of name clashes. In particular, we can use $x \odot \mathsf{root}$ to generate a fresh name for a fresh variable if we ensure that x is distinct from the other local names.

6.5 CHECKING TYPES

In this section, we shall show how to synthesise the types of expressions and check that they are correct. Typechecking makes essential use of the semantics of terms. We defer our implementation of this semantics until section 6.6: here we indicate our *requirements* for our representation of Values.

    The typing rules are realized by three functions infer, synth and check. Firstly, infer infers the type of its argument in a syntax-directed manner.

infer :: Term $\rightarrow$ Checking Value

Secondly, synth calls infer to check that its argument has a type and, *safe in this knowledge*, returns both its value and the inferred type.

synth :: Term $\rightarrow$ Checking (Typed Value)
synth $t = $ **do**
  $ty \leftarrow $ `"ty"` $\odot$ infer t
  return (val $t :\in ty$)
val :: Term $\rightarrow$ Value   -- must only be used with well-typed terms
syn :: Value $\rightarrow$ Term   -- recovers the syntax from a Value

Note that `"ty"` $\odot$ infer t performs the inference in the namespace extended by `"ty"` ensuring that name choices made by infer t are local to the new namespace. Thirdly, check takes a Value representing a *required* type and a Term. It synthesises the value and type of the latter, then checks that types coincide, in accordance with the conversion rule.

check :: Value $\rightarrow$ Term $\rightarrow$ Checking Value
check $ty\ t = $ **do**
  $(tv :\in sty) \leftarrow $ `"sy"` $\odot$ synth t
  `"eq"` $\odot$ areEqual $((ty, sty) :\in \text{vStar})$
  return tv

Type checking will require us to ask the following questions about values:

areEqual :: Typed (Value, Value) $\rightarrow$ Checking ()
isZero :: Value $\rightarrow$ Checking ()
isPi, isSi :: Value $\rightarrow$ Checking (Value, ScoVal)

We have just seen that we need to check when types are equal. We also need to determine whether a type matches the right pattern for a given elimination form, extracting the components in the case of Π- and Σ-types. The ScoVal type gives the semantics of Scopes, with val and syn correspondingly overloaded, as we shall see in section 6.6.

In order to synthesise types, we shall need to construct values from checked components returned by infer, synth and check, isPi and isSi. We thus define 'smart constructors' which assemble Values from the semantic counterparts of the corrresponding Term constructors.

vStar, vAbsurd :: Value
vStar $=$ val (C Star)
vAbsurd $=$ val (Pi (C Star) (`"T"` $:.$ V 0))
vPi, vSi :: Value $\rightarrow$ ScoVal $\rightarrow$ Value
vLet   :: Typed Value $\rightarrow$ ScoVal $\rightarrow$ Value
vdefn   :: Typed (Name, Value) $\rightarrow$ Value
vpara   :: (Typed Name) $\rightarrow$ Value

6.5.1 Implementing the Typing Rules

We will now define infer in accordance with the typing rules from figure 6.2. We match on the syntax of the term and in each case implement the rule with the corresponding conclusion, performing the checks in the hypotheses, then constructing the type from checked components. The base cases are easy: references cache their types and constants have constant types—we just give the case for $\star$.

$$\text{infer } (\mathsf{R} \ (\_ := (\_ :\in ty))) = \text{return } ty$$
$$\text{infer } (\mathsf{C} \ \mathsf{Star}) = \text{return } \mathsf{vStar}$$

The case for bound variables $\mathsf{V} \ i$ never arises. We always work with *closed* terms, instantiating a bound variable as we enter its Scope, abstracting it when we leave. Local definition is a case in point:

$$
\begin{aligned}
&\text{infer } (\mathsf{Let} \ (s, sty) \ t) = \textbf{do} \\
&\quad styv \leftarrow \text{"sty"} \odot \text{check vStar } sty \\
&\quad sv \ \ \ \leftarrow \text{"s"} \ \ \ \ \odot \text{check } styv \ s \\
&\quad x \ \ \ \ \leftarrow \text{"x"} \ \ \ \odot \text{root} \\
&\quad ttyv \leftarrow \text{"tty"} \odot \text{infer } (t /\!\!/ \mathsf{vdefn} \ ((x, sv) :\in styv)) \\
&\quad \text{return } (\mathsf{vLet} \ (sv :\in styv) \ (\mathsf{val} \ ((x, \mathsf{adv} \ t) \backslash\!\backslash \mathsf{syn} \ ttyv)))
\end{aligned}
$$

We check that ty is a type and that s inhabits it. The rules achieve this indirectly via context validity at each leaf of the typing derivation; we perform the check once, before vdefn creates the reference value which realises the extension of the context. The new variable gets its fresh name from "x" $\odot$ root, and the corresponding value is used to instantiate the bound variable of t. Once we have t's type, $ttyv$, we use vLet to build the type of the whole thing from checked components. Values do not support the $(\backslash\!\backslash)$ operation, so we abstract x from the syntax of $ttyv$, then generate a semantic scope with val. Checking a Π-type requires a similar journey under a binder, but the resulting type is a simple $\star$.

$$
\begin{aligned}
&\text{infer } (\mathsf{Pi} \ dom \ ran) = \textbf{do} \\
&\quad domv \leftarrow \text{"dom"} \odot \text{check vStar } dom \\
&\quad x \ \ \ \ \leftarrow \text{"x"} \ \ \ \odot \text{root} \\
&\quad \_ \ \ \ \ \leftarrow \text{"ran"} \odot \text{check vStar } (ran /\!\!/ \mathsf{vpara} \ (x :\in domv)) \\
&\quad \text{return vStar}
\end{aligned}
$$

We check that dom is a type, then create a fresh variable and instantiate the range, ensuring that it also is a type. Checking a Σ-type works the same way. Meanwhile, to typecheck a λ, we must use the type inferred under the binder to generate the Π-type of the function, abstracting a scope from its syntax as we did for Let.

$$
\begin{aligned}
&\text{infer } (\mathsf{L} \ dom \ t) = \textbf{do} \\
&\quad domv \leftarrow \text{"dom"} \odot \text{check vStar } dom \\
&\quad x \ \ \ \ \leftarrow \text{"x"} \ \ \ \odot \text{root} \\
&\quad ranv \leftarrow \text{"ran"} \odot \text{infer } (t /\!\!/ \mathsf{vpara} \ (x :\in domv)) \\
&\quad \text{return } (\mathsf{vPi} \ domv \ (\mathsf{val} \ ((x, \mathsf{adv} \ t) \backslash\!\backslash \mathsf{syn} \ ranv)))
\end{aligned}
$$

To infer the type of an application we check that the 'function' actually has a Π-type, revealing the domain type for which to check the argument. If all is well we let-bind the return type, corresponding to the rule exactly.

> infer (f :$ A a) = **do**
>   fty ← "f" ⊙ infer f
>   (dom, ran) ← isPi fty
>   av ← "a" ⊙ check dom a
>   return (vLet (av :∈ dom) ran)

Here is how we infer the type of pairs:

> infer (P s (t, ran)) = **do**
>   tys@(sv :∈ domv) ← "s"   ⊙ synth s
>   x   ← "x"   ⊙ root
>   _   ← "ran" ⊙ check vStar (ran∥vpara (x :∈ domv))
>   _   ← "t"   ⊙ check (vLet tys (val ran)) t
>   return (vSi domv (val ran))

First, we ensure that s is well typed yielding the domain of the Σ-type. Next, we check that the supplied range ran is a type in the context extended with the parameter of the domain type. Then we check t in the appropriately let bound range. We then deliver the Σ-type. Meanwhile, projections are straightforward.

> infer (p :$ P0) = **do**   infer (p :$ P1) = **do**
>   pty   ← "p" ⊙ infer p   pty   ← "p" ⊙ infer p
>   (dom, _) ← isSi pty   (dom, ran) ← isSi pty
>   return dom   return (vLet ((val (p :$ P0)) :∈ dom) ran)

Finally, eliminating the empty type always yields absurdity!

> infer (z :$ OE) = **do**
>   zty ← "z" ⊙ infer z
>   isZero zty
>   return vAbsurd

6.6   FROM SYNTAX TO SEMANTICS

We shall now give a definition of Value which satisfies the requirements of our checker. Other definitions are certainly possible, but this one has the merit of allowing considerable control over which computations happen.

> **data** Glued t w = (:⇓){syn :: t, sem :: w}
> **type** Value   = Glued Term Whnf
> **type** ScoVal   = Glued Scope (Value → Whnf)

A Value glues a Term to a functional representation of its weak head normal form (Whnf). The semantic counterpart of a Scope is a ScoVal, which affixes a Haskell function, delivering the meaning of the scope with its bound variable instantiated.

Just as in 'normalisation-by-evaluation' [6], the behaviour of scopes (for Π and Σ, not just λ) is delivered by the implementation language, but if we want to read a Value, we just project its syntax. Whnfs are given as follows:

data Whnf = WR Reference (BList (Elim Value))   -- Spine
      | WPi Value ScoVal | WSi Value ScoVal   -- Π-type, Σ-type
      | WL ScoVal | WP Value Value   -- λ-abstraction, pair
      | WC Const   -- Constant

The only elimination forms we need to represent are those which operate on an inert parameter, hence we pack them together, with the WR constructor. Bound variables do not occur, except within the Scope part of a ScoVal. We drop the type annotations on λ-abstractions and pairs as they have no operational use. With this definition, operations such as isPi, isSi and isZero can be implemented directly by pattern matching on Whnf. Meanwhile, the computational behaviour of Values is given by the overloaded \$ operator:

class Eliminable t **where**
    (\$) :: $t \rightarrow$ (Elim Value) $\rightarrow t$
instance Eliminable Value **where**
    t \$ e = (syn t :\$ fmap syn e) :$\Downarrow$ (sem t \$ e)
instance Eliminable Whnf **where**
    WL ($\_$:$\Downarrow f$) \$ A $v = f\, v$ -- β-reduction by Haskell application
    WP $x\, \_$ \$ P0 = sem x -- projections
    WP $\_\, y$ \$ P1 = sem y
    WR $x\, es$ \$ e = WR x ($es \lhd e$)   -- inert computations

We shall now use \$ to deliver the function eval which makes values from checked syntax. This too is overloaded, and its syntactic aspect relies on the availability of substitution of *closed* terms for bound variables.

type Env = BList Value
bproj :: BList $x \rightarrow$ Int $\rightarrow x$

class Close t **where**
    close :: $t \rightarrow$ Env $\rightarrow$ Int $\rightarrow t$ -- the Int is the first bound variable to replace

class Close $t \Rightarrow$ Whnv $t\, w$ | $t \rightarrow w$ **where**
    whnv :: $t \rightarrow$ Env $\rightarrow w$
    eval :: $t \rightarrow$ Env $\rightarrow$ Glued $t\, w$
    eval $t\, \gamma$ = (close $t\, \gamma$ 0) :$\Downarrow$ (whnv $t\, \gamma$)
    val :: $t \rightarrow$ Glued $t\, w$
    val $t = t$:$\Downarrow$ whnv t B0

We export val, for closed terms, to the typechecker. However, eval and whnv, defined mutually, thread an environment γ explaining the bound variables. By separating Scope from Term, we can say how to go under a binder once, for all.

instance Close Scope **where**
    close $(s :. t)\, \gamma\, i = s :.$ close $t\, \gamma\, (i + 1)$ -- start γ further out

instance Whnv Scope (Value → Whnf) **where**
    whnv $(\_::t)\,\gamma = \lambda x \rightarrow$ whnv $t\,(\gamma \lhd x)$ -- extend the environment

Meanwhile, whnv for Term traverses the syntax, delivering the semantics.

instance Whnv Term Whnf **where**
    whnv $(\mathsf{R}\,(\_ := (\mathsf{Defn}\,v :\in \_)))\,\_ = \mathsf{sem}\,v$
    whnv $(\mathsf{R}\,r)$ $\_ = \mathsf{WR}\,r\,\mathsf{B0}$
    whnv $(\mathsf{V}\,i)$ $\gamma = \mathsf{sem}\,(\mathsf{bproj}\,\gamma\,i)$
    whnv $(\mathsf{Pi}\,d\,r)$ $\gamma = \mathsf{WPi}\,(\mathsf{eval}\,d\,\gamma)\,(\mathsf{eval}\,r\,\gamma)$
    whnv $(\mathsf{Si}\,d\,r)$ $\gamma = \mathsf{WSi}\,(\mathsf{eval}\,d\,\gamma)\,(\mathsf{eval}\,r\,\gamma)$
    whnv $(\mathsf{L}\,\_\,r)$ $\gamma = \mathsf{WL}\,(\mathsf{eval}\,r\,\gamma)$
    whnv $(\mathsf{P}\,x\,(y,\_))$ $\gamma = \mathsf{WP}\,(\mathsf{eval}\,x\,\gamma)\,(\mathsf{eval}\,y\,\gamma)$
    whnv $(t :\$\,e)$ $\gamma = \mathsf{whnv}\,t\,\gamma\,\$\$\,\mathsf{fmap}\,(`\mathsf{eval}`\gamma)\,e$
    whnv $(\mathsf{C}\,c)$ $\_ = \mathsf{WC}\,c$
    whnv $(\mathsf{Let}\,(t,\_)\,s)$ $\gamma = \mathsf{whnv}\,s\,\gamma\,(\mathsf{eval}\,t\,\gamma)$

Defined free variables are expanded; parameters gain an empty spine; γ explains bound variables. We interpret $(:\$)$ with $(\$\$)$. Lets directly exploit the their bodies' functional meaning. Everything else is structural.

The close operation just substitutes the environment for the bound variables, without further evaluation. The Int counts the binders crossed, hence the number of variables which should stay bound. We give only the interesting cases:

instance Close Term **where**
    close t $\mathsf{B0}\,\_ = t$
    close $(\mathsf{V}\,j)\,\gamma$ $i = $ **if** $j < i$ **then** $\mathsf{V}\,j$ **else** $\mathsf{syn}\,(\mathsf{bproj}\,\gamma\,(j-i))$

6.7 CHECKING EQUALITY

Our equality algorithm does 'on-the-fly' η-expansion on weak-head β-normal forms, directed by their types. The observational rules for elements of Π and Σ-types perform the η-expansion to yield η-long normal forms at ground type ($\star$,1 or *Zero*). We now define areEqual skipping the structural cases for constant types, WPi, WSi, and going straight to the interaction between the the observational rules and checking equality on spines.

We do not need to look at elements of type 1 to know that they are equal to $\langle\rangle$. Elements of O (hypothetical, of course) are also equal. We compare functions by applying them to a fresh parameter and pairs by comparing their projections.

    areEqual :: Typed (Value, Value) → Checking ()
    areEqual $(\_ :\in (\_ :\Downarrow \mathsf{WC}\,\mathsf{One}\,)) = \mathsf{return}\,()$
    areEqual $(\_ :\in (\_ :\Downarrow \mathsf{WC}\,\mathsf{Zero})) = \mathsf{return}\,()$
    areEqual $((f,g) :\in (_ :\Downarrow \mathsf{WPi}\,dom\,ran)) = $ **do**
      $x \leftarrow$ "x" $\odot$ root
      let $v = \mathsf{vpara}\,(x :\in dom)$
      "ran" $\odot$ areEqual $((f\,\$\$\,\mathsf{A}\,v, f\,\$\$\,\mathsf{A}\,v) :\in \mathsf{vLet}\,(v :\in dom)\,ran)$

areEqual $((p,q) :\in (\_ :\Downarrow \mathsf{WSi}\ dom\ ran)) = \mathbf{do}$
   "fst" $\odot$ areEqual $((p\,\$\$\,\mathsf{P0}, q\,\$\$\,\mathsf{P0}) :\in dom)$
   "snd" $\odot$ areEqual $((p\,\$\$\,\mathsf{P1}, q\,\$\$\,\mathsf{P1}) :\in (\mathsf{vLet}\ (p\,\$\$\,\mathsf{P0} :\in dom)\ ran))$

For ground terms of types other than 1 and O, we can only have inert references with spines, which we compare in accordance with the structural rules. We rebuild the type of a spine as we process it, in order to compare its components correctly.

areEqual $((\_ :\Downarrow \mathsf{WR}\ r1\ @(\_ := (\_ :\in ty))\ as, \_ :\Downarrow \mathsf{WR}\ r2\ bs) :\in \_) =$
  spineEq (as, bs) **where**
    spineEq :: $(\mathsf{Elim}\ \mathsf{Value}, \mathsf{Elim}\ \mathsf{Value}) \rightarrow \mathsf{Checking}\ \mathsf{Value}$

We peel eliminators until we reach the reference, whose type we pass back.

  spineEq $(\mathsf{B0}, \mathsf{B0}) = \mathsf{guard}\ (r1 \equiv r2) \gg \mathsf{return}\ ty$

For applications, we check that preceding spines are equal and analyse the Π-type they deliver; we then confirm that the arguments are equal elements of its domain and pass on the instantiated range.

  spineEq $(as \lhd\mathsf{A}\ a, bs \lhd\mathsf{A}\ b) = \mathbf{do}$
    $sty \leftarrow$ spineEq (as, bs)
    $(dom, ran) \leftarrow$ isPi sty
    "eqargs" $\odot$ areEqual $((a, b) :\in dom)$
    return $(\mathsf{vLet}\ (a :\in dom)\ ran)$

For like projections from pairs we analyse the Σ-type from the preceding spines and pass on the appropriate component, instantiated if need be.

  spineEq $(as \lhd\mathsf{P0}, bs \lhd\mathsf{P0}) = \mathbf{do}$
    $sty \leftarrow$ spineEq (as, bs)
    $(dom, \_) \leftarrow$ isSi sty
    return dom
  spineEq $(as \lhd\mathsf{P1}, bs \lhd\mathsf{P1}) = \mathbf{do}$
    $sty \leftarrow$ spineEq (as, bs)
    $(dom, ran) \leftarrow$ isSi sty
    return $(\mathsf{vLet}\ ((\mathsf{spine}\ (as \lhd\mathsf{P0})) :\in dom)\ ran)$

For 'naught E', we need look no further!

  spineEq $(as \lhd\mathsf{OE}, bs \lhd\mathsf{OE}) = \mathsf{return}\ \mathsf{vAbsurd}$
  spine :: $(\mathsf{Elim}\ \mathsf{Value}) \rightarrow \mathsf{Value}$
  spine $\mathsf{B0} = \mathsf{val}\ (\mathsf{R}\ r1)$
  spine $(es \lhd e) = \mathsf{spine}\ r1\ es\,\$\$\,e$

6.8 RELATED WORK

Type checking algorithms for dependent types are at the core of systems like Lego [17] and Coq [9] (which have only β-equality) and Agda [10], for which Coquand's simple algorithm with βη-equality for Π-types [12] forms the core; he and Abel have recently extended this to Σ-types [1]. Our more liberal equality makes it easy to import developments from these systems, but harder to export to them.

Coquand's and Abel's algorithms are syntax-directed: comparison proceeds structurally on β-normal forms, except when comparing $\lambda x.\,t$ with some variable-headed (or 'neutral') f, which gets expanded to $\lambda x.\,f\,x$. Also, when comparing $\langle s, t \rangle$ with neutral p, the latter expands to $\langle p\,\pi_0, p\,\pi_1 \rangle$. Leaving two neutral functions or pairs unexpanded cannot make them appear different, so this 'tit-for-tat' η-expansion suffices. However, there is no such syntactic cue for 1 or O: apparently distinct neutral terms can be equal, if they have a proof-irrelevant type.

We have taken type-directed η-expansion from normalisation-by-evaluation [6, 3], fusing it with the conversion check. Our whnv is untyped and lazy, but compilation in the manner of Gregoire and Leroy [14] would certainly pay off for heavy type-level computations, especially if enhanced by Brady's optimisations [7, 8].

6.9 CONCLUSIONS AND FURTHER WORK

The main deliverable of our work is a standalone typechecker for ETT which plays an important rôle in the overall architecture of Epigram. We have addressed a number of challenges in implementing a stronger conversion incorporating observational rules. These simplify elaboration and will play a vital rôle in our project to implement Observational Type Theory[4] whose equality judgement remains decidable, but which supports *reasoning* up to observation as in [2].

REFERENCES

[1] Andreas Abel and Thierry Coquand. Untyped algorithmic equality for Martin-Löf's logical framework with surjective pairs. In *Typed Lambda Calculus and Applications*, pages 23–38, 2005.

[2] Thorsten Altenkirch. Extensional equality in intensional type theory. In *LICS 99*, 1999.

[3] Thorsten Altenkirch, Martin Hofmann, and Thomas Streicher. Categorical reconstruction of a reduction free normalization proof. In David Pitt, David E. Rydeheard, and Peter Johnstone, editors, *Category Theory and Computer Science*, LNCS 953, pages 182–199, 1995.

[4] Thorsten Altenkirch and Conor McBride. Towards observational type theory. Manuscript, available online, February 2006.

[5] Thorsten Altenkirch, Conor McBride, and James McKinna. Why dependent types matter. Manuscript, available online, April 2005.

[6] Ulrich Berger and Helmut Schwichtenberg. An inverse of the evaluation functional for typed λ–calculus. In R. Vemuri, editor, *Proceedings of the Sixth Annual IEEE Symposium on Logic in Computer Science*, pages 203–211. IEEE Computer Science Press, Los Alamitos, 1991.

[7] Edwin Brady. *Practical Implementation of a Dependently Typed Functional Programming Language*. PhD thesis, University of Durham, 2005.

[8] Edwin Brady, Conor McBride, and James McKinna. Inductive families need not store their indices. In Stefano Berardi, Mario Coppo, and Ferrucio Damiani, editors, *Types for Proofs and Programs, Torino, 2003*, volume 3085 of *LNCS*, pages 115–129. Springer-Verlag, 2004.

[9] L'Équipe Coq. The Coq Proof Assistant Reference Manual. http://pauillac.inria.fr/coq/doc/main.html, 2001.

[10] Catarina Coquand and Thierry Coquand. Structured Type Theory. In *Workshop on Logical Frameworks and Metalanguages*, 1999.

[11] Thierry Coquand. An analysis of Girard's paradox. In *Proceedings of the First IEEE Symposium on Logic in Computer Science, Cambridge, Massachussetts*, pages 227–236, 1986.

[12] Thierry Coquand. An algorithm for testing conversion in type theory. In Gérard Huet and Gordon Plotkin, editors, *Logical Frameworks*. CUP, 1991.

[13] Nicolas G. de Bruijn. Lambda Calculus notation with nameless dummies: a tool for automatic formula manipulation. *Indagationes Mathematicæ*, 34:381–392, 1972.

[14] Benjamin Grégoire and Xavier Leroy. A compiled implementation of strong reduction. In *International Conference on Functional Programming 2002*, pages 235–246. ACM Press, 2002.

[15] Robert Harper and Randy Pollack. Type checking with universes. *Theoretical Computer Science*, 89:107–136, 1991.

[16] Zhaohui Luo. *Computation and Reasoning: A Type Theory for Computer Science*. Oxford University Press, 1994.

[17] Zhaohui Luo and Robert Pollack. LEGO Proof Development System: User's Manual. Technical Report ECS-LFCS-92-211, LFCS, 1992.

[18] Per Martin-Löf. *Intuitionistic Type Theory*. Bibliopolis·Napoli, 1984.

[19] Conor McBride. Elimination with a Motive. In Paul Callaghan, Zhaohui Luo, James McKinna, and Robert Pollack, editors, *Types for Proofs and Programs (Proceedings of the International Workshop, TYPES'00)*, volume 2277 of *LNCS*. Springer-Verlag, 2002.

[20] Conor McBride, Healfdene Goguen, and James McKinna. A Few Constructions on Constructors. In *Types for Proofs and Programs, Paris, 2004*, LNCS. Springer-Verlag, 2005. accepted; to appear.

[21] Conor McBride and James McKinna. Functional Pearl: I am not a Number: I am a Free Variable. In Henrik Nilsson, editor, *Proceedings of the ACM SIGPLAN Haskell Workshop 2004, Snowbird, Utah*. ACM, 2004.

[22] Conor McBride and James McKinna. The view from the left. *Journal of Functional Programming*, 14(1), 2004.

[23] James McKinna. *Deliverables: A Categorical Approach to Program Development in Type Theory*. PhD thesis, LFCS, 1992.

[24] George C. Necula. Proof-carrying code. In *Proceedings of the 24th ACM SIGPLAN-SIGACT Symposium on Principles of Programming Languages*, pages 106–119, Paris, January 1997.

Chapter 7

Formalisation of Haskell Refactorings

Huiqing Li[1], Simon Thompson[1]

Abstract: Refactoring is a technique for improving the design of existing programs without changing their external behaviour. HaRe is the refactoring tool we have built to support refactoring Haskell 98 programs. Along with the development of HaRe, we have also investigated the formal specification and proof of validity of refactorings. This formalisation process helps to clarify the meaning of refactorings, improves our confidence in the behaviour-preservation of refactorings, and reduces the need for testing. This paper gives an overview of HaRe, and shows our approach to the formalisation of refactorings.

7.1 INTRODUCTION

Refactoring [4] is about improving the design of a program without changing its external behaviour. Behaviour preservation guarantees that refactoring does not introduce (nor remove) any bugs. Separating general software updates into functionality changes and refactorings has well-known benefits. While it is possible to refactor a program by hand, tool support is considered invaluable as it is more reliable and allows refactorings to be done (and undone) easily. Tools can ensure the validity of refactoring steps by automating both the checking of the conditions for the refactoring and the application of the refactoring itself, thus making refactoring less painful and less error-prone.

As part of our project 'Refactoring Functional Programs' [15], we have developed the Haskell Refactorer, HaRe [7], providing support for refactoring Haskell programs. HaRe covers the full Haskell 98 standard language, and is integrated with two development environments: Vim and (X)Emacs. Apart from preserving behaviour, HaRe preserves both the comments and layout of the refactored

---

[1]Conputing Laboratory, University of Kent, UK; Email: H.Li@kent.ac.uk, S.J.Thompson@kent.ac.uk

```
-- Test.hs                          -- Test.hs
module Test where                   module Test where

f [] = 0                            f m [] = 0
f (h:t) = h^2 + f t                 f m (h:t) = h^m + f m t

-- Main.hs                          -- Main.hs
module Main where                   module Main where
import Test                         import Test

main = print $ f [1..5]             main = print $ f 2 [1..5]
```

FIGURE 7.1.   Generalise function **f** over the subexpression 2.

programs as much as possible. HaRe is itself implemented in Haskell. The first version of HaRe was released in October 2003, and since then more features have been added to make it more usable. The third release of HaRe supports 24 refactorings, and also exposes an API [8] for defining refactorings or more general program transformations.

The refactorings implemented in HaRe fall into three categories: **structural** refactorings, **module** refactorings, and **data-oriented** refactorings. **Structural** refactorings, such as generalising a definition, renaming a definition, unfolding a definition and changing the scope of a definition, mainly concern the name and scope of the entities defined in a program and the structure of definitions. **Module** refactorings, such as moving a definition from one module to another, removing redundant imports, etc, concern the imports and exports of individual modules, and the relocation of definitions among modules. **Data-oriented** refactorings, such as from concrete to abstract data type, are associated with data type definitions. Apart from implementing HaRe, we have also examined the formal specification and proof of correctness of various refactorings.

A number of tools [11] have been developed to automate the application of refactorings, especially for object-oriented(OO) programming languages. However the study of formalisation and proof of refactorings has been lagging behind system development mostly due to the complexity of programming language semantics. In comparison with imperative languages, pure functional languages have a stronger theoretical basis, and reasoning about programs written in pure functional languages is less complicated due to the referential transparency [5] property. This is also manifested by the collection of related work in the functional programming paradigm where functionality-preserving program transformations are used for reasoning about programs [14], for deriving efficient implementations from program specifications [2, 13], and for compiler optimisation [6].

This paper investigates the formal specification of refactorings as well as the proof of their functionality preservation within our context of refactoring. Two representative refactorings are examined in detail, and they are *generalise a def-*

```
-- Test1.hs                          -- Test1.hs
module Test1(foo,sq) where           module Test1(sq) where

sq x = x ^ 2                         sq x = x ^ 2

foo x y = sq x + sq y                -- Test2.hs
                                     module Test2 where
-- Test2.hs                          import Test1(sq)
module Test2 where
import Test1(sq)                      foo x y = sq x + sq y

bar x y = x + y                      bar x y = x + y

-- Main.hs                            -- Main.hs
module Main where                    module Main where
import Test1                         import Test1
import Test2(bar)                    import Test2(bar,foo)

main x y                             main x y
  = print $ foo x y + bar x y          = print $ foo x y + bar x y
```

FIGURE 7.2. **Move the definition of** *foo* **to module** M2

inition and *move a definition from one module to another.* The former, which is typical of the class of **structural** refactorings, generalises a definition by making an identified expression of its right-hand side into a value passed into the function via a new formal parameter, thereby improving the usability of the definition illustrated by the example shown in Figure 7.1, where the program before generalisation appears in the left-hand column and the program after generalisation appears in the right-hand column.

The second example, which is typical of the class of **module** refactorings, moves a top-level definition from its current module to a specified module. Associated with the definition move is the modification of the imports/exports of the affected modules, which compensates for the changes caused by moving the definition, as shown in the example in Figure 7.2. These two refactorings are typical, so by treating these we aim to illustrate how other refactorings can be formalised in a similar way. The formalisation of **data-oriented** refactorings and how type information can be used in the formalisation need further research, and are not covered in this paper.

For each refactoring, we give its formal definition consisting of the representations of the program before and after the refactoring, the side-conditions that should be met by the program in order for the refactoring to preserve behaviour, and prove that the programs before and after the refactoring are equivalent in functionality under the given side-conditions.

While HaRe is targeted at Haskell 98, our first formalisation of refactorings is based on the simple λ-calculus augmented with letrec-expressions (denoted as λ_{Letrec}). By starting from λ_{Letrec}, we keep our specifications and proofs simple and manageable, but still reflect the essential characteristics of refactorings. In the case that a refactoring involves features not covered by λ_{Letrec}, such as data constructors, the type system, etc, we could extend λ_{Letrec} accordingly. Another reason for choosing λ_{Letrec} is that although Haskell has been evolved to maturity in the last two decades, an officially defined, widely accepted semantics, for this language does not exist yet.

In the remainder of this paper, Section 7.2 gives an overview of related work. Section 7.3 introduces λ_{Letrec}. Section 7.4 presents some definitions and lemmas needed for working with λ_{Letrec} and for the specification of refactorings. Section 7.5 studies the formalisation of the *generalise a definition* refactoring. In Section 7.6 , we extend λ_{Letrec} to λ_M to accommodate a simple module system. Some fundamental definitions for the simple module system are given in Section 7.7. Then the formalisation of *move a definition from one module to another* is given in Section 7.8, and some conclusions are drawn in Section 7.9.

7.2 RELATED WORK

Refactorings should preserve the behaviour of software. Ideally, the most fundamental approach is to prove formally that refactorings preserve the full program semantics. This requires a formal semantics for the target language to be defined. However, for most complex languages such as C++, it is very difficult to define a formal semantics.

Opdyke [12] proposed a set of seven invariants to preserve behaviour for object-oriented programming language refactorings. These invariants are: unique superclass, distinct class names, distinct member names, inherited member variables not redefined, compatible signatures in member function redefinition, type-safe assignments and semantically equivalent reference and operations[2] . Opdyke's refactorings were accompanied by proofs demonstrating that the enabling conditions he identified for each refactoring preserved the invariants. Opdyke did not prove that preserving these invariants preserves program behaviour. Similar work by Tokuda *et al* is reported in [18].

In [17], Tip *et al.* explored the use of type constraints to verify the preconditions and to determine the allowable source code modifications for a number of generalisation-related refactorings in an OO programming language context.

Using a different approach, Mens *et al.* [10] explored the idea of using graph transformation to formalise the effect of refactorings and prove behaviour preservation in the object-oriented programming paradigm. This approach proposed to use graphs to represent those aspects (access relation, update relation and call relation) of the source code that should be preserved by a refactoring, and graph rewriting rules as a formal specification for the refactoring transformations.

---

[1]Note that Opdyke's final invariant is a catch-all "preserve semantics", with the others identifying particular ways that the (static) semantics can be preserved.

7.3 THE λ-CALCULUS WITH LETREC (λ_{LETREC})

The syntax of λ_{Letrec} terms is:

$$V ::= x \mid \lambda x.E$$
$$E ::= V \mid E_1\, E_2 \mid \text{letrec } D \text{ in } E$$
$$D ::= \varepsilon \mid x_i = E_i \mid D,D$$

where x, x_i represent variables, V represents the set of values, E represents expressions, and D is a sequence of bindings. A value is a variable or an abstraction. For letrec D in E, we require that the variables x_i defined in D are pairwise distinct. Recursion is allowed in a **letrec** expression and the scope of x_i in the expression

$$\text{letrec } x_1 = E_1, ..., x_n = E_n \text{ in } E$$

is E and all the E_is. No ordering among the bindings in a **letrec** expression is assumed. As a notation, we use $\equiv$ to represent syntactical equivalence, and $\doteq$ to represent semantic equivalence.

As to the reduction strategy, one option for calculating lambda expressions with **letrec** is call-by-need [9], which is an implementation technique for the call-by-name [14] semantics that avoids re-evaluating expressions multiple times by memorising the result of the first evaluation. In the case that behaviour-preservation allows introducing/removing sharing of computation, call-by-need interpretation might invalidate many refactorings which preserve the observable behaviour but change the sharing of computation. In this study, we use call-by-name for reasoning about program transformations, so that sharing could be lost or gained during the transformation. However, comments about the change of sharing during a refactoring will be given when appropriate.

Instead of developing the call-by-name calculus for λ_{Letrec} from scratch, we make use of the results from the paper *Lambda Calculi plus Letrec* [19], in which Ariola and Blom developed a call-by-name cyclic calculus ($\lambda\circ_{name}$) where *cyclic* implies that recursion is handled in this calculus. $\lambda\circ_{name}$ defines exactly the same set of terms as λ_{Letrec} does, only with slightly different notation. Figure 7.3 lists the axioms of $\lambda\circ_{name}$ expressed using the λ_{Letrec} notation.

In the axioms shown in Figure 7.3, a / attached to a term indicates that some bound variables in the term might have been renamed to avoid name capture during the transformation. Name capture and other standard definitions in λ-calculus can be found in [1]. A context $C[]$ is a term with a hole in the place of one sub-term. The operation of filling the context C with a term M yields the term $C[M]$. The two substitution axioms require that the x (x_1 is the second axiom) in the hole occurs free in $C[x]$. $FV(E)$ means the set of free variables in term E. $D_1 \perp D_2$ means that the set of variables that occur on the left-hand side of of a definition in D_1 does not intersect with the set of free variables of D_2. In the *copying* axiom, σ is a function from recursion variables to recursion variables, and E^{σ} is the term obtained by replacing all occurrences of recursion variables x by $\sigma(x)$ (leaving the free variables of E unchanged), followed by a reduction to normal form with the

$\beta\circ$:

$\quad (\lambda x.\, E)\, E_1 \;\doteq\; \text{letrec } x = E_1 \text{ in } E, \quad \text{if } x \notin FV(E_1).$

Substitution :

$\quad \text{letrec } x = E, D \text{ in } C[x] \;\doteq\; \text{letrec } x = E, D \text{ in } C'[E]$

$\quad \text{letrec } x = C[x_1], x_1 = E_1, D \text{ in } E \;\doteq\; \text{letrec } x = C'[E_1], x_1 = E_1, D \text{ in } E$

Lift :

$\quad (\text{letrec } D \text{ in } E)\, E_1 \;\doteq\; \text{letrec } D' \text{ in } (E'\, E_1)$

$\quad E_1\, (\text{letrec } D \text{ in } E) \;\doteq\; \text{letrec } D' \text{ in } (E_1\, E')$

$\quad \lambda x.(\text{letrec } D_1, D_2 \text{ in } E)$

$\quad\quad \doteq\; \text{letrec } D_2 \text{ in } \lambda x.(\text{letrec } D_1 \text{ in } E), \quad \text{if } D_1 \perp D_2 \text{ and } x \notin FV(D_2).$

Merge :

$\quad \text{letrec } x = \text{letrec } D \text{ in } E_1, D_1 \text{ in } E \;\doteq\; \text{letrec } x = E_1', D', D_1 \text{ in } E$

$\quad \text{letrec } D_1 \text{ in } (\text{ letrec } D \text{ in } E) \;\doteq\; \text{letrec } D_1, D' \text{ in } E'$

Garbage collection :

$\quad \text{letrec } \varepsilon \text{ in } E \;\doteq\; E$

$\quad \text{letrec } D, D_1 \text{ in } E \;\doteq\; \text{letrec } D \text{ in } E, \quad \text{if } D_1 \perp D \text{ and } D_1 \perp E.$

Copying :

$\quad E \;\doteq\; E_1, \quad \text{if } \exists \sigma : \nu \to \nu, E^\sigma \equiv E_1.$

FIGURE 7.3. **The call-by-name cyclic calculus axioms in the λ_{Letrec} notation**

unification rule: $x = E, x = E \to x = E$ within the resulting **letrec** bindings [19]. These rules, together with the definitions and lemmas given in the next section, form the basis of the proof of correctness of structural refactorings, as will be shown in section 7.5.

7.4 THE FUNDAMENTALS OF λ_{LETREC}

Definition 1 *Given two expressions E and E', E' is a sub-expression of E (notation $E' \subseteq E$), if $E' \in sub(E)$, where $sub(E)$, the collection of sub-expressions of E, is defined inductively as follows:*

$\quad sub(x) = \{x\}$

$\quad sub(\lambda x.E) = \{\lambda x.E\} \cup sub(E)$

$\quad sub(E_1\, E_2) = \{E_1\, E_2\} \cup sub(E_1) \cup sub(E_2)$

$\quad sub(\text{ letrec } x_1 = E_1, ..., x_n = E_n \text{ in } E) =$

$\quad \{ \text{ letrec } x_1 = E_1, ..., x_n = E_n \text{ in } E\} \cup sub(E) \cup sub(E_1) \cup ... \cup sub(E_n)$

Definition 2 *Given an expression E and a context C[ ], we define $sub(E,C)$ as those sub-expressions of C[E], including C[E] itself, which contain the hole filled* with the expression E, that is: $e \in Sub(E, C)$ iff $\exists C_1[\ ], C_2[\ ]$, such that $e \equiv C_2[E] \wedge C[\ ] \equiv C_1[C_2[\ ]]$.

Definition 3 *The result of substituting N for the free occurrences of x in E with automatic renaming is defined as:*

$x[x := N] = N$

$y[x := N] = y;$ *where* $y \not\equiv x$

$(E_1 E_2)[x := N] = E_1[x := N]E_2[x := N]$

$(\lambda x.E)[x := N] = \lambda x.E$

$(\lambda y.E)[x := N] = \lambda z.E[y := z][x := N]$, *where* $(y \not\equiv x)$, *and* $z \equiv y$ *if*
  $x \notin FV(E)$ *or* $y \notin FV(N)$, *otherwise* z *is a fresh variable.*

$(\text{letrec } x_1 = E_1, ..., x_n = E_n \text{ in } E)[x := N]$

$\quad = \text{letrec } z_1 = E_1[\vec{x_i} := \vec{z_i}][x := N], ..., z_n = E_n[\vec{x_i} := \vec{z_i}][x := N]$

$\quad \text{in } E[\vec{x_i} := \vec{z_i}][x := N],$

where $z_i \equiv x_i$ *if* $x \notin FV(\text{letrec } x_1 = E_1, ..., x_n = E_n \text{ in } E)$ *or* $x_i \notin FV(N)$,
otherwise z_i *is a fresh variable* $(i = 1..n)$.

Definition 4 *Given $x \in FV(E)$ and a context $C[\ ]$, we say that x is free over $C[E]$ if and only if* $\forall e, e \in sub(E, C) \Rightarrow x \in FV(e)$. *Otherwise we say that x becomes bound over $C[E]$.*

Lemma 1 *Let E_1, E_2 be expressions, and $E_2 \equiv C[z]$, where z is a free variable in E_2 and does not occur free in $C[\ ]$. If none of the free variables in E_1 will become bound over $C[E_1]$, then $E_2[z := E_1] \equiv C[E_1]$.*

Proof. Proof by induction on the structure of E_2.

7.5 FORMALISATION OF *GENERALISING A DEFINITION*

7.5.1 Definition of *generalise a definition*

Definition 5 *Given an expression*

$$\text{letrec } x_1 = E_1, ..., x_i = E_i, ..., x_n = E_n \text{ in } E_0$$

Assume E is a sub-expression of E_i, and $E_i \equiv C[E]$, then the condition for generalising the definition $x_i = E_i$ on E is:

$$x_i \notin FV(E) \wedge \forall x, e : (x \in FV(E) \wedge e \in sub(E_i, C) \Rightarrow x \in FV(e)).$$

After generalisation, the original expression becomes:

$\text{letrec } x_1 = E_1[x_i := x_i E], ..., x_i = \lambda z.C[z][x_i := x_i z], ..., x_n = E_n[x_i := x_i E]$
$\text{in } E_0[x_i := x_i E], \quad$ *where z is a fresh variable*

What follows provides some explanation of the above definition:

- The condition $x_i \notin FV(E)$ means that there should be no recursive calls to x_i within the identified sub-expression E. Allowing recursive calls in the identified expression would need extra care to make sure that the generalised function has the correct number of parameters at its call-sites.

- This specification replaces only the identified occurrence of E in the definition $x_i = E_i$ by the formal parameter z. Another variant is to replace all the occurrences of E in $x_i = E_i$ by z. This does not change the side-conditions for the refactoring, but it does change the transformation within $x_i = E_i$.

- According to this definition of generalising a definition, the refactoring could introduce duplicated computation. One way to avoid duplicating the computation of $x_i E$ is to introduce a new binding into the **letrec** expression to represent the expression, instead of duplicating it at each call-site of x_i. This discussion reflects the general observation that under the same refactoring name, for instance *generalising a definition*, different people may mean different things, and there is no unique way of resolving this choice.

7.5.2 Behaviour-preservation of *generalising a definition*

In order to prove that this refactoring is behaviour-preserving, we decompose the transformation into a number of steps. If each step is behaviour-preserving, then we can conclude that the whole transformation is behaviour-preserving. An example showing the application of the following proof to a Haskell program is available at *http://www.cs.kent.ac.uk/projects/refactor-fp/presentations/TFP2005.ppt*.

Proof. Given the original expression:

$$\text{letrec } x_1 = E_1, \ldots, x_i = E_i, \ldots, x_n = E_n \text{ in } E_0$$

Generalising the definition $x_i = E_i$ on the sub-expression E can be decomposed into the following steps:

Step 1. add definition $x_i' = \lambda z.C[z]$, where x_i' and z are fresh variables, and $C[E] = E_i$, we get

$$\text{letrec } x_1 = E_1, \ldots, x_i = E_i, x_i' = \lambda z.C[z], \ldots, x_n = E_n \text{ in } E_0$$

The equivalence of semantics is guaranteed by the garbage collection rule and the commutability of bindings within **letrec**.

Step 2. By the side-conditions and axioms, in the context of the definition of x_i', we can prove

$$
\begin{aligned}
x_i' E &\equiv (\lambda z.C[z])E \\
&= \text{letrec } z = E \text{ in } C[z] \quad \text{by } \beta \circ \\
&= \text{letrec } z = E \text{ in } C[E] \quad \text{by } \textit{substitution} \text{ axiom and side-conditions} \\
&= C[E] \quad \text{by } \textit{garbage collection} \text{ axioms} \\
&\equiv E_i
\end{aligned}
$$

Therefore replacing E_i with $x_i' E$ in the context of this definition does not change its semantics, so the original expression is equivalent to:

$$\text{letrec } x_1 = E_1, \ldots, x_i = x_i' E, x_i' = \lambda z.C[z], \ldots, x_n = E_n \text{ in } E_0$$

Step 3. Using the second *substitution axiom*, it is trivial to prove that substituting $x_i'E$ for the free occurrences of x_i in the right-hand-side of x_i' does not change the semantics of x_i'. We get

$$\text{letrec } x_1 = E_1, \ldots, x_i = x_i'E, x_i' = (\lambda z.C[z])[x_i := x_i'E], \ldots, x_n = E_n \text{ in } E_0$$

As $z \notin FV(x_i'E)$, we have:

$$\text{letrec } x_1 = E_1, \ldots, x_i = x_i'E, x_i' = \lambda z.C[z][x_i := x_i'E], \ldots, x_n = E_n \text{ in } E_0$$

Step 4. In the definition of x_i', replace E with z. we get:

$$\text{letrec } x_1 = E_1, \ldots, x_i = x_i'E, x_i' = \lambda z.C[z][x_i := x_i'z], \ldots, x_n = E_n \text{ in } E_0$$

It is evident that the right-hand-side (RHS) of the definition of x_i' in this step is not semantically equal to the RHS defined in step 3. However, we can prove the equivalence of $x_i'E$ from step 3 to step 4 in the context of the bindings for $x_1, \ldots, x_n$ (note that x_i' does not depend on the definition of x_i, so there is no mutual dependency between x_i and x_i').

Step 5. Substituting $x_i'E$ for the free occurrences of x_i outside the definition of x_i and x_i' does not change the semantics of the let-expression, as $x_i = x_i'E$ from step 4.

$$\text{letrec } x_1 = E_1[x_i := x_i'E], \ldots, x_i = x_i'E, x_i' = \lambda z.C[z][x_i := x_i'z], \ldots, x_n = E_n[x_i := x_i'E]$$
$$\text{in } E_0[x_i := x_i'E]$$

Step 6. Removing the unused definition of x_i does not change the semantics according to the garbage collection rules, and we get

$$\text{letrec } x_1 = E_1[x_i := x_i'E], \ldots, x_i' = \lambda z.C[z][x_i := x_i'z], \ldots, x_n = E_n[x_i := x_i'E] \text{ in } E_0[x_i := x_i'E]$$

Step 7. Renaming x_i' to x_i, we have

$$\text{letrec } x_1 = E_1[x_i := x_i'E][x_i' := x_i], \ldots, x_i = \lambda z.C[z][x_i := x_i'z][x_i' := x_i],$$
$$\ldots, x_n = E_n[x_i := x_i'E][x_i' := x_i]$$
$$\text{in } E_0[x_i := x_i'E][x_i' := x_i]$$

Capture-free renaming of bound variables, i.e. α-renaming, does not change the semantics. Finally, by the substitution lemma, we have

$$\text{letrec } x_1 = E_1[x_i := x_iE], \ldots, x_i = \lambda z.C[z][x_i := x_iz], \ldots, x_n = E_n[x_i := x_iE] \text{ in } E_0[x_i := x_iE]$$

as required.

7.6 FORMALISATION OF A SIMPLE MODULE SYSTEM λ_M

A module-aware refactoring normally affects not only the definitions in a module, but also the imports and exports of the module. More than that, it may potentially affect every module in the system. In order to formalise module-aware refactorings, we extend λ_{Letrec} with a simple module system. The definition of the new language, which is called λ_M, is given next.

7.6.1   The Simple Module System λ_M

The syntax of λ_M terms is defined as:

$$Program ::= \text{let } Mod \text{ in } (Exp; Imp; \text{ letrec } D \text{ in } E)$$
$$Mod ::= \varepsilon \mid Modid = (Exp; Imp; D) \mid Mod; Mod$$
$$Exp ::= \varepsilon \mid (Ep_1, ..., Ep_n) \ (n0)$$
$$Ep = x \mid Modid.x \mid \text{ module } Modid$$
$$Imp ::= (Ip_1, ..., Ip_n) \ (n \geq 0)$$
$$Ip = \text{ import } Qual \ Modid \ Alias \ ImpSpec$$
$$Modid ::= M_i \ (i \geq 0)$$
$$Qual ::= \varepsilon \mid \text{qualified}$$
$$ImpSpec ::= \varepsilon \mid (x_1, ..., x_n) \mid \text{ hiding } (x_1, ..., x_n) \ (n \geq 0)$$
$$Alias ::= \varepsilon \mid \text{ as } Modid$$
$$V ::= x \mid Modid.x \mid \lambda x.E$$
$$E ::= V \mid E_1 \ E_2 \mid \text{ letrec } D \text{ in } E$$
$$D ::= \varepsilon \mid x = E \mid D, D$$

In the above definition, *Program* represents a program and *Mod* is a sequence of modules. Each module has a unique name in the program. A module consists of three parts: *Exp*, which exports some of the locally available identifiers for use by other modules; *Imp*, which imports identifiers defined in other modules, and *D*, which defines a number of value identifiers. The $(Exp; Imp;$ letrec D in $E)$ part of the definition of *Program* represents the *Main* module of the program, and the expression E represents the *main* expression. ε means an null export list or entity list in the definitions of *Exp* and *ImpSpec*, and *empty* in other definitions. Qualified names are allowed, and we assume that the usage of qualified names follows the rules specified in the Haskell 98 Report [16].

The module system has been defined to model aspects of the Haskell 98 module system. Because only value identifiers can be defined in λ_M, λ_M's module system is actually a subset of the Haskell 98 module system. We assume that the semantics of this simple module system follows the semantics of the Haskell 98 module system.

A formal specification of the Haskell 98 module system has been described in [3], where the semantics of a Haskell program with regard to the module system is a mapping from the collection of modules to their corresponding *in-scope* and *export* relations. The *in-scope* relation of a module represents the set of names (with the represented entities) that are visible to this module, and this forms the top-level environment of the module. The *export* relation of a module represents the set of names (also with the represented entities) that are made available by this module for other modules to use; in other words, it defines the interface of the module.

In the following specification of module-aware refactorings, we assume that, using the module system analysis algorithm from the formal specification given in [3], we are able to get the *in-scope* and *export* relation of each module, and for each identifier in the *in-scope/export* relation, we can infer the name of the module in which the identifier is defined. In fact, the same module analysis system is used in the implementation of HaRe.

When only module-level information is relevant, i.e. the exact definition of entities is not of concern, we can view a multi-module program in this way: a program P consists of a set of modules and each module consists of four parts: the module name, M, the set of identifiers defined by this module, D, the set of identifiers imported by this module, I, and the set of identifiers exported by this module, E. Each top-level identifier can be uniquely identified by the combination of the identifier's name and its defining module as *(modid, id)*, where *modid* is the name of the identifier's defining module and *id* is the name of the identifier. Two identifiers are the same if they have the same name and defining module. Accordingly, we can use $P = \{(M_i, D_i, I_i, E_i)\}_{i=1..n}$ to denote the program.

7.7 FUNDAMENTALS OF λ_M

Definition 6 *A* client module *of module M is a module which imports M either directly or indirectly; A* server module *of module M is a module which is imported by module M either directly or indirectly.*

Definition 7 *Given a module M=(Exp, Imp, D), we say that module M is exported by itself if Exp is* ε *or* module M *occurs in Exp as an element of the export list.*

Definition 8 *The* defining module *of an identifier is the name of the module in which the identifier is defined.*

Definition 9 *Suppose v is an identifier that is in scope in module M, we use* defineMod(v, M) *to represent the name of the module in which the identifier is defined.*

Definition 10 *We say that the identifier x defined in module N is used by module M=(Exp, Imp, D) (M ≠ N) if DefineMod(x,M) = N and either x ∈ FV(D) or x is exported by module M, otherwise we say that the x defined in module N is not used by module M.*

Definition 11 Binding structure *refers to the association of uses of identifiers with their definitions in a program. Binding structure involves both top-level variables and local variables. When analysing module-level phenomena, it is only the top-level bindings that are relevant, in which case we define the binding structure, B, of a program $P = \{(M_i, D_i, I_i, E_i)\}_{i=1..n}$ as: $B \subset \cup(D_i \times (D_i \cup I_i))_{i=1..n}$, so that $\{((m_1, id_1), (m_2, id_2)) \in B \mid id_2$ occurs free in the definition of id_1; id_1's defining module is m_1, and id_2's defining module is m_2 \}.*

The following five definitions involve syntactical manipulations of the import/export list. Due to the limits on space, we give their descriptions, but omit the full definitions.

Definition 12 *Given a set of identifiers Y and an export list Exp, rmFromExp(Exp,Y) is the export list Exp with the occurrences of the identifiers from Y removed.*

Definition 13 *Given an identifier y which is defined in module M, and the export list, Exp, of module M, addToExp (Exp, y, M) is the export list with y added if it is not already exported by Exp.*

Definition 14 *Given an identifier y which is exported by module M and Imp which is a sequence of imports, rmFromImp (Imp, y, M) is the import sequence Imp with the occurrences of y removed. The function can be used to remove the uses of y in import declarations that import module M when y is no longer exported by M.*

Definition 15 *Given an identifier y which is exported by module M (M is not necessarily the module where y is defined) and Imp which is a sequence of imports, then hideInImp(Imp, y, M) is the import sequence Imp with y removed from the explicit entity list or added to the explicit hiding enity list in the import declarations wich import module M, so that the resulting Imp does not bring this identifier into scope by importing it from module M.*

Definition 16 *Suppose the same binding, say y, is exported by both module M_1 and M_2, and Imp is a sequence of import declarations, then chgImpPath(Imp, y, M_1, M_2) is the import sequence Imp with the importing of y from M_1 changed to from M_2.*

7.8 FORMALISATION OF *MOVE A DEFINITION FROM ONE MODULE TO ANOTHER* IN λ_M

Like other refactorings, the realisation of *Move a definition from one module to another* is not unique. Suppose we would like to move the definition of *foo* from module *M* to module *N*, the following design decisions were made in the implementation of this refactoring in HaRe.

- If a variable which is free in the definition of *foo* is not in scope in module *N*, then the refactorer will ask the user to refactor the program to make the variable visible to module *N* first.

- If the identifier *foo* is already in scope in module *N* (either defined by module *N* or imported from other modules), but it refers to a definition of *foo* other than that in module *M*, the user will be prompted to do renaming first.

- We do not allow the introduction of during a refactoring due to the fact that transparent compilation of mutually recursive modules are not yet supported by the current working Haskell compilers/interpreters.

- Module *N* will export *foo* after the refactoring only if *foo* is either exported by module *M* or used by the other definitions in module *M* before the refactoring. The imports of *foo* will be via *M* if module *M* still exports *foo* after the refactoring; otherwise via *N*.

7.8.1 Definition of *move a definition from one module to another*

The definition of this refactoring and a commentary on the definition follows.

Definition 17 *Given a valid program P:*

$$P = \text{let } M_1 = (Exp_1; Imp_1; x_1 = E_1, ..., x_i = E_i, ..., x_n = E_n);$$
$$M_2 = (Exp_2; Imp_2; D_2); ...; M_m = (Exp_m; Imp_m; D_m)$$
$$\text{in } (Exp_0; Imp_0; \text{letrec } D_0 \text{ in } E)$$

The conditions for moving the definition $x_i = E_i$ from module M_1 to another module, M_2, are:

1. *If x_i is in scope at the top level of M_2, then $DefineMod(x_i, M_2) = M_1$.*

2. *$\forall v \in FV(x_i = E_i)$, if $DefineMod(v, M_1)=N$, then v is in scope in M_2 and $DefineMod(v, M_2)=N$.*

3. *If M_1 is a server module of M_2, then $\{x_i, M_1.x_i\} \cap FV(E_{j(j \neq i)}) = \emptyset$.*

4. *If module $M_{j(j \neq 1)}$ is a server module of M_2, and $x_i \in FV(D_j)$, then $DefineMod(x_i, M_j) \neq M_1$ (x_i could be qualified or not).*

After moving the definition to module M_2, the original program becomes:

$$P' = \text{let } M_1 = (Exp_1'; Imp_1'; x_1 = E_1, ..., x_{i-1} = E_{i-1}, x_{i+1} = E_{i+1}, ..., x_n = E_n);$$
$$M_2 = (Exp_2'; Imp_2'; x_i = E_i[M_1.x_i := M_2.x_i], D_2); ...;$$
$$M_m = (Exp_m; Imp_m'; D_m)$$
$$\text{in } (Exp_0; Imp_0'; \text{letrec } D_0 \text{ in } E)$$

In the above definition, a $\prime$ attached to an export/import indicates that this export/import might have been changed after the refactoring. In what follows, the changes to those exports/imports are given according to whether x_i is exported by M_1, and different situations are considered in each case. Only those imports/exports which are actually changed are given in each case.

Case 1. x_i is not exported by M_1.
Case 1.1. x_i is not used by other definitions in M_1: $\{x_i, M_1.x_i\} \cap FV(E_{j(j \neq i)}) = \emptyset$.
  $Imp_j' = hideInImp(Imp_j, x_i, M_2)$ if M_2 is exported by itself;
    Imp_j otherwise. $(3 \leq j \leq m)$

Case 1.2. x_i is used by other definitions in M_1.
  $Imp_1' = hideInImp(Imp_1, x_i, M_2)$; import M_2 as $M_1(x_i)$
  $Exp_2' = addToExp(Exp_2, x_i, M_2)$
  $Imp_j' = hideInImp(Imp_j, x_i, M_2)$ $(3 \leq j \leq m)$

Case 2. x_i is exported by M_1.
Case 2.1. M_2 is not a client module of M_1.

107

$$Imp'_1 = Imp1; \text{ import } M_2 \text{ as } M_1(x_i)$$
$$Exp'_2 = addToExp\ (Exp_2, x_i, M_2)$$
$$Imp'_j = hideInImp\ (Imp_j, x_i, M_2)\ (3 \leq j \leq m)$$

Case 2.2. M_2 is a client module of M_1.
$$Exp'_1 = rmFromExport\ (Exp_1, x_i, M_1)$$
$$Exp'_2 = addToExp\ (Exp_2, x_i, M_2)$$
$$Imp'_2 = rmFromImp\ (Imp_2, x_i, M_1)$$
$$Imp'_j = if\ M_j \text{ is a server module of } M_2 \text{ then } rmFromImp\ (Imp_j, x_i, M_1)$$
$$\quad else\ rmFromImp\ (chgImportPath\ (Imp''_j, x_i, M_1, M_2), x_i, M_1)\ (3 \leq j \leq m)$$
$$Imp''_j = if\ x_i \text{ is exported by } M_2 \text{ before refactoring, then } Imp_j;$$
$$\quad hideInImp\ (Imp_j, x_i, M_2) \text{ otherwise. } (3 \leq j \leq m)$$

What follows is some explanation about the above definition:

- As to the side-conditions, condition 1) means that if x_i is in scope in the target module, M_2, then this x_i should be the same as the x_i whose definition is to be moved, in order to avoid conflict/ambiguous occurrence [16] in M_2; condition 2) requires that all the free variables used in the definition of x_i are in scope in M_2. Conditions 3) and 4) guarantee that mutual recursive modules won't be introduced during the refactoring process.

- The transformation rules are complicated mainly due to the Haskell 98 module system's lack of control in the export list. For example, when a new identifier is brought into scope in a module, the identifier could also be exported automatically by this module, and then further exported by other modules if this module is imported and exported by those modules. However, this is dangerous in some cases as the new entity could cause name conflict/ambiguity in modules which import it either directly or indirectly. Two strategies are used in the transformation in order to overcome this problem: the first strategy is to use `hiding` to exclude an identifier from being imported by another module when we are unable to exclude it from being exported, as in case 1.1; the second strategy is to use *alias* in the import declaration to avoid the changes to the export list as in case 1.2.

7.8.2 Behaviour-preservation of *move a definition from one module to another*

We prove the correctness of this refactoring from four aspects: the refactoring does not change the structure of individual definitions; the refactoring creates a binding structure which is isomorphic to the one before the refactoring; the refactoring does not introduce mutually recursive modules; and the refactoring does not violate any syntactic rules. More details follow.

- The refactoring does not change the structure of individual definitions. This is obvious from the transformation rules. Inside the definition of $x_i = E_i$, the uses of $M_1.x_i$ have been changed to $M_2.x_i$, this is necessary as x_i is now defined in module M_2. We keep the qualified names qualified in order to avoid name capture inside the E_i. The uses of x_i in module M_2 will not cause ambiguous reference due to condition a).

- The refactoring creates a binding structure which is isomorphic to the one before the refactoring. Suppose the binding structures before and after the refactoring are B and B' respectively, then B and B' satisfy:

$$B' = \{(fx, fy) | (x,y) \in B\},$$
where $f(M,x) = (M_2, x_i)$ if $(M,x) \equiv (M_1, x_i)$; (M,x) otherwise.

The only change from B to B' is that the defining module of x_i has been changed from the M_1 to M_2. This is guaranteed by conditions a) and b).

- The refactoring does not introduce recursive modules. On one hand, moving the definition does not add any import declarations to M_2, therefore, there is no chance for M_2 to import any of its client modules. On the other hand, an import declaration importing M_2 is added to other modules only when it is necessary and M_2 is not a client module of them because of conditions c), d) and the condition checking in case 2.2.

- The refactoring does not violate any syntactic rules. The only remaining potential violations exist in the import/export lists of the modules involved. In case 1.1, case 1.2 and case 2.1, except module M_2, none of the modules' in scope/export relations have been changed; in case 2.2, M_1 no longer exports x_i, and those modules which use x_i now get it from module M_2. *rmFromExport*, *addToExp*, *rmFromImp*, and *hideInImport* are used to manipulate the program syntactically to ensure the program's syntactic correctness.

7.9 CONCLUSIONS AND FUTURE WORK

Behaviour preservation is the key criterion of refactorings, therefore the assurance of behaviour preservation is indispensable during the refactoring process. This paper explores the specification and proof of behaviour preservation of refactorings in the context of refactoring Haskell programs in a formal way. To this purpose, we first defined the simple lambda-calculus, λ_{Letrec}, then augmented it with a simple module system. Two representative refactorings are examined in this paper: *generalise a definition* and *move a definition from one module to another*. For future work, more structural or module-related refactorings, such as, *renaming*, *lifting a definition*, *specialise a definition*, *add an item to the export list*, etc[15], can be formalised in this framework without difficulty.

This framework need to be extended to accommodate more features from the Haskell 98 language, such as constants, case-expressions, data types, etc, so that more complex refactorings, such as data refactorings, can be formalised. Nevertheless, this work provides a foundation for the further study of formalisation of Haskell refactorings. Finally, a formally defined semantics for Haskell could help the (potentially automate) verifications of Haskell refactorings.

REFERENCES

[1] H. P. Barendregt. *The Lambda Calculus – Its Syntax and Semantics*, volume 103 of *Studies in Logic and the Foundations of Mathematics*. North-Holland, 1984.

[2] R. M. Burstall and J. Darlington. A Transformation System for Developing Recursive Programs. *Journal of the ACM*, 24(1):44–67, 1977.

[3] I. S. Diatchki, M. P. Jones, and T. Hallgren. A Formal Specification for the Haskell 98 Module System. In *ACM Sigplan Haskell Workshop*, 2002.

[4] M. Fowler, K. Beck, J. Brant, W. Opdyke, and D. Roberts. *Refactoring: Improving the Design of Existing Code*. Addison-Wesley, 1999.

[5] J. Hughes. Why Functional Programming Matters. *Computer Journal*, 32(2):98–107, 1989.

[6] S. P. Jones. Compiling Haskell by Program Transformation: A Report from the Trenches. In *ESOP*, pages 18–44, 1996.

[7] H. Li, C. Reinke, and S. Thompson. Tool Support for Refactoring Functional Programs. In Johan Jeuring, editor, *ACM SIGPLAN Haskell Workshop, Uppsala, Sweden*, August 2003.

[8] Huiqing Li, Simon Thompson, and Claus Reinke. The Haskell Refactorer: HaRe, and its API. In John Boyland and Grel Hedin, editors, *Proceedings of the 5th workshop on Language Descriptions, Tools and Applications (LDTA 2005)*, April 2005.

[9] Manfred Schmidt-Schauß and Michael Huber. A Lambda-Calculus with letrec, case, constructors and non-determinism. *CoRR*, cs.PL/0011008, 2000.

[10] T. Mens, S. Demeyer, and D. Janssens. Formalising Behaviour Preserving Program Transformations. In *ICGT '02: Proceedings of the First International Conference on Graph Transformation*, pages 286–301. Springer-Verlag, 2002.

[11] T. Mens and T. Tourwé. A Survey of Software Refactoring. *IEEE Trans. Software Eng.*, 30(2):126–139, 2004.

[12] W. F. Opdyke. *Refactoring Object-Oriented Frameworks*. PhD thesis, Univ. of Illinois, 1992.

[13] H. Partsch and R. Steinbrüggen. Program Transformation Systems. *ACM Computing Surveys*, 15(3), September 1983.

[14] G. D. Plotkin. Call-by-name, call-by-value and the λ-calculus. *Theoretical Computer Science*, 1:125–159, 1975.

[15] Refactor-fp. Refactoring Functional Programs. `http://www.cs.kent.ac.uk/projects/refactor-fp/`.

[16] S.Peyton Jones, editor. *Haskell 98 Language and Libraries: the Revised Report*. Cambridge University Press, 2003.

[17] F. Tip, A. Kiezun, and D. Bäumer. Refactoring for Generalization Using Type Constraints. In *Object-Oriented Programming Systems, Languages, and Applications (OOPSLA 2003)*, pages 13–26, Anaheim, CA, USA, November 6–8, 2003.

[18] L. Tokuda and D. Batory. Evolving Object-Oriented Applications with Refactorings. Technical Report CS-TR-99-09, University of Texas, Austin, March 1, 1999.

[19] Z. M. Ariola and S. Blom. Lambda Calculi plus Letrec. Technical report, July 1997.

Chapter 8

Systematic Search for Lambda Expressions

Susumu Katayama[1]

Abstract: We present a system for inductive synthesis of small functional programs by trial and error, or just by generating a stream of all the type-correct programs in a systematic and exhaustive manner and evaluating them. The main goal of this line of research is to ease functional programming, to provide an axis to evaluate heuristic approaches to inductive program synthesis such as genetic programming by investigating the best performance possible by exhaustive search algorithms, and to provide a basis on which to build heuristics in a more modular way. While the previous approach to that goal used combinatory expressions in order to simplify the synthesis process, which led to redundant combinatory expressions with complex types, this research uses de Bruijn lambda expressions and enjoys improved results.

8.1 INTRODUCTION

Type systems are by nature tools for sound programming that constrain programs to help identifying errors. On the other hand, by exploiting strong typing, functional programming can be done in a way like solving a jigsaw puzzle, by repetition of combining unifying functions and their arguments until the programmer eventually obtains the intended program. Search-based approach to inductive program synthesis, or program synthesis from incomplete specification, can be viewed as automation of this process.

This research proposes an algorithm that searches for the type-consistent small functional programs from an incomplete specification rather in a systematic and exhaustive way, that is, by generating all the programs from small to infinitely

[1]Department of Computer Science and Systems Engineering, University of Miyazaki, Miyazaki, Miyazaki 889-2155, Japan; Phone: +81 (985)58-7941; Email: skata@cs.miyazaki-u.ac.jp

111

large that match the given type and checking if they satisfy the specification. Note that due to the incompleteness in the specification the synthesized programs may not conform the users' intentions, like other inductive programming methods. The correctness of the synthesized programs could be assured through tests during or after the synthesis. Also, for the above reason it is desirable that synthesized programs are easy to understand and pretty printed.

The proposed algorithm improves the efficiency of the previous algorithm [Kat04] by doing the following:

- it searches for de Bruijn lambda expressions, while the old one obtains combinatory expressions which is more redundant;

- the function taking the set of available atom expressions and a type t and returning the prioritized set of synthesized expressions[2] whose type and t unify is now memoized;

- more equivalent expressions which cause redundancy in the search space and multiple counting are excluded.

8.1.1 Perspective applications

One obvious effect of this research is to programming. Readers may gain more concrete impression from Subsection 8.2.1, although further rearrangement of the obtained expressions may be desired.

Another application can be auto-completion in functional shells (e.g. Esther [vWP03]).

8.1.2 Related work

Conventional research on inductive synthesis of functional programs can be categorized into two styles. One approach is via computational traces. The other uses genetic programming, which is a search-based heuristic approach.

Synthesis via computational traces There is a long history of this line of research. Typically they first generate computational traces and then fold them into a recursive program. Although the second folding step can be done by simple pattern matching, the first step is more difficult, and as a result there have been various approaches.

- Summers [Sum77] did that by limiting the scope to list functions and enforcing partial orders.

- Later some people noticed that in some cases creating traces by hand is not a great burden for users. This is called programming by demonstration, and is actively explored by many scientists [Cyp93].

---

[2]More exactly it returns the prioritized set of tuples of synthesized expressions and a unifier substitution.

- Recently Schmid and her people have been working on search-based trace generation [Sch01][SW04].

One point of these approaches is that they modularize their algorithms into two. However, we think that the search space of the unfolded traces is much greater than that of recursive programs, because the latter is much more compact and the search space can bloat exponentially in the program length.

Genetic Programming   Genetic Programming (GP) also searches for functional programs. It is a kind of heuristic approach to search for programs by maintaining a set of "promising programs" and by exchanging and varying their subexpressions, based on the assumption that *promising programs should include useful, reusable subexpressions*. Although GP is heuristic, researchers of GP tend not to compare their algorithms with non-heuristic approaches, leaving it unclear whether the heuristic works or not, and how much it improves the efficiency. This paper focuses on efficient implementation of exhaustive enumeration of expressions, and provides a basis on which to build heuristic approaches in future.

8.2   IMPLEMENTED SYSTEM

This section details the implemented system, whose latest version is available from

`http://nautilus.cs.miyazaki-u.ac.jp/~skata/MagicHaskeller.html`.

8.2.1   Overview

User interface   The implemented system has a user interface that looks like Haskell interpreters. Figure 8.1 and Figure 8.2 show sample interactions with the implemented system, where each > represents a command line prompt.

When the user types from the console a boolean function as the *constraint*, the system tries to synthesize an expression which satisfies it, i.e., which makes the function return *True*. The constraint can be any unary predicate in theory because it just filters the generated programs, although currently the interpreter only supports a subset of the Haskell language.[3] Then it prints the expression converted into the usual lambda expression acceptable by Haskell interpreters and compilers. Optionally the user may provide the type of the desired expression, or otherwise it is inferred. The line beginning with :load loads the *component library file* written in Haskell subset with the Hindley-Milner type system, and the system generates all the type-correct lambda expressions using variables defined there as primitives. Here is an example component library file, defining constructors and curried paramorphisms of natural numbers and lists, and thus covering

---

[3]Also, it is desirable if the predicate always terminates within a short time. However, sometimes it is more realistic to tell non-termination by trying the synthesis than to assume such prior knowledge.

113

a lot of useful total functions on them. Some discussion on library design and termination can be found in the previous work. [Kat04]

module *Library* **where**

```
zero :: Int
zero = 0
inc  :: Int→Int
inc  = λx → x+1

nat_para :: Int → a → (Int → a → a) → a
nat_para = λi x f → if i ≡ 0 then x
                             else f (i-1) (nat_para (i-1) x f)

nil  :: [a]
nil  = []
cons :: a → [a] → [a]
cons = (:)

list_para :: [b] → a → (b → [b] → a → a) → a
list_para = λl x f → case l of []  → x
                               a:m → f a m (list_para m x f)
```

Although the above specification may look natural, it is not common among GP systems solving the same kind of problems. Each time synthesizing a function, they require a file with tens of lines written, which describes:

- which primitive functions/terminals to use,

- what constraints to satisfy,

- what fitness function to use as heuristic, and

- what values of the parameters to use.

This usually means that synthesizing a function requires more skills and labors than those for implementing the function by hand. Unlike those systems, we make only realistic requirements in order to create a useful system.

Language Currently the language is a Haskell subset without most of the syntactic sugars. The Hindley-Milner type system can be supported, but for efficiency reasons we prohibit compound data types containing functions such as [a->b], (a, b->c), etc. Thus, for example, catamorphisms have to be defined in their curried form, e.g.

```
curried_list_cata :: a → (b→a→a) → [b] → a
```

instead of

```
list_cata :: (a, b→a→a)  →  [b]  →  a
```

where a tuple contains a function. (This conversion could be done internally, but it is not yet done for now.) The program generator can deal with any data type including user-defined ones in theory, but the interpreter does not support them yet.

The system structure   Figure 8.3 shows the rough structure of the implemented system. The component library file is read beforehand, and when the user inputs a constraint (and optionally a type), internally the system generates all the type-correct expressions that can be expressed by the combinators in the component library, and then, they are filtered by the constraint and the first expression is printed.[4] Note that currently there is no feedback from the interpreter result to the generator — the generator literally exhausts all the expressions except those which are semantically equivalent.

8.2.2   The old algorithm

This section describes the implementation used in the previous work [Kat04], which did not elaborate on the implementation detail.

Monad for breadth-first search

Spivey [Spi00] devised a monad that abstracts and thus eases implementation of breadth-first search algorithms. The ideas are:

- a value in the monad is defined as a stream of bags, representing a prioritized bag of alternatives, where the n-th element of the stream represents the alternatives that reside at the depth n of the search tree and have the n-th priority,

- the depth n of the direct product of two of such monadic values can be defined using the i-th bag of the first monadic value and the j-th of the second monadic value for all the i and j combinations such that $i + j = n$, and

- the direct sum of such monadic values can be defined as concatenation of bags at the same depth.

Once this monad is defined, one can easily define breadth-first algorithms using the direct sum and product, or just by replacing the monad for depth-first search in the source code of algorithms with the above one.

Preliminary experiments showed that using Spivey's monad without change for our algorithm causes huge consumption of the heap space. Changing the definition of the monad to recompute everything as the focus goes deeper in the search tree solved the problem:

---

[4]Strictly speaking, such filtering is defined rather in a depth-wise manner, using the *Recomp* monad introduced later.

115

```
newtype Recomp a = Rc {unRc :: Int → Bag a}
instance Monad Recomp where
    return x   = Rc f where f 0 = [x]
                            f _ = []
    Rc f >>= g = Rc (λn → [ y | i ← [0..n]
                              , x ← f i
                              , y ← unRc (g x) (n-i) ])
instance MonadPlus Recomp where
    mzero = Rc (const [])
    Rc f 'mplus' Rc g = Rc (λi → f i ++ g i)
```

In order to represent alternative substitutions and infer consistent types during search, *Recomp* monad is usually used in combination with monad transformer [LHJ95] for type inference defined as

```
newtype Monad m =>
        TI m a = TI (Subst → Int → m (a, Subst, Int))
```

where *Subst*s represent the current substitution and *Int*s represent the ID number of the next fresh variable.

The expression construction

The old algorithm enumerates type-correct combinatory expressions that match the requested type, and for representing lambda abstractions it heavily depends on primitive *SKIBC* combinators. It works as follows: let us assume expressions with type, say, $\forall a\, b.\, [a] \to b \to Int$ are requested. Firstly, the type variables, which are assumed to be universally quantified under the Hindley-Milner type system, are replaced with non-existent type constructor names, say, $G0$ and $G1$ for the above case. Then a function named unifyingExprs is invoked to obtain the prioritized bags of expressions whose types and the requested type $[G0] \to G1 \to Int$ unify. It has the following type:

```
unifyingExprs
      :: [(Expression, Type)]  →  Type  →  TI Recomp Expression
```

where the first argument represents variables and their types from the component library, and the second represents the requested type.

For an intuitive explanation of the implementation of unifyingExprs, we use simpler type as an example, namely *Int*, instead of $[G0] \to G1 \to Int$ in order to avoid complication. When expressions with type *Int* are to be generated, first unifyingExprs generates a list of components whose return type and *Int* unify, i.e., zero :: *Int*, succ :: *Int* → *Int*, nat_para :: *Int* → a → (*Int* → a → a) → a, and list_para :: $[b]$ → a → $(b \to [b] \to a \to a)$ → a if the component library shown in Section 8.2.1 is used as the primitive set. Let us call them *head candidates*. Then, for each of their types, the algorithm applies the most general unifier substitution, so in the case of list_para the substitution is $[\,a \mapsto Int\,]$ and now list_para has type $[b] \to Int \to (b \to [b] \to Int \to Int) \to Int$.

Then for each of its argument types, i.e. $[b]$, *Int*, and $b \rightarrow [b] \rightarrow Int \rightarrow Int$, the algorithm generates a prioritized bag of expressions with the type, which can be done by recursive call of `unifyingExprs`. Elements of the generated prioritized bag are called *spine candidates*. Finally, all the combinations of the spine candidates applied to the corresponding head candidates are generated as a prioritized bag.

8.2.3 Improvements

de Bruijn lambda calculus

The old primitive combinatory approach is inefficient because the polymorphism loosens the restrictions over the search domain, that is,

- expressions become redundant: polymorphic primitive combinators permit combinatory expressions such as $B\,C\,C$ which can also be implemented by I, and such polymorphic combinators can appear everywhere including places that have nothing to do with the program structure;

- undecided type variables make the shallow nodes in the search tree branch many times: because type variables are replaced too late after being passed through computations, branching is not restricted enough while computing the program candidates, even in the cases where eventually at the leaf of the search tree the algorithm finds out that there is no type-consistent expression below that node;

- the complexity of the request type bloats rapidly as the program size increases.

A solution to the above problems could be use of director strings [KS88]. In this paper we go further to search over the de Bruijn lambda expressions in the η-long β-normal form equivalent to the expressions using director strings.

In the rest of this section we first present an unoptimized implementation of the algorithm and then introduce efficiency improvements.

Unoptimized implementation

lambda expressions in de Bruijn notation can be defined as follows:

```
data Expression = Lambda Expression        -- lambda abstraction
               | X       Int               -- de Bruijn variable
               | Expression :$ Expression   -- function application
               | Prim    Int               -- component
```

Types in the Hindley-Milner type system can be defined in the usual way, except that the function type constructor ($\rightarrow$) should receive special treatment:

```
data Type = TV TVar | TC TCon | TA Type Type | Type :-> Type
```

117

i.e., a *Type* is either a type variable, a type constructor, application of another type to a higher-order type, or a function type, where the function type constructor is not considered as a higher-order type.

The type of unifyingExprs is updated to use the above definition of *Expression*.

```
unifyingExprs
    :: [([Expression],Type)]  →
       [Type]  →  Type  →  TI Recomp [Expression]
```

This definition takes an additional argument avails::[*Type*] which represents the types of usable de Bruijn variables, where the n-th of the avails represents the type of the de Bruijn variable x_n; Another change is that *Expression*s with the same type are put together to form a list for reducing unnecessary type inference. The effect of doing this becomes more obvious when we reorganize avails for effective memoization as explained later.

When the requested type is a function type, the resulting expressions have to be lambda abstracted as many times as its arity, because we generate η-expanded forms. Since the abstracted variables are usable within the abstractions, we can safely

- push the argument types at the beginning of avails in the reverse order,

- invoke unifyingExprs with the resulting avails as the first argument and the return type of the requested type as the second argument, and

- lambda abstract each of the resulting expressions as many times as the arity of the requested type.

Thus,

```
unifyingExprs prims avails (t0:->t1)
  = do result ← unifyingExprs prims (t0:avails) t1
       return (map Lambda result)
```

For non-function types, the behavior of unifyingExprs is not very different from that of the old algorithm. It makes head candidates, i.e., a set of the expressions from the component library and avails whose return types and the requested type reqret unify. Then, spine candidates are computed and combined with the head candidates.

```
unifyingExprs prims avails reqret
  = do (exprs,typ) ←
         msum (zipWith (λ i t → return ([X i], t)) [0..] avails
               ++ map fresh prims)
       unify (returnTypeOf typ) reqret
       formSpine prims avails typ exprs
returnTypeOf (_:->t) = returnTypeOf t
returnTypeOf t       = t
```

where unify :: *MonadPlus* m => *Type* → *Type* → *TI* m () extends the current substitution with a most general unifier of its arguments if the two arguments unify, or otherwise it returns mzero. fresh introduces fresh variables to universally quantified variables, which exist only in prims because we use Hindley-Milner system:

```
fresh :: Monad m => (e,Type) → TI m (e,Type)
fresh (expr,typ) = do typ' ← freshVariablesForForalls typ
                      return (expr,typ')
```

The spine is formed by invoking unifyingExprs recursively using each argument type as the request type; then it returns the combination of the head with the results of the recursive calls.

```
formSpine
  :: [([Expression],Type)] →
     [Type] → Type → [Expression] → TI Recomp [Expression]
formSpine prims avails (t:->ts) funs
  = delayTI (do args ← applyAndUnifyingExprs prims avails t
                formSpine prims avails ts (liftM2 (:$) funs args))
formSpine prims avails _          funs = return funs
delayTI (TI f) = TI g where g s i = delay (f s i)
```

where applyAndUnifyingExprs applies the current substitution to types in avails and the requested type.

```
applyAndUnifyingExprs prims avails t
  = do subst ← getSubst
       unifyingExprs prims (map (apply subst) avails)
                     (apply subst t)
```

Dealing with functions returning a type variable

The actual implementation of unifyingExprs has to be more complicated than the above definition, because the return type of the head can be a type variable, in which case the number of its arguments can be arbitrarily large. Our current approach to this problem is rather naive, trying the infinite number of alternative substitutions $[X/a], [b → X/a], [b → c → X/a], [b → c → d → X/a], \ldots$ where X is the requested return type, a is the return type of the head, and $b, c, \ldots$ are fresh variables.

Note that the above approach is quite inefficient in some ways, preventing the algorithm from being applied to synthesis of larger programs. For example, when the type variable a is replaced with an n-ary function type, by permuting the arguments there are $n!$ equivalent expressions. Currently we are fixing this problem.

Also note that the arguments newly introduced by the substitutions have to be used, or they introduce another redundancy. Because this can easily be tested by seeing if all the fresh variables are replaced, the idea is already implemented in the proposed algorithm.

Memoization

The proposed algorithm often tries to synthesize the prioritized set of subexpressions on requests of the same type. In such cases memoization often works.

Although lazy memoization that hashes the pointers of objects is quite commonly known in functional programming, for our algorithm it is not a good option, because pointer equality makes little sense here, and there is no need of lazy memoization. We implemented a trie-based memoization by

- defining the data type of lazy infinite trie indexed by the arguments of the memo function,

- putting the return value of the memo function at each leaf node of the trie, and

- looking up the trie instead of computing the function value whenever the return value for any argument is required.

How to implement the generalized trie indexed by any data type is detailed in [Hin00].[5] When memoizing `unifyingExprs`, the trie is indexed by `avails::[`*Type*`]` and `reqret::`*Type*, and has a Spivey's monad instead of *Recomp* at each leaf node. The type variable names in `avails` and `reqret` should be normalized before the look up, or e.g. $\forall a.\,[a]$ and $\forall b.\,[b]$ would be regarded as different types.

One problem is that although the same types are often requested, the set of available variables change from time to time. Especially because the set of available variables increases monotonically as the position of the spine in question goes deeper in the syntax tree, it is quite likely that the memoization rarely hits if its argument is the naive combination of the requested return type and the set of the available expressions.

A hint on this problem is: "when constructing a type-consistent expression we are only interested in the types of the available variables, not those variables themselves", or in other words, "available variables of the same type are alternative in the sense of type-consistency." Thus, instead of just looking up the memo trie one should do the following to make memo trie hit more often and to save the heap space for memoization:

- reorganize the set of available variables by classifying them by type, and assign new variable number for each class,

- look up the return value from the trie using the reorganized list of such classes, and

- replace all the variable numbers introduced above in the obtained expressions with the available expressions.

---

[5]Note that a lazy infinite trie instead of a growing finite trie has to be used here, and thus unlike the implementation in [Hin00] Patricia tree implementation (e.g. [OG98]) is not fitted for the integer-indexed tries. However, because the only integers used as indexes are the identification numbers for type variables and type constructors, which are usually small below ten, usual lazy lists can be used instead of Patricia tree without outstanding loss of efficiency.

Because memoization costs the heap space, the values that are rarely looked up should rather be recomputed than memoized. In the case of memoizing unifyingExprs, it is effective to look up only small expressions from the memo because they are requested many times.

Excluding unoptimized expressions

Every known optimization rule suggests when equivalent programs can be synthesized, and helps to avoid such redundant synthesis. For example, from the *foldr/nil* rule we know that *foldr op x* $[]$ $= x$, and thus we should always avoid synthesis of expressions including *foldr* ? ? $[]$ pattern as a subexpression. Failure to exploit such rules can cause a tremendous loss to our algorithm because without doing so *foldr* ? ? $[]$ pattern can appear everywhere even when the requested type has nothing to do with lists at all.

Currently we use only the following heuristic to capture them:

- identify beforehand the library functions that consume some data type; whether a function is a consumer or not is currently just guessed from its type;

- prohibit constants as the consumed strict parameter.

This is not enough to capture all the cases, and a lot of expressions which generate and then consume lists are generated even when synthesizing an *Int* → *Int* function. However, there has been a long line of literature on identification of fusion points by general rules (e.g. [OHIT97]), which could also be exploited for further narrowing of the search space.

8.3 EFFICIENCY EVALUATION

Honestly speaking, the current system requires further improvements in efficiency to become very useful. Although synthesis of simple functions consisting of several primitive expressions requires only a few seconds, synthesis of functions consisting of more than twelve primitive expressions usually requires more than a minute, and may not finish the synthesis within an hour. Still, there is large room for improvements by suppressing redundant expressions before trying heuristic approaches. In fact, the efficiency keeps improving.

In addition to the old system, this research is related to GP algorithms such as PolyGP [YC98], [Yu01] that is GP under polymorphic higher-order type system, and ADATE [Ols95] that uses monomorphic first-order type system. Although it is usually desirable to compare the proposed method with such algorithms, here we do not compare efficiency with them for the reasons below.

Comparison with PolyGP should be unnecessary, because the comparison between PolyGP and the old system was made in [Kat04], where the latter showed better results on all problems there, and thus if the current system shows improvements from the old system on those problems, that should be enough.

The ADATE system has two releases: version 0.3 and 0.41, but unfortunately on our computers both of them could not reproduce the interesting results from

TABLE 8.1.   Computation time (sec.) of the old and the new algorithms.

	nth	map	length
computation time for the old system (real)	5.3	2.2	0.03
(user)	5.1	2.2	0.02
	nth	map	length
computation time for the new system (real)	0.8	1.9	0.03
(user)	0.6	1.2	0.02

the literature. Version 0.3 is released only in the binary form, compiled with legacy libraries, and thus is not runnable in our recent Linux systems. Although Version 0.41 seems runnable, it does not show the reported efficiency even from the sample specifications that come with the release — for example, the list sorting problem, which can reportedly be solved in 1529 seconds on 200MHz Pentium III, cannot be solved in five days on our 3GHz Pentium 4 machine. (In addition, when given other problems than the samples, it aborts because of lack in error handling.)

One possible reason of the above discouraging result might be as follows: although in usual GP some descendants of parent individuals who are stuck at local minima are dropped to minima at some interpolating positions by the crossover operator, since ADATE lacks in any crossover it is likely that without good luck in the random number seed it is difficult for any individual program to get out of local minima.

It is unknown how often ADATE fails, when it should be restarted if it seems to have failed, and how long it takes in average to obtain a desired result finally after the failures.

Improvements from the old algorithm   Table 8.1 shows the execution time of synthesizing the same functions in the same environment as in [Kat04], i.e. on Pentium4 2.00GHz machine with the Glasgow Haskell Compiler ver. 6.2 on Linux 2.4.22, with the -O optimization flag.

For the new algorithm, we used an adapted version of the original library file excluding *SKIBC* combinators and specialized variants of paramorphisms that are no longer necessary. In other words, we added dec = subtract 1, head, and tail to the example library file in Section 8.2.1.

In all the experiments performance improvements are observed.

8.4   DISCUSSIONS FOR FURTHER IMPROVEMENTS

8.4.1   Number of equivalent programs

Although the current version of the implemented system can synthesize many interesting expressions consisted of around twelve components within a minute, the efficiency has to be further improved for the serious purpose of reducing programmers' burden. One question here for such improvement is how redundant

122

the search space is, i.e., how many equivalent programs are tried. Whether we should focus on eliminating equivalent programs or we should proceed to trying heuristics depends on the answer to the question.

In order to tell a quite rough estimate of this amount, we tried a very lightweight random testing for synthesis of $take :: Int \rightarrow [a] \rightarrow [a]$. For all the expressions generated until the $take$ function is obtained in f, we computed $(f\ 2\ "12332", f\ 0\ "56789", f\ 2\ "k", f\ 0\ "")$, where the integers and the strings are selected randomly while covering different cases. Then we compared the number of expressions generated and that of different expressions generated. The former was 251940, while the latter was 514. This result suggests potentially the synthesis might be improved to about 500 times faster, and thus eliminating equivalent programs further is still worth trying.

Another question is whether such equivalent programs can be eliminated only by known optimization rules. One alternative approach might be to apply the same kind of random testing to small expressions and eliminate or lower the priorities of expressions that seem to be equivalent.

8.4.2 Should there be a timeout?

In the component libraries shown so far, expressions like fixpoint combinator that cause programs to enter an infinite loop did not appear. For this reason, the current version of the interpreter does without a timeout.

However, while the number of programs increases exponentially in the program size at most, there is no limit in the interpretation time. We can verify this fact by considering the program which takes n and applies $(1+)$ to 0, say, $2^{(2^n)}$ times. Hence, eventually the interpreter needs the timeout facility.

8.5 CONCLUSIONS

An algorithm that searches for the type-consistent functional programs from an incomplete set of constraints in a systematic and exhaustive way is proposed. It improves the efficiency of the previous algorithm by using de Bruijn lambda calculus at the back end, memoization, and some rules to avoid multiple counting of the equivalent expressions.

ACKNOWLEDGEMENTS

The author would like to thank Zhenjiang Hu, Pieter Koopman and anonymous reviewers for various comments.

REFERENCES

[Cyp93]   A. Cypher, editor. *Watch What I Do: Programming by Demonstration*. MIT Press, Cambridge, 1993.

[Hin00]   Ranf Hinze. Generalizing generalized tries. *Journal of Functional Programming*, 10(4):327–351, 2000.

[Kat04]   Susumu Katayama. Power of brute-force search in strongly-typed inductive functional programming automation. In *PRICAI 2004: Trends in Artificial Intelligence, 8th Pacific Rim International Conference on Artificial Intelligence, LNAI 3157*, pages 75–84, August 2004.

[KS88]   Richard Kennaway and Ronan Sleep. Director strings as combinators. *ACM Transactions on Programming Languages and Systems*, 10(4):602–626, 1988.

[LHJ95]   Sheng Liang, Paul Hudak, and Mark P. Jones. Monad transformers and modular interpreters. In *POPL'95: 22nd ACM SIGPLAN-SIGACT Symposium on Principles of Programming Languages*, 1995.

[OG98]   C. Okasaki and A. Gill. Fast mergeable integer maps. In *Workshop on ML*, pages 77–86, 1998.

[OHIT97]   Yoshiyuki Onoue, Zhenjiang Hu, Hideya Iwasaki, and Masato Takeichi. A calculational fusion system HYLO. In *Algorithmic Languages and Calculi*, pages 76–106, 1997.

[Ols95]   Roland Olsson. Inductive functional programming using incremental program transformation. *Artificial Intelligence*, 74(1):55–81, 1995.

[Sch01]   Ute Schmid. *Inductive Synthesis of Functional Programs – Learning Domain-Specific Control Rules and Abstract Schemes*. Springer, 2001. Habilitation thesis.

[Spi00]   M. Spivey. Combinators for breadth-first search. *Journal of Functional Programming*, 10(4):397–408, 2000.

[Sum77]   P. D. Summers. A methodology for lisp program construction from examples. *Journal ACM*, 24(1):162–175, 1977.

[SW04]   U. Schmid and J. Waltermann. Automatic synthesis of XSL-transformations from example documents. In *IASTED International Conference on Artificial Intelligence and Applications*, 2004.

[vWP03]   A. van Weelden and R Plasmeijer. A functional shell that dynamically combines compiled code. In *Proceedings on 15th international workshop on the implementation of functional languages*, Scotland, September 2003. Springer Verlag.

[YC98]   Tina Yu and Chris Clack. PolyGP: A polymorphic genetic programming system in haskell. In John R. Koza, Wolfgang Banzhaf, Kumar Chellapilla, Kalyanmoy Deb, Marco Dorigo, David B. Fogel, Max H. Garzon, David E. Goldberg, Hitoshi Iba, and Rick Riolo, editors, *Genetic Programming 1998: Proceedings of the Third Annual Conference*, pages 416–421, University of Wisconsin, Madison, Wisconsin, USA, 22-25 July 1998. Morgan Kaufmann.

[Yu01]   Tina Yu. Polymorphism and genetic programming. In Julian F. Miller, Marco Tomassini, Pier Luca Lanzi, Conor Ryan, Andrea G. B. Tettamanzi, and William B. Langdon, editors, *Genetic Programming, Proceedings of EuroGP'2001*, volume 2038 of *LNCS*, pages 218–233, Lake Como, Italy, 18-20 April 2001. Springer-Verlag.

```
> :set --quiet
> :load Library.hs
> \f -> f ["sldkfj","","324oj","wekljr3","43sld"] == "s3w4"
The inferred type is: (([] ([] Char)) -> ([] Char)).
Looking for the correct expression.
current program size = 1
current program size = 2
current program size = 3
current program size = 4
current program size = 5
current program size = 6
current program size = 7
current program size = 8
current program size = 9
Found!
(\ a -> list_para a nil (\ b c d -> list_para b d (\ e f g -> cons e d)))
1 sec in real,
0.28 seconds in CPU time spent.
> \f -> f (\x -> x+2) [1,2,3,4] == [3,4,5,6] ;; (a->a)->[a]->[a]
Looking for the correct expression.
current program size = 1
current program size = 2
current program size = 3
current program size = 4
current program size = 5
current program size = 6
current program size = 7
Found!
(\ a b -> list_para b nil (\ c d e -> cons (a c) e))
 in real,
0.04 seconds in CPU time spent.
> \f -> f "qwerty" == "ytrewq"
The inferred type is: (([] Char) -> ([] Char)).
Looking for the correct expression.
current program size = 1
current program size = 2
current program size = 3
current program size = 4
current program size = 5
current program size = 6
current program size = 7
current program size = 8
Found!
(\ a -> list_para a (\ b -> b) (\ b c d e -> d (cons b e)) nil)
 in real,
0.11 seconds in CPU time spent.
>
```

FIGURE 8.1. Sample user interaction. Program size is measured by the number of function applications plus one.

```
> :set --quiet
> \f -> f 3 "abcde" == 'c'
The inferred type is: (Int -> (([] Char) -> Char)).
Looking for the correct expression.
current program size = 1
current program size = 2
current program size = 3
current program size = 4
Found!
(\ a b -> hd (tl (tl b)))
 in real,
0.000000000000 seconds in CPU time spent.
> \f -> (f 3 "abcde" == 'c') && (f 4 "qwerty" == 'r')
The inferred type is: (Int -> (([] Char) -> Char)).
Looking for the correct expression.
current program size = 1
current program size = 2
current program size = 3
current program size = 4
current program size = 5
current program size = 6
current program size = 7
current program size = 8
Found!
(\ a b -> hd (nat_para a nil (\ c d -> list_para d b (\ e f g -> f))))
 in real,
0.23 seconds in CPU time spent.
>
```

FIGURE 8.2. Another sample user interaction. When the constraint is not strong enough one can obtain wrong answers. Because the number of examples required cannot be told before synthesis, one good policy is to start with a weak constraint and then add examples for the failed cases lazily.

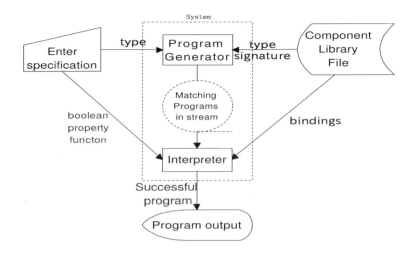

FIGURE 8.3. The system structure

126

Chapter 9

First-Class Open and Closed Code Fragments

Morten Rhiger[1]

Abstract: Multi-stage languages that allow "evaluation under lambdas" are excellent implementation languages for programs that manipulate, specialize, and execute code at runtime. In statically typed multi-stage languages, the existence of staging primitives demands a sound distinction between open code, which may be manipulated under lambdas, and closed code, which may be executed. We present $\lambda^{[]}$, a monomorphic type-safe multi-staged language for manipulating code with free identifiers. It differs from most existing multi-stage languages (such as, for example, derivatives of MetaML) in that its dynamic fragment is not hygienic; in other words, dynamic identifiers are not renamed during substitution. $\lambda^{[]}$ contains a first-class run operation, supports mutable cells (and other computational effects), and has decidable type inference. As such, it is a promising first step towards a practical multi-stage programming language.

9.1 INTRODUCTION

Programs that manipulate code fragments abound. Compilers, interpreters, and tools performing program optimization, program analysis, code refactoring, or program specialization all accept code as input, produce code as output, or both. In addition to these traditional examples, there is an increasing tendency to structure modern software development into two separate *stages*, namely (1) the implementation of generic software components and (2) the instantiation of these components to parameters that suit a specific group of customers [2]. Such generic software components can be implemented as *multi-stage programs* that produce the customized, or specialized, software component when given a set of customer-specific parameters. Therefore, program specialization techniques, and hence also

---
[1]Department of Computer Science, Roskilde University, P. O. Box 260, DK-4000 Roskilde, Denmark. E-mail: mir@ruc.dk. Homepage: www.ruc.dk/~mir/.

127

programming languages that support code manipulation and generation, may play an important role in the development of off-the-shelf application packages in the future.

Program manipulation is one of the oldest disciplines of programming and has been applied in practice at least since the development of the first Fortran compiler in 1957 [1]. Due to the work by the artificial-intelligence community in the 1960s and 1970s and the partial-evaluation community in the 1980s, *quasi-quotations* have become the dominant program constructs supporting code generation [4]. As an example of their use, consider the following procedure implemented in the Lisp-dialect Scheme [23].

```
(define (calc_gen tax)
  `(define (calc amount) (* amount ,(/ tax 100)))))
```

This procedure represents a generic tax-calculation module parameterized over a tax rate. It uses a backquote (`) to mark code that should be generated and a comma (,) to mark a computation whose result should be inserted in the generated code. When applied to a specific tax rate, it yields (the text of) a customized function computing taxes of income amounts. For example, running (calc_gen 13.5) yields (the text of) the program

```
(define (calc amount) (* amount 0.135))
```

The following common programming mistakes often arise in programs that use quasi-quotation to generate code fragments.

- The staging of the program is incorrect either because a code fragment is used as a value (for example as an argument to an arithmetic operation) or because a compound value (such as a closure) is used as a code fragment [14, Section 2.4].

- The staging of the program is correct, but the generated code fragments are illegal programs. This situation may arise if the generated programs contain unbound variables. For example, if we had accidentally replaced the second occurrence of amount by value in the above program, then the following program containing an undefined variable would have been generated.

```
(define (calc amount) (* value 0.135))
```

These programming mistakes are purposely not caught by implementations of Lisp and Scheme. In statically typed languages, additional errors may arise when the generated program fragments are not well-typed. It is the goal of typesafe multi-stage programming languages to catch all these mistakes during the type-checking of the original multi-stage program [35].

9.1.1 Multi-stage languages

The field of multi-stage programming grew out of the studies of offline partial evaluation conducted by Jones's group in the late 1980s [5, 18, 22]. Offline partial evaluation is a technique for specializing programs to parts of their inputs [11].

In offline partial evaluation, a program subject to specialization is first binding-time separated by differentiating between its static program parts (those that can be "specialized away" when the static inputs are supplied) and dynamic program parts (those that must remain in the specialized program). The binding-time separated program is then executed on its static inputs by interpreting the dynamic program parts as code generating primitives. The output of such a multi-stage program is (the text of) the specialized program. When viewed operationally like this, a binding-time separated program is called a generating extension [17]. In offline partial evaluation, binding times are statically verifiable properties that play the same role as types in statically typed languages [30].

In the mid-1990s, Davies [15] and Davies and Pfenning [16] established the logical connections between types and binding times. They showed that in the two calculi $\lambda^{\bigcirc}$ and $\lambda^{\square}$, images of, respectively, linear-time temporal logic and the intuitionistic modal logic S4 under the Curry-Howard isomorphism, type correctness corresponds to binding-time correctness. These calculi extend the lambda calculus with types $\bigcirc\tau$ and $\square\tau$ of dynamic program parts of type τ. The primary operational difference between the two calculi is that $\lambda^{\bigcirc}$ allows manipulation of open code fragments while $\lambda^{\square}$ only allows manipulation of closed code fragments. On the other hand, a first-class eval-like operation is definable in terms of existing primitives in $\lambda^{\square}$ while $\lambda^{\bigcirc}$ becomes unsound in the presence of such an operation. Neither of these calculi was designed to handle imperative features.

Following Davies and Pfenning, the multi-stage programming language community was established, one of whose aims was to combine the advantageous features of $\lambda^{\bigcirc}$ and $\lambda^{\square}$ in one language. The effort of the community has led to the development of multi-stage dialects of ML [8, 9, 38] and to much research in static type systems for multi-stage languages [6, 7, 24, 29, 35–39]. All existing multi-stage languages extend a core type system with a type constructor of code, similar in purpose to $\bigcirc\tau$ and $\square\tau$ of $\lambda^{\bigcirc}$ and $\lambda^{\square}$. The primary challenge that multi-stage languages must address is probably the combination of open-code manipulations on one hand and a first-class run operation and imperative features on the other. For example, the following staged-correct program should be rejected since it evaluates an open code fragment x.

```
`(lambda (x) ,(eval `x))
```

As another example, after evaluating the following stage-correct program, the cell cell contains an open code fragment.

```
(define cell (box `1))
(define code `(lambda (x)
              ,(begin (set-box! cell `x)
                      `x)))
```

The programmer may later attempt to introduce this code fragment under a binder of its free variable x. A static type system should handle this situation correctly. One approach to guarantee type safety under these circumstances has been to count the number of occurrences of eval that "surrounds" a term [29]. However, this results in a system in which eval can not be lambda abstracted an hence is not a first-class operation. Another approach have been to introduce a separate type of *second-class* closed code [6]. The latest version of MetaOCaml [27], a multistage dialect of the OCaml language, uses *environment classifiers* to decorate code type with a symbolic classifier that constraints the variables that may occur free in a code fragment [7].

9.1.2 Hygienic languages

Most existing multi-stage languages, such as those mentioned above, are *hygienic* [25]. That is, dynamic (or future-stage) program parts are lexically scoped. Hygiene is required to guarantee confluence for rewriting systems where a term carrying free variables may be substituted under a binder for one of its free variables. Examples include rewriting systems that performs (full) β-normalization (such as, e.g, partial evaluation [22], type-directed partial evaluation [12, 13], Barendregt et al's innermost spine reduction [3], and many other program optimizations), macro systems, multi-stage languages, and variants of Scheme where globally defined symbols are not reduced until they are needed (facilitating incrementally defined mutually recursive procedures [23, Section 5.2.1]).

In macro systems and in multi-stage languages, lexically scoped dynamic identifiers are often implemented by consistently renaming them using, e.g., a gensym-like operation [26]. However, in the presence of side effects and of an eval-like operation it has turned out to be somewhat challenging to design languages that account for renaming of dynamic identifiers in their type systems.

9.1.3 Contributions

Many of the existing multi-stage calculi mentioned above have evolved out of studying *the interplay between open and closed code*. In the present work, we propose to take *non-hygiene* as the primary principle for designing the multistage language $\lambda^{[]}$. We foresee that new statically typed multi-stage languages may evolve out of studying *the interplay between hygiene and non-hygiene*.

In a non-hygienic language, future-stage variables are not renamed during substitutions. Therefore, a type system can explicitly mention free variables in the type of dynamic code. In this article we hope to establish convincing evidences demonstrating that the resulting type system treats code and stages in a fairly straightforward manner.

An immediate and intriguing consequence of our design is that the type system enables a uniform treatment of open and closed program fragments as *first-class data*. The type system of $\lambda^{[]}$ extends the simply-typed lambda calculus with a type $[\gamma]\tau$ of code. Intuitively, an expression has type $[\gamma]\tau$ if it evaluates to a code fragment which has type τ in type environment γ. The language also contains two staging primitives, $\uparrow$ and $\downarrow$, similar to those found in existing multi-stage languages [15, 38] and to quasiquote and unquote in Lisp and Scheme [4].

In $\lambda^{[]}$, source identifiers occur in type environments and hence also in types.

As an extreme example, the expression $\uparrow x$ is a legal closed program of type $[x : \text{int}]\text{int}$; indeed $\uparrow x$ evaluates to the program fragment x which certainly has type int in the type environment $x : \text{int}$. The type $[x : \text{int}]\text{int}$ is not the principal type of $\uparrow x$: This expression also has type, say, $[x : \text{bool}, y : \beta]\text{bool}$ and neither of these types appear to be more general than the other. This is mirrored by the fact that neither $x : \text{int} \vdash x : \text{int}$ nor $x : \text{bool}, y : \beta \vdash x : \text{bool}$ are *principal typings* [21] of the expression x. Principal types that involve code types use *type environment variables* γ in a way similar to the use of traditional *type variables*. For example, the principal type of $\uparrow x$ is $[x : \alpha, \gamma]\alpha$; indeed $\uparrow x$ evaluates to the program fragment x which has type α in *any* type environment of shape $x : \alpha, \gamma$. We can replace γ and α by int and $\emptyset$ (where $\emptyset$ denotes the empty type environment) or by $y : \beta$ and bool to obtain the types shown above. We do not study principality in this article. Since type environments occur in the type of code, the type of *closed code* of type τ is easily expressible as $[\emptyset]\tau$ which we also write as $[\,]\tau$. Therefore, the first-class operation run has type $[\,]\tau \rightarrow \tau$.

The type system alleviates some of the weaknesses of non-hygiene: It is sometimes possible to read from the types reported by the type system, the variables that may be captured during evaluation. For example, the type $[x : \text{int}, \gamma]\tau \rightarrow [\gamma]\tau$ of the term $\lambda c. \uparrow (\text{let} x = 42 \,\text{in}\, \downarrow c)$, shows that this expression denotes a function that maps code into code, and that any free x's in the input will be captured in the output.

9.1.4 Outline

The rest of this article is organized as follows. We present the terms, type system, and operational semantics of $\lambda^{[]}$ in Section 9.2. In Section 9.3 we present a proof of type safety. In Section 9.4 we demonstrate the capabilities of the proposed language using examples. In Section 9.5 we outline related work in the area of multi-stage programming and in Section 9.6 we conclude.

9.2 OPEN AND CLOSED CODE FRAGMENTS

In this section we introduce the syntax, the type system, and an operational semantics of the monomorphic multi-stage language $\lambda^{[]}$. We let x, y, z range over an infinite set $\mathbf{V}$ of identifiers. Furthermore we let i range over the set $\mathbf{Z}$ of integers and n over the set $\mathbf{N} = \{0, 1, \cdots\}$ of natural numbers. Finally, ℓ ranges over an infinite supply of names of reference cells.

The terms of $\lambda^{[]}$ are defined by the following grammar.

$$
\begin{aligned}
e, E \quad \in \quad \text{EXPR} \quad ::= \quad & i \mid x \mid \lambda x.e \mid e_1 e_2 & \text{— pure fragment} \\
\mid \quad & \uparrow e \mid \downarrow e \mid \text{lift}(e) \mid \text{run}(e) & \text{— staged fragment} \\
\mid \quad & \text{ref}(e) \mid \text{get}(e) \mid \text{set}(e_1, e_2) \mid \ell & \text{— imperative fragment}
\end{aligned}
$$

The staging operations $\uparrow$, $\downarrow$, and run correspond, respectively, to quasiquote (` ), unquote ( , ), and `eval` in Lisp and Scheme. The expression $\text{lift}(e)$ injects the value of e into a future stage. There is no general lifting operation in Lisp and

Scheme; instead, the value of any "self-evaluating" constant expression is treated (by `eval`) as the constant expression itself [23]. The operations ref, get, and set correspond to the operations `ref`, `!`, and `:=` on reference cells in Standard ML [28] and `box`, `unbox`, and `set-box!` in many implementations of Scheme. Since the language presented in this article is monomorphic, there are no polymorphic references requiring special treatment [40, 41]. Terms containing reference cells ℓ may arise during reduction (as a result of creating new cells using ref) but reference cells are not intended to occur in source terms.

9.2.1 Type system

The types of the multi-stage language consist of base types (here restricted to one type int of integers), function types, types of reference cells, and a type $[\gamma]\tau$ for code fragments of type τ in type environment γ.

$$
\begin{array}{rcll}
\tau & \in & \text{TYPE} & ::= \quad \text{int} \mid \tau_1 \to \tau_2 \mid \tau\,\text{ref} \mid [\gamma]\tau \\
\gamma & \in & \text{ENV} & ::= \quad \emptyset \mid x : \tau, \gamma \\
& & \Gamma & ::= \quad \gamma_1, \cdots, \gamma_n \\
& & \Sigma & ::= \quad \ell_1 : \tau_1, \cdots, \ell_n : \tau_n
\end{array}
$$

In the type rules and during type checking, a stack Γ contains type environments mapping free identifiers to types. Free static identifiers are at the bottom of the stack (to the left) while dynamic identifiers are further towards the top (to the right). In contrast to traditional typed lambda calculi, type environments not only exists during type checking but may also appear in the final types assigned to terms. During type checking, a location typing Σ assigns types to locations.

In the presentation of the type system, we represent type environments uniformly as elements of the inductively defined set ENV. In order to achieve principality [20], however, care must be taken to identify type environments that contain re-ordered bindings rather than only syntactically identical type environments. For example, the term $\uparrow(fx)$ can be assigned both of the types $[x : \tau_1, f : \tau_1 \to \tau_2]t_2$ and $[f : \tau_1 \to \tau_2, x : \tau_1]\tau_2$ both of which we treat as principal type of $\uparrow(fx)$. Technically, we define an equivalence relation on types and type environment that take re-ordering of bindings into account and we work on the equivalence classes induced by this relation instead of directly on the inductively defined elements.

Definition 9.1. *We obtain a finite mapping* $\mathbf{V} \to \text{TYPE}$, *here expressed as a subset of* $\mathbf{V} \times \text{TYPE}$, *from a type environment as follows.*

$$
\begin{array}{rcl}
\bar{\emptyset} & = & \{\} \\
\overline{x : \tau, \gamma} & = & \{(x, \tau)\} \cup \{(y, \tau') \in \bar{\gamma} \mid y \neq x\}
\end{array}
$$

This definition guarantees that $\bar{\gamma}$ is a function, i.e., a subset of $\mathbf{V} \times \text{TYPE}$ for which $(x, \tau_1) \in \bar{\gamma}$ and $(x, \tau_2) \in \bar{\gamma}$ implies $\tau_1 = \tau_2$. Note that bindings to the left take precedence over bindings to the right.

We treat two type environments as equivalent if they denote the same finite mapping. This notion of equivalence is extended to types as follows.

Definition 9.2 (Type equivalence). *We define an equivalence relation $\approx$ on types and type environments as follows.*

$$\frac{\begin{array}{c}\mathrm{dom}(\overline{\gamma_1}) = \mathrm{dom}(\overline{\gamma_2})\\ \textit{For all } x \in \mathrm{dom}(\overline{\gamma_1}), \overline{\gamma_1}(x) \approx \overline{\gamma_2}(x)\end{array}}{\gamma_1 \approx \gamma_2} \qquad \frac{}{\mathsf{int} \approx \mathsf{int}}$$

$$\frac{\tau_1 \approx \tau_2 \quad \tau_1' \approx \tau_2'}{\tau_1 \to \tau_1' \approx \tau_2 \to \tau_2'} \qquad \frac{\tau \approx \tau'}{\tau\,\mathsf{ref} \approx \tau'\,\mathsf{ref}} \qquad \frac{\gamma_1 \approx \gamma_2 \quad \tau_1 \approx \tau_2}{[\gamma_1]\tau_1 \approx [\gamma_2]\tau_2}$$

Note that $\approx$ is indeed an equivalence relation. We extend this notion of equivalence to stacks of type environments and to location typings as follows: Two stacks of type environments (two location typings) are equivalent, written $\Gamma_1 \approx \Gamma_2$ ($\Sigma_1 \approx \Sigma_2$) if their elements are point-wise equivalent.

In the rest of this article, we make frequent use of the construction of finite mappings from type environments and of the equality relation. For example, a γ that satisfies the equation $[x : \tau_1, \gamma]\tau \approx [y : \tau_2, \gamma]\tau$ for $x \neq y$, must have $\{x, y\} \subseteq \mathrm{dom}(\gamma)$ and must already assign τ_1 to x and τ_2 to y. In other words, we must have $\gamma \approx x : \tau_1, y : \tau_2, \gamma'$ for some γ'.

We use the following notational conventions. We omit the empty type environment $\emptyset$ and write, for example, $[\,]\tau$ and $[x : \tau]\tau$ instead of $[\emptyset]\tau$ and $[x : \tau, \emptyset]\tau$. The code-type constructor $[-]-$ has higher precedence than function arrows, so, for example, the types $[\,]\tau \to \tau$ and $([\,]\tau) \to \tau$ are identical and both different from $[\,](\tau \to \tau)$. We write ε for the empty stack of type environments. We allow access to elements at both end of the stack; thus γ, Γ denotes a stack with γ at the bottom while Γ, γ denotes a stack with γ at the top. The operation $|-|$ yields the height of a stack of type environments, i.e., $|\gamma_1, \cdots, \gamma_n| = n$ and $|\varepsilon| = 0$.

To account for reference cells that occur in terms, a typing judgment carries a finite mapping Σ from names of reference cells to types. (Harper calls such mappings *location typings* to distinguish them from *variable typings*, or type environments, mapping variables to types [19].) We write $\Sigma(\ell)$ for the type associated with ℓ in Σ and we use the construction $\Sigma[\ell : \tau]$ to denote the result of updating location typing Σ with a binding of ℓ to τ. In other words, $(\Sigma[\ell : \tau])(\ell) = \tau$ and $(\Sigma[\ell : \tau])(\ell') = \Sigma(\ell')$ if $\ell \neq \ell'$. We write $\Sigma \subseteq \Sigma'$ if and only if for any $\ell \in \mathrm{dom}(\Sigma)$, $\ell \in \mathrm{dom}(\Sigma')$ and $\Sigma(\ell) \approx \Sigma'(\ell)$.

The type system for the monomorphic languages is given in Figure 9.1. A typing judgment $\Gamma; \Sigma' \vdash e : \tau$ may be read "under the stack of type environments Γ and given a location typing Σ, the term e has type τ." (A type system for the subset of the language without mutable references can be obtained simply by removing all occurrences of Σ in the first eight rules in Figure 9.1 and discarding the remaining four rules.)

Modulo type equivalence, the premise of the rule 3 in Figure 9.1 may be read simply as $\Gamma, (x : \tau', \gamma); \Sigma \vdash e : \tau$. Rule 8 states that running a term of code type $[\,]\tau$ yields a value of type τ. It is intended to guarantee that only closed and well-typed code fragments can be executed at runtime. The symbol run may be abstracted,

Pure fragment:

$$\frac{}{\Gamma,\gamma;\Sigma \vdash i : \mathsf{int}} \quad (1)$$

$$\frac{\overline{\gamma}(x) \approx \tau}{\Gamma,\gamma;\Sigma \vdash x : \tau} \quad (2)$$

$$\frac{\Gamma,\gamma';\Sigma \vdash e : \tau \quad \gamma' \approx (x:\tau',\gamma)}{\Gamma,\gamma;\Sigma \vdash \lambda x.e : \tau' \to \tau} \quad (3)$$

$$\frac{\Gamma,\gamma;\Sigma \vdash e_1 : \tau_2 \to \tau \quad \Gamma,\gamma;\Sigma \vdash e_2 : \tau_2}{\Gamma,\gamma;\Sigma \vdash e_1 e_2 : \tau} \quad (4)$$

Staged fragment:

$$\frac{\Gamma,\gamma;\Sigma \vdash e : \tau}{\Gamma;\Sigma \vdash {\uparrow} e : [\gamma]\tau} \quad (5)$$

$$\frac{\Gamma;\Sigma \vdash e : [\gamma]\tau}{\Gamma,\gamma;\Sigma \vdash {\downarrow} e : \tau} \quad (6)$$

$$\frac{\Gamma;\Sigma \vdash e : \tau}{\Gamma;\Sigma \vdash \mathsf{lift}(e) : [\gamma]\tau} \quad (7)$$

$$\frac{\Gamma;\Sigma \vdash e : [\,]\tau}{\Gamma;\Sigma \vdash \mathsf{run}(e) : \tau} \quad (8)$$

Imperative fragment:

$$\frac{\Sigma(\ell) \approx \tau}{\Gamma;\Sigma \vdash \ell : \tau\,\mathsf{ref}} \quad (9)$$

$$\frac{\Gamma;\Sigma \vdash e : \tau}{\Gamma;\Sigma \vdash \mathsf{ref}(e) : \tau\,\mathsf{ref}} \quad (10)$$

$$\frac{\Gamma;\Sigma \vdash e : \tau\,\mathsf{ref}}{\Gamma;\Sigma \vdash \mathsf{get}(e) : \tau} \quad (11)$$

$$\frac{\Gamma;\Sigma \vdash e_1 : \tau\,\mathsf{ref} \quad \Gamma;\Sigma \vdash e_2 : \tau}{\Gamma;\Sigma \vdash \mathsf{set}(e_1,e_2) : \tau} \quad (12)$$

FIGURE 9.1. Typing rules for the monomorphic, multi-stage language $\lambda^{[\,]}$.

as in $\lambda x.\mathsf{run}(x)$, but, like any other function, the result of type $[\,]\tau \to \tau$ cannot be used polymorphically in this monomorphic language. Note that stages participate in relating the definition and the uses of a variable in the sense that identifiers at different stages are always different. For example, the expression $\lambda x.\,{\uparrow}x$ contains two distinct identifiers of name x, the rightmost unbound. This expressions is semantically equivalent to $\lambda y.\,{\uparrow}x$. Similarly, $\lambda x.\,{\downarrow}x$ contains two distinct identifiers of name x. (This expression is not equivalent to $\lambda y.\,{\downarrow}x$, however.) Therefore, $(\lambda x.\,{\downarrow}x)E$ does not reduce to ${\downarrow}E$.

To justify the definition of type equivalence, we show that if a term can be given a type then it can also be given any equivalent type.

Lemma 9.3. *Assume* $\Gamma_1;\Sigma_1 \vdash e : \tau_1$. *If furthermore* $\Gamma_1 \approx \Gamma_2$, $\Sigma_1 \approx \Sigma_2$, *and* $\tau_1 \approx \tau_2$ *then* $\Gamma_2;\Sigma_2 \vdash e : \tau_2$.

Proof. By induction on the derivation of $\Gamma_1;\Sigma_1 \vdash e : \tau_1$.

9.2.2 Operational semantics

We present a left-to-right, call-by-value, small-step operational semantics of $\lambda^{[\,]}$ below. The key difference between this semantics and the semantics of hygienic multi-stage languages is that substitution does not rename bound dynamic identifiers. (It does rename bound static identifiers, however.)

We first need the following auxiliary definition.

Definition 9.4 (Free variables). $\mathrm{FV}(e)_n$ denotes the set of free static identifiers in the stage-n term e.

$$\mathrm{FV}(i)_n = \{\}$$
$$\mathrm{FV}(x)_0 = \{x\} \qquad\qquad \mathrm{FV}(x)_{n+1} = \{\}$$
$$\mathrm{FV}(\lambda x.e)_0 = \mathrm{FV}(e)_0\backslash\{x\} \qquad \mathrm{FV}(\lambda x.e)_{n+1} = \mathrm{FV}(e)_{n+1}$$
$$\mathrm{FV}(e_1\,e_2)_n = \mathrm{FV}(e_1)_n \cup \mathrm{FV}(e_2)_n$$
$$\mathrm{FV}(\uparrow e)_n = \mathrm{FV}(e)_{n+1} \qquad\qquad \mathrm{FV}(\downarrow e)_{n+1} = \mathrm{FV}(e)_n$$
$$\mathrm{FV}(\mathsf{lift}(e))_n = \mathrm{FV}(e)_n \qquad\qquad \mathrm{FV}(\mathsf{run}(e))_n = \mathrm{FV}(e)_n$$
$$\mathrm{FV}(\mathsf{ref}(e))_n = \mathrm{FV}(e)_n \qquad\qquad \mathrm{FV}(\ell)_n = \{\}$$
$$\mathrm{FV}(\mathsf{set}(e_1,e_2))_n = \mathrm{FV}(e_1)_n \cup \mathrm{FV}(e_2)_n \qquad \mathrm{FV}(\mathsf{get}(e))_n = \mathrm{FV}(e)_n$$

In order to treat the manipulation of identifiers carefully, substitution is defined as a relation on raw terms rather than as a function on α-equivalence classes as follows. As in traditional λ-calculi, fresh static identifiers are introduced to avoid capturing free static variables.

Definition 9.5 (Substitution).

$$i\{E/x\}_n = i \qquad\qquad x\{E/x\}_0 = E$$
$$y\{E/x\}_0 = y,\ \text{for } x \neq y \qquad y\{E/x\}_{n+1} = y$$

$$(\lambda x.e)\{E/x\}_0 = \lambda x.e$$
$$(\lambda z.e)\{E/x\}_{n+1} = \lambda z.e\{E/x\}_{n+1}$$
$$(\lambda z.e)\{E/x\}_0 = \lambda y.e\{y/z\}_0\{E/x\}_0,$$
$$\qquad\qquad \text{for } z \neq x \text{ and } y \notin (\mathrm{FV}(e)_0\backslash\{z\}) \cup \mathrm{FV}(E)_0$$
$$(e_1\,e_2)\{E/x\}_n = (e_1\{E/x\}_n)\,(e_2\{E/x\}_n)$$

$$(\uparrow e)\{E/x\}_n = \uparrow e\{E/x\}_{n+1} \qquad (\downarrow e)\{E/x\}_{n+1} = \downarrow e\{E/x\}_n$$
$$(\mathsf{lift}(e))\{E/x\}_n = \mathsf{lift}(e\{E/x\}_n) \qquad (\mathsf{run}(e))\{E/x\}_n = \mathsf{run}(e\{E/x\}_n)$$
$$(\mathsf{ref}(e))\{E/x\}_n = \mathsf{ref}(e\{E/x\}_n) \qquad (\mathsf{get}(e))\{E/x\}_n = \mathsf{get}(e\{E/x\}_n)$$
$$\ell\{E/x\}_n = \ell \qquad (\mathsf{set}(e_1,e_2))\{E/x\}_n = \mathsf{set}(e_1\{E/x\}_n, e_2\{E/x\}_n)$$

Restricted to operate on static terms (e.g., considering only the operation $-\{-/-\}_0$), this notion of substitution is capture avoiding and coincides with the traditional substitution for the λ-calculus. For the dynamic fragment, identifiers are dynamically bound in that they are not renamed during substitution. For example, substituting $\uparrow y$ for the free static identifier x in $\uparrow (\lambda y.\downarrow x)$ does not rename the bound dynamic identifier y: $(\uparrow (\lambda y.\downarrow x))\{\uparrow y/x\}_0 = \uparrow (\lambda y.\downarrow\uparrow y)$.

The following two fundamental properties of the simply-typed λ-calculus also hold for $\lambda^{[]}$.

Lemma 9.6 (Weakening). *Assume* $\gamma, \Gamma; \Sigma \vdash e : \tau$. *If furthermore* $x \notin \mathrm{FV}(e)_{|\Gamma|}$ *then*

$$(x : \tau', \gamma), \Gamma; \Sigma \vdash e : \tau.$$

Pure (and staged) fragment:

$$\frac{}{\mathcal{V} \vdash_n i} \quad (1)$$

$$\frac{\mathcal{V} \vdash_{n+1} e}{\mathcal{V} \vdash_n \uparrow e} \quad (6)$$

$$\frac{}{\mathcal{V} \vdash_{n+1} x} \quad (2)$$

$$\frac{\mathcal{V} \vdash_{n+1} e}{\mathcal{V} \vdash_{n+2} \downarrow e} \quad (7)$$

$$\frac{}{\mathcal{V} \vdash_0 \lambda x.e} \quad (3)$$

$$\frac{\mathcal{V} \vdash_{n+1} e}{\mathcal{V} \vdash_{n+1} \mathsf{lift}(e)} \quad (8)$$

$$\frac{\mathcal{V} \vdash_{n+1} e}{\mathcal{V} \vdash_{n+1} \lambda x.e} \quad (4)$$

$$\frac{\mathcal{V} \vdash_{n+1} e}{\mathcal{V} \vdash_{n+1} \mathsf{run}(e)} \quad (9)$$

$$\frac{\mathcal{V} \vdash_{n+1} e_1 \quad \mathcal{V} \vdash_{n+1} e_2}{\mathcal{V} \vdash_{n+1} e_1 e_2} \quad (5)$$

Imperative (and staged) fragment:

$$\frac{}{\mathcal{V} \vdash_n \ell} \quad (10)$$

$$\frac{\mathcal{V} \vdash_{n+1} e}{\mathcal{V} \vdash_{n+1} \mathsf{get}(e)} \quad (12)$$

$$\frac{\mathcal{V} \vdash_{n+1} e}{\mathcal{V} \vdash_{n+1} \mathsf{ref}(e)} \quad (11)$$

$$\frac{\mathcal{V} \vdash_{n+1} e_1 \quad \mathcal{V} \vdash_{n+1} e_2}{\mathcal{V} \vdash_{n+1} \mathsf{set}(e_1, e_2)} \quad (13)$$

FIGURE 9.2. Values of $\lambda^{[]}$.

Proof. By induction on the derivation of $\gamma, \Gamma; \Sigma \vdash e : t$.

Lemma 9.7 (Substitution). *If* $(x : \tau', \gamma), \Gamma; \Sigma \vdash e : t$ *and* $\gamma, \Gamma; \Sigma \vdash e' : \tau'$ *then*

$$\gamma, \Gamma; \Sigma \vdash e\{e'/x\}_{|G|} : t.$$

Proof. By induction on the derivation of $x : \tau', \gamma), \Gamma; \Sigma \vdash e : \tau$. Lemma 9.6 (Weakening) is used in the case $(x : \tau', \gamma); \Sigma \vdash \lambda z.e : \tau'' \to \tau$ for $z \neq x$.

Figure 9.2 characterizes the values that can result from evaluating a stage-n term. In the following section we show that only these values can be the final results of evaluation well-typed $\lambda^{[]}$-terms. But first we need a representation of stores (or memories) and a characterization of when a store is well-typed with respect to a location type Σ: A store σ is a finite mapping from reference cells to values at stage 0 (i.e., expressions e satisfying $\mathcal{V} \vdash_0 e$). We write $\sigma[\ell := e]$ for the operation that updates the store σ with a binding of ℓ to e.

Definition 9.8. *A store* σ *has location type* Σ, *written* $\sigma : \Sigma$, *if for any* $\ell \in \mathrm{dom}(\sigma)$,

$$\emptyset; \Sigma \vdash \sigma(\ell) : \Sigma(\ell).$$

The left-to-right, call-by-value, small-step operational semantics is presented in Figure 9.3. In this figure, rule 1 represents evaluation under (dynamic) lambdas.

Contextual rules:

$$\frac{S \vdash_{n+1} \langle e, \sigma \rangle \longrightarrow \langle e', \sigma' \rangle}{S \vdash_{n+1} \langle \lambda x.e, \sigma \rangle \longrightarrow \langle \lambda x.e', \sigma' \rangle} \quad (1)$$

$$\frac{S \vdash_{n+1} \langle e, \sigma \rangle \longrightarrow \langle e', \sigma' \rangle}{S \vdash_n \langle \uparrow e, \sigma \rangle \longrightarrow \langle \uparrow e', \sigma' \rangle} \quad (4)$$

$$\frac{S \vdash_n \langle e_1, \sigma \rangle \longrightarrow \langle e_1', \sigma' \rangle}{S \vdash_n \langle e_1 e_2, \sigma \rangle \longrightarrow \langle e_1' e_2, \sigma' \rangle} \quad (2)$$

$$\frac{S \vdash_n \langle e, \sigma \rangle \longrightarrow \langle e', \sigma' \rangle}{S \vdash_{n+1} \langle \downarrow e, \sigma \rangle \longrightarrow \langle \downarrow e', \sigma' \rangle} \quad (5)$$

$$\frac{\mathcal{V} \vdash_n e_1 \quad S \vdash_n \langle e_2, \sigma \rangle \longrightarrow \langle e_2', \sigma' \rangle}{S \vdash_n \langle e_1 e_2, \sigma \rangle \longrightarrow \langle e_1 e_2', \sigma' \rangle} \quad (3)$$

$$\frac{S \vdash_n \langle e, \sigma \rangle \longrightarrow \langle e', \sigma' \rangle}{S \vdash_n \langle \mathsf{lift}(e), \sigma \rangle \longrightarrow \langle \mathsf{lift}(e'), \sigma' \rangle} \quad (6)$$

$$\frac{S \vdash_n \langle e, \sigma \rangle \longrightarrow \langle e', \sigma' \rangle}{S \vdash_n \langle \mathsf{run}(e), \sigma \rangle \longrightarrow \langle \mathsf{run}(e'), \sigma' \rangle} \quad (7)$$

$$\frac{S \vdash_n \langle e, \sigma \rangle \longrightarrow \langle e', \sigma' \rangle}{S \vdash_n \langle \mathsf{ref}(e), \sigma \rangle \longrightarrow \langle \mathsf{ref}(e'), \sigma' \rangle} \quad (8)$$

$$\frac{S \vdash_n \langle e, \sigma \rangle \longrightarrow \langle e', \sigma' \rangle}{S \vdash_n \langle \mathsf{get}(e), \sigma \rangle \longrightarrow \langle \mathsf{get}(e'), \sigma' \rangle} \quad (9)$$

$$\frac{S \vdash_n \langle e_1, \sigma \rangle \longrightarrow \langle e_1', \sigma' \rangle}{S \vdash_n \langle \mathsf{set}(e_1, e_2), \sigma \rangle \longrightarrow \langle \mathsf{set}(e_1', e_2), \sigma' \rangle} \quad (10)$$

$$\frac{\mathcal{V} \vdash_n e_1 \quad S \vdash_n \langle e_2, \sigma \rangle \longrightarrow \langle e_2', \sigma' \rangle}{S \vdash_n \langle \mathsf{set}(e_1, e_2), \sigma \rangle \longrightarrow \langle \mathsf{set}(e_1, e_2'), \sigma' \rangle} \quad (11)$$

Reduction rules:

$$\frac{\mathcal{V} \vdash_0 e_2}{S \vdash_0 \langle (\lambda x.e_1) e_2, \sigma \rangle \longrightarrow \langle e_1\{e_2/x\}, \sigma \rangle} \quad (12)$$

$$\frac{\mathcal{V} \vdash_1 e}{S \vdash_0 \langle \mathsf{run}(\uparrow e), \sigma \rangle \longrightarrow \langle e, \sigma \rangle} \quad (16)$$

$$\frac{\mathcal{V} \vdash_0 e \quad \ell \notin \mathrm{dom}(\sigma)}{S \vdash_0 \langle \mathsf{ref}(e), \sigma \rangle \longrightarrow \langle \ell, \sigma[\ell := e] \rangle} \quad (13)$$

$$\frac{\mathcal{V} \vdash_0 e}{S \vdash_0 \langle \mathsf{lift}(e), \sigma \rangle \longrightarrow \langle \uparrow e, \sigma \rangle} \quad (17)$$

$$\frac{}{S \vdash_0 \langle \mathsf{get}(\ell), \sigma \rangle \longrightarrow \langle \sigma(\ell), \sigma \rangle} \quad (14)$$

$$\frac{\mathcal{V} \vdash_1 e}{S \vdash_1 \langle \downarrow (\uparrow e), \sigma \rangle \longrightarrow \langle e, \sigma \rangle} \quad (18)$$

$$\frac{\mathcal{V} \vdash_0 e}{S \vdash_0 \langle \mathsf{set}(\ell, e), \sigma \rangle \longrightarrow \langle e, \sigma[\ell := e] \rangle} \quad (15)$$

FIGURE 9.3. **Left-to-right, call-by-value, small-step operational semantics.**

9.3 SYNTACTIC TYPE SOUNDNESS

The following auxiliary result states that a well-typed value at stage $n+1$ is also a well-typed expression at stage n. In that respect, it serves the same purpose as the demotion operation defined for MetaML [29, 36].

Lemma 9.9 (Demotion). *If* $\emptyset, \Gamma, \gamma; \Sigma \vdash e : \tau$ *and* $\mathcal{V} \vdash_{|\Gamma|+1} e$ *then* $\Gamma, \gamma; \Sigma \vdash e : \tau$.

Proof. By induction on the derivation of $\emptyset, \Gamma, \gamma; \Sigma \vdash e : \tau$.

137

We also need the following result stating that a well-typed value at stage 0 is also a well-typed value at stage 1.

Lemma 9.10 (Promotion at stage 0). *If* $\emptyset; \Sigma \vdash e : \tau$ *and* $\mathcal{V} \vdash_0 e$ *then* $\emptyset, \gamma; \Sigma \vdash e : \tau$.

Proof. Since e is a value at stage 0, e is closed. Hence, by repeating Lemma 9.6 (Weakening), $\gamma; \Sigma \vdash e : \tau$. Then we also have (by a straightforward separate lemma) that $\emptyset, \gamma; \Sigma \vdash e : \tau$ as required.

Lemma 9.11 (Subject reduction). *Assume* $\emptyset, \Gamma; \Sigma \vdash e : \tau$. *If furthermore* $\sigma : \Sigma$ *and* $\mathcal{S} \vdash_{|\Gamma|} \langle e, \sigma \rangle \longrightarrow \langle e', \sigma' \rangle$ *then there exists a location typing* $\Sigma' \supseteq \Sigma$ *such that* $\sigma' : \Sigma'$ *and* $\emptyset, \Gamma; \Sigma' \vdash e' : \tau$.

Proof. By induction on the derivation of $\mathcal{S} \vdash_{|\Gamma|} \langle e, \sigma \rangle \longrightarrow \langle e', \sigma' \rangle$. Lemmas 9.7 (Substitution), 9.9 (Demotion), and 9.10 (Promotion) are used in the cases where the redex is $(\lambda x.e_1) e_2$, $\mathsf{run}(\uparrow e)$, and $\mathsf{lift}(e)$, respectively.

Lemma 9.12 (Well-typed terms are not stuck). *If* $\emptyset, \Gamma; \Sigma \vdash e : \tau$ *then either*

1. $\mathcal{V} \vdash_{|G|} e$, *or*

2. for any $\sigma : \Sigma$ *there exists* e' *and* σ' *such that* $\mathcal{S} \vdash_{|\Gamma|} \langle e, \sigma \rangle \longrightarrow \langle e', \sigma \rangle$.

Proof. By induction on the derivation of $\emptyset, \Gamma; \Sigma \vdash e : \tau$. A simple type inversion result stating that abstractions are the only values of type $\tau_1 \to \tau_2$, that reference cells are the only values of type $\tau\,\mathsf{ref}$, and that quoted terms are the only values of type $[\gamma]\tau$ is used in the three cases corresponding to the reduction rules 12, 16, and 18 in Figure 9.3.

Definition 9.13 (Evaluation). *We define an iterated reduction relation inductively as follows.*

$$\frac{\text{There are no } e', \sigma' \text{ such that } \mathcal{S} \vdash_0 \langle e, \sigma \rangle \longrightarrow \langle e', \sigma' \rangle}{\langle e, \sigma \rangle \longrightarrow^* \langle e, \sigma \rangle}$$

$$\frac{\mathcal{S} \vdash_0 \langle e, \sigma \rangle \longrightarrow \langle e'', \sigma'' \rangle \qquad \langle e'', \sigma'' \rangle \longrightarrow^* \langle e', \sigma' \rangle}{\langle e, \sigma \rangle \longrightarrow^* \langle e', \sigma' \rangle}$$

We define a partial function EXPR $\to$ EXPR *as follows.*

$$\mathrm{eval}(e) = \begin{cases} e', & \text{if } \langle e, \emptyset \rangle \longrightarrow^* \langle e', \sigma' \rangle \text{ and } \mathcal{V} \vdash_0 e' \\ \text{undefined}, & \text{otherwise} \end{cases}$$

The following main result states that a well-typed term either diverges or yields a value of the same type.

Theorem 9.14 (Strong type safety). *If* $\emptyset; \emptyset \vdash e : t$ *and* $\mathrm{eval}(e) = e'$ *then* $\mathcal{V} \vdash_0 e'$ *and there exists a location typing* Σ *such that* $\emptyset; \Sigma \vdash e' : t$.

9.4 EXAMPLES

Generating extensions can be implemented in $\lambda^{[]}$ using the staging primitives $\uparrow$ and $\downarrow$. The specialized programs output by generating extensions can be evaluated using run to produce first-class functions. As an example, consider the following implementation of the linear integer exponentiation function.[2] (The logarithmic exponentiation function is subject to the same considerations [14] but is left out for pedagogical purposes.)

$$\mathbf{fun}\ \exp(n,x)\ =\ \mathbf{if}\ n = 0\ \mathbf{then}\ 1\ \mathbf{else}\ x \times (\exp(n-1,x))$$

A generating extension of this function is a program that, given an integer n, yields (the text of) a program that computes x^n. A standard binding-time analysis of the exponentiation function with respect to n being static and x dynamic reveals that the integer constant 1 and the multiplication are dynamic. The rest of the program is static. These annotations give rise to following the staged exponentiation function.

$$\mathbf{fun}\ \exp_{\mathrm{bta}}(n,x)\ =\ \mathbf{if}\ n = 0\ \mathbf{then}\ \uparrow 1\ \mathbf{else}\ \uparrow(\downarrow x \times \downarrow(\exp_{\mathrm{bta}}(n-1,x)))$$

This function has principal type $\mathrm{int} \times [\gamma]\mathrm{int} \to [\gamma]\mathrm{int}$. It will be used at type $\mathrm{int} \times [z:\mathrm{int}]\mathrm{int} \to [z:\mathrm{int}]\mathrm{int}$ below. The generating extension is defined as the following two-level eta-expansion of the staged exponentiation function.

$$\mathbf{fun}\ \exp_{\mathrm{gen}}(n)\ =\ \uparrow(\lambda z.\ \downarrow(\exp_{\mathrm{bta}}(n,\uparrow z)))$$

The generating extension $\exp_{\mathrm{gen}}$ has type $\mathrm{int} \to [](\mathrm{int} \to \mathrm{int})$. This type shows that $\exp_{\mathrm{gen}}$ produces closed code fragments. For example, $\exp_{\mathrm{gen}}(3)$ has type $[](\mathrm{int} \to \mathrm{int})$ and evaluates to the program fragment $\lambda z.z \times z \times z \times 1$. This code fragment can be executed using the operator run. Hence, $\mathrm{run}(\exp_{\mathrm{gen}}(3))$ has type $\mathrm{int} \to \mathrm{int}$ and yields a first-class cube operation.

The example above is a standard application of multi-stage languages but it demonstrates an important practical property of multi-stage programs: By erasing the staging primitives one obtains the original unstaged program. In order to apply this principle to programs using mutable cells, the multi-stage program must be able to store open code fragments in mutable cells. Consider the following imperative exponentiation function of type $\mathrm{int} \times \mathrm{int} \to \mathrm{int}$.

$$
\begin{aligned}
&\mathbf{fun}\ \mathrm{impexp}(n,x)\ =\\
&\quad \mathbf{let\ val}\ m = \mathbf{ref}\ n\\
&\qquad\ \ \mathbf{val}\ r\ = \mathbf{ref}\ 1\\
&\quad \mathbf{in\ while}\ !m > 0\ \mathbf{do}\ (r := x \times !r;\, m := !m - 1);\\
&\qquad\ \ !r\\
&\quad \mathbf{end}
\end{aligned}
$$

A multi-stage version of this functions looks as follows.

---

[2]In the rest of this paper, we use an ML-like notation. We also assume the existence of recursion, conditionals, monomorphic let-expressions, tuples, etc. These extensions are straightforward to add to $\lambda^{[]}$.

```
fun impexp_bta(n, x) =
    let val m = ref n
        val r = ref ↑1
    in while !m > 0 do (r := ↑(↓x× ↓!r); m := !m−1);
       !r
    end
```

This multi-stage function has principal type $\text{int} \times [\gamma]\text{int} \to [\gamma]\text{int}$. It is, as in the functional case above, used at type $\text{int} \times [z : \text{int}]\text{int} \to [z : \text{int}]\text{int}$ below. The generating extension is defined as above, using a two-level eta-expansion of the binding-time annotated function.

$$\textbf{fun } \text{impexp}_{\text{gen}}(n) = \uparrow(\lambda z. \downarrow(\text{impexp}_{\text{bta}}(n, \uparrow z)))$$

In the function $\text{impexp}_{\text{bta}}$, the variable r has type $([z : \text{int}]\text{int})\,\text{ref}$. During specialization, this cell contains the sequence of dynamic terms 1, $z \times 1$, $z \times z \times 1$, $z \times z \times z \times 1$, etc.

The two examples above motivate the introduction of a general two-level eta expansion

$$\textbf{fun } \text{eta}(f) = \uparrow(\lambda z. \downarrow(f \uparrow z))$$

of principal type $([z : \alpha, \gamma']\alpha \to [z : \beta, \gamma]\delta) \to [\gamma](\beta \to \delta)$. The expression

$$\text{eta}(\lambda x.\text{exp}_{\text{bta}}(3, x))$$

of type $[\,](\text{int} \to \text{int})$ yields the (text of the) cube function. Note that eta can also be used "non-hygienically:" Given $f = \lambda c. \uparrow(\lambda z. \downarrow c)$ of principal type $[z : \alpha, \gamma']\beta \to [\gamma'](\alpha \to \beta)$, $\text{eta}(f)$ evaluates to a representation of the code fragment $\lambda z.\lambda z.z$ in which the inner lambda (supplied by f) shadows the outer lambda (supplied by eta). It is (correctly) assigned the principal type $[\gamma'](\alpha \to \beta \to \beta)$.

9.5 RELATED WORK

Pfenning and Elliott have used higher-order abstract syntax as a representation of programs (and other entities) with bound variables [32]. Higher-order abstract syntax also enables an embedded lightweight type system for programs that generate code fragments [33].

The observation that a naive hygienic multi-stage programming language becomes unsound in the presence of a first-class eval operation is due to Rowan Davies, in the context of MetaML. Safe type systems have been designed that combine types for open code and types for closed code and that contain an eval-like operation [6, 29]. We have avoided the complexities of these languages by taking non-hygiene as a primary design principle of $\lambda^{[]}$.

Chen and Xi take a first-order unstaged abstract syntax as the starting point for defining the multi-stage type-safe calculus $\lambda^{+}_{\text{code}}$ [10]. Like $\lambda^{[]}$, $\lambda^{+}_{\text{code}}$ contains a type of code parameterized by a type environment. $\lambda^{+}_{\text{code}}$ is defined by a translation into λ_{code}, a nameless unstaged extension of the second-order polymorphic λ-calculus. In contrast, $\lambda^{[]}$ is a direct extension of the simply-typed

λ-calculus, it does not require polymorphism, and it does not assume de Bruijn-indexed terms. More seriously, dynamic λ^+_{code}-terms must be closed. For example, the term $\text{let } c = \uparrow (x,y) \text{ in } (\lambda x.\lambda y. \downarrow c, \lambda y.\lambda x. \downarrow c)$ is ill-typed in λ^+_{code} (because the dynamic sub-term $\uparrow (x,y)$ contains free identifiers) but has type

$$[\gamma](\tau_1 \rightarrow \tau_2 \rightarrow \tau_1 \times \tau_2) \times [\gamma](\tau_2 \rightarrow \tau_1 \rightarrow \tau_1 \times \tau_2)$$

in $\lambda^{[]}$.

DynJava, an extension of Java with dynamic compilation, is another type-safe multi-stage language that builds on the principles of non-hygiene [31]. DynJava has only two stages and its code type eliminator (@, which corresponds to $\downarrow$ of $\lambda^{[]}$) only applies to variables. Furthermore, DynJava is an extension of an imperative, explicitly typed language whereas $\lambda^{[]}$ is an extension of an implicitly typed, higher-order language.

Recently, Kim, Yi, and Calcagno have presented a multi-stage calculus which extends $\lambda^{[]}$ with polymorphism and with additional support for type-safe generation of fresh dynamic identifiers during substitution [24]. Therefore, their calculus supports both hygienic and non-hygienic manipulation of code fragments. They prove the type system sound with respect to a big-step operational semantics. They also prove that type-inference is decidable.

9.6 CONCLUSIONS

Well-designed languages balance concise specifications against expressive features and safe execution. We have demonstrated that by liberating a multi-stage language from the demand of *hygiene*, it can be given a type system that safely handles mutable cells (and other effects) and a first-class run operation while requiring only a minimum of extra type constructors and type rules. We have thus provided a first step towards a practical higher-order multi-stage programming language whose type system supports the implementation of run-time specialization and execution and other partial evaluation techniques. The extensions proposed by Kim, Yi, and Calcagno [24] take our work one step further and answers to our vision that useful multi-stage languages may grow out of the study of the interplay between hygiene and non-hygiene.

9.7 ACKNOWLEDGMENTS

The work presented in this article was inspired by a series of discussions the author had with Peter Sestoft at the IT-University of Copenhagen during the fall of 2002.

REFERENCES

[1] J. W. Backus, R. J. Beeber, S. Best, R. Goldberg, L. M. Haibt, H. L. Herrick, R. A. Nelson, D. Sayre, P. B. Sheridan, H. Stern, I. Ziller, R. A. Hughes, and R. Nutt.

The Fortran automatic coding system. In *Proceedings of the Western Joint Computer Conference*, pages 188–198, 1957.

[2] Jørgen P. Bansler and Erling C. Havn. Information system development with generic systems. In Walter R. J. Baets, editor, *Proceedings of the Second Conference on Information Systems*, pages 707–715, Breukelen, The Netherlands, May 1994. Nijenrode University Press.

[3] Henk P. Barendregt, Richard Kennaway, Jan Willem Klop, and M. Ronan Sleep. Needed reduction and spine strategies for the lambda calculus. *Journal of Functional Programming*, 75(3):191–231, 1987.

[4] Alan Bawden. Quasiquotation in Lisp. In Olivier Danvy, editor, *Proceedings of the ACM SIGPLAN Workshop on Partial Evaluation and Semantics-Based Program Manipulation*, number NS–99–1 in BRICS Note Series, pages 4–12, San Antonio, Texas, January 1999.

[5] Anders Bondorf, Neil D. Jones, Torben Mogensen, and Peter Sestoft. Binding time analysis and the taming of self-application. Diku rapport, University of Copenhagen, Copenhagen, Denmark, 1988.

[6] Cristiano Calcagno, Eugenio Moggi, and Walid Taha. Closed types as a simple approach to safe imperative multi-stage programming. In Ugo Montanari, José D. P. Rolim, and Emo Welzl, editors, *Proceedings of the 27th International Colloquium on Automata, Languages and Programming*, number 1853 in Lecture Notes in Computer Science, pages 25–36, Geneva, Switzerland, July 2000. Springer-Verlag.

[7] Cristiano Calcagno, Eugenio Moggi, and Walid Taha. ML-like inference for classifiers. In David A. Schmidt, editor, *Proceedings of the Thirteenth European Symposium on Programming*, number 2986 in Lecture Notes in Computer Science, pages 79–93, Barcelona, Spain, March 2004. Springer-Verlag.

[8] Cristiano Calcagno, Walid Taha, Liwen Huang, and Xavier Leroy. A bytecode-compiled, type-safe, multi-stage language. Technical report, Rice University, 2002.

[9] Cristiano Calcagno, Walid Taha, Liwen Huang, and Xavier Leroy. Implementing multi-stage languages using ASTs, gensym, and reflection. In Frank Pfenning and Yannis Smaragdakis, editors, *Proceedings of the Second International Conference on Generative Programming and Component Engineering*, number 2830 in Lecture Notes in Computer Science, pages 57–76, Erfurt, Germany, September 2003.

[10] Chiyan Chen and Hongwei Xi. Meta-programming through typeful code representation. *Journal of Functional Programming*, 15(6):797–835, 2005.

[11] Charles Consel and Olivier Danvy. Tutorial notes on partial evaluation. In Susan L. Graham, editor, *Proceedings of the Twentieth Annual ACM Symposium on Principles of Programming Languages*, pages 493–501, Charleston, South Carolina, January 1993. ACM Press.

[12] Olivier Danvy. Type-directed partial evaluation. In Steele [34], pages 242–257.

[13] Olivier Danvy. Type-directed partial evaluation. In John Hatcliff, Torben Æ. Mogensen, and Peter Thiemann, editors, *Partial Evaluation – Practice and Theory; Proceedings of the 1998 DIKU Summer School*, number 1706 in Lecture Notes in Computer Science, pages 367–411, Copenhagen, Denmark, July 1998. Springer-Verlag.

[14] Olivier Danvy. Programming techniques for partial evaluation. In Friedrich L. Bauer and Ralf Steinbrüggen, editors, *Foundations of Secure Computation*, NATO Science series, pages 287–318. IOS Press Ohmsha, 2000.

[15] Rowan Davies. A temporal-logic approach to binding-time analysis. In Edmund M. Clarke, editor, *Proceedings of the Eleventh Annual IEEE Symposium on Logic in Computer Science*, pages 184–195, New Brunswick, New Jersey, July 1996. IEEE Computer Society Press.

[16] Rowan Davies and Frank Pfenning. A modal analysis of staged computation. *Journal of the ACM*, 48(3):555–604, 2001.

[17] Andrei P. Ershov. On the essence of compilation. In E. J. Neuhold, editor, *Formal Description of Programming Concepts*, pages 391–420. North-Holland, 1978.

[18] Carsten K. Gomard and Neil D. Jones. A partial evaluator for the untyped lambda-calculus. *Journal of Functional Programming*, 1(1):21–69, 1991.

[19] Robert Harper. A simplified account of polymorphic references. *Information Processing Letters*, 51(4):201–206, August 1994.

[20] J. Roger Hindley. *Basic Simple Type Theory*, volume 42 of *Cambridge Tracts in Theoretical Computer Science*. Cambridge University Press, 1997.

[21] Trevor Jim. What are principal typings and what are they good for? In Steele [34], pages 42–53.

[22] Neil D. Jones, Carsten K. Gomard, and Peter Sestoft. *Partial Evaluation and Automatic Program Generation*. Prentice Hall International Series in Computer Science. Prentice-Hall, 1993. Available online at http://www.dina.kvl.dk/~sestoft/pebook/pebook.html.

[23] Richard Kelsey, William Clinger, and Jonathan Rees, editors. Revised[5] report on the algorithmic language Scheme. *Higher-Order and Symbolic Computation*, 11(1):7–105, 1998. Also appears in ACM SIGPLAN Notices 33(9), September 1998.

[24] Ik-Soon Kim, Kwangkeun Yi, and Cristiano Calcagno. A polymorphic modal type system for Lisp-like multi-staged languages. In Simon Peyton Jones, editor, *Proceedings of the Thirty-Third Annual ACM Symposium on Principles of Programming Languages*, pages 257–268, Charleston, South Carolina, January 2006. ACM Press.

[25] Eugene E. Kohlbecker. *Syntactic Extensions in the Programming Language Lisp*. PhD thesis, Indiana University, Bloomington, Indiana, 1986.

[26] Eugene E. Kohlbecker, Daniel P. Friedman, Matthias Felleisen, and Bruce Duba. Hygienic macro expansion. In William L. Scherlis and John H. Williams, editors, *Proceedings of the 1986 ACM Conference on Lisp and Functional Programming*, pages 151–161, Cambridge, Massachusetts, August 1986. ACM Press.

[27] The MetaOCaml homepage. http://www.metaocaml.org.

[28] Robin Milner, Mads Tofte, Robert Harper, and David MacQueen. *The Definition of Standard ML (Revised)*. The MIT Press, 1997.

[29] Eugenio Moggi, Walid Taha, Zine-El-Abidine Benaissa, and Tim Sheard. An idealized MetaML: Simpler, and more expressive. In S. Doaitse Swierstra, editor, *Proceedings of the Eighth European Symposium on Programming*, number 1576 in Lecture Notes in Computer Science, pages 193–207, Amsterdam, The Netherlands, March 1999. Springer-Verlag.

[30] Flemming Nielson and Hanne Riis Nielson. *Two-Level Functional Languages*, volume 34 of *Cambridge Tracts in Theoretical Computer Science*. Cambridge University Press, 1992.

[31] Yutaka Oiwa, Hidehiko Masuhara, and Akinori Yonezawa. DynJava: Type safe dynamic code generation in Java. In *The 3rd JSSST Workshop on Programming and Programming Languages*, Tokyo, Japan, 2001.

[32] Frank Pfenning and Conal Elliott. Higher-order abstract syntax. In Mayer D. Schwartz, editor, *Proceedings of the ACM SIGPLAN'88 Conference on Programming Languages Design and Implementation*, SIGPLAN Notices, Vol. 23, No 7, pages 199–208, Atlanta, Georgia, June 1988. ACM Press.

[33] Morten Rhiger. A foundation for embedded languages. *ACM Transactions on Programming Languages and Systems*, 25(3):291–315, May 2003.

[34] Guy L. Steele, editor. *Proceedings of the Twenty-Third Annual ACM Symposium on Principles of Programming Languages*, St. Petersburg Beach, Florida, January 1996. ACM Press.

[35] Walid Taha. *Multi-Stage programming: Its Theory and Applications*. PhD thesis, Oregon Graduate Institute of Science and Technology, 1999.

[36] Walid Taha, Zine-El-Abidine Benaissa, and Tim Sheard. Multi-stage programming: Axiomatization and type safety. In Kim G. Larsen, Sven Skyum, and Glynn Winskel, editors, *Proceedings of the 25th International Colloquium on Automata, Languages, and Programming*, number 1443 in Lecture Notes in Computer Science, pages 918–929. Springer-Verlag, 1998.

[37] Walid Taha and Michael Florentin Nielsen. Environment classifiers. In Greg Morrisett, editor, *Proceedings of the Thirtieth Annual ACM Symposium on Principles of Programming Languages*, pages 26–37, New Orleans, Louisiana, January 2003. ACM Press.

[38] Walid Taha and Tim Sheard. Multi-stage programming with explicit annotations. In Charles Consel, editor, *Proceedings of the ACM SIGPLAN Symposium on Partial Evaluation and Semantics-Based Program Manipulation*, pages 203–217, Amsterdam, The Netherlands, June 1997. ACM Press.

[39] Walid Taha and Tim Sheard. MetaML and multi-stage programming with explicit annotations. *Theoretical Computer Science*, 248(1-2):211–242, 2000.

[40] Mads Tofte. Type inference for polymorphic references. *Information and Computation*, 89(1):1–34, November 1990.

[41] Andrew K. Wright. Simple imperative polymorphism. *Lisp and Symbolic Computation*, 8(4):343–355, December 1995.

Chapter 10

Comonadic functional attribute evaluation

Tarmo Uustalu[1] and Varmo Vene[2]

Abstract: We have previously demonstrated that dataflow computation is comonadic. Here we argue that attribute evaluation has a lot in common with
dataflow computation and admits a similar analysis. We claim that this yields
a new, modular way to organize both attribute evaluation programs written directly in a functional language as well as attribute grammar processors. This is
analogous to the monadic approach to effects. In particular, we advocate it as a
technology of executable specification, not as one of efficient implementation.

10.1 INTRODUCTION

Following on from the seminal works of Moggi [Mog91] and Wadler [Wad92],
monads have become a standard tool in functional programming for structuring
effectful computations that are used both directly in programming and in language
processors. In order to be able to go also beyond what is covered by monads,
Power and Robinson [PR97] invented the concept of Freyd categories. Hughes
[Hug00] proposed the same, unaware of their work, under the name of arrow
types. The showcase application example of Freyd categories/arrow types has
been dataflow computation, which, for us, is an umbrella name for various forms
of computation based on streams or timed versions thereof and characterizes, in
particular, languages like Lucid [AW85], Lustre [HCRP91] and Lucid Synchrone
[CP96].

In two recent papers [UV05a, UV05b], we argued that, as far as dataflow
computation is concerned, a viable alternative to Freyd categories is provided by

---

[1]Inst. of Cybernetics at Tallinn Univ. of Technology, Akadeemia tee 21, EE-12618
Tallinn, Estonia; Email `tarmo@cs.ioc.ee`

[2]Dept. of Computer Science, Univ. of Tartu, J. Liivi 2, EE-50409 Tartu, Estonia; Email
`varmo@cs.ut.ee`

something considerably more basic and standard, namely comonads, the formal dual of monads. In fact, comonads are even better, as they explicate more of the structure present in dataflow computations than the laxer Freyd categories. Comonads in general should be suitable to describe computations that depend on an implicit context. Stream functions as abstractions of transformers of discrete-time signals turn out to be a perfect example of such computations: the value of the result stream in a position of interest (the present of the result signal) may depend not only on the value in the argument stream in the same position (the present of the argument signal), but also on other values in it (its past or future or both). We showed that general, causal and anticausal stream functions are described by comonads and that explicit use of the appropriate comonad modularizes both stream-based programs written in a functional language and processors of stream-based languages.

In this paper, we demonstrate that attribute evaluation from attribute grammars admits a similar comonadic analysis. In attribute grammars [Knu68], the value of an attribute at a given node in a syntax tree is defined by the values of other attributes at this and other nodes. Also, an attribute definition only makes sense relative to a suitable node in a tree, but nodes are never referenced explicitly in such definitions: context access happens solely via operations for relative local navigation. This hints that attribute grammars exhibit a form of dependence on an implicit context which is quite similar to that present in dataflow programming. We establish that this form of context-dependence is comonadic and discuss the implications. In particular, we obtain a new, modular way to organize attribute evaluation programs, which is radically different from the approaches that only use the initial-algebraic structure of tree types.

Similarly to the monadic approach to effects, this is primarily to be seen as an executable specification approach. As implementations, our evaluators will normally be grossly inefficient, unless specifically fine-tuned, but as specifications, they are of a very good format: they are concise and, because of their per-attribute organization, smoothly composable (in the dimension of composing several attribute grammars over the same underlying context-free grammar). Systematic transformation of these reference evaluators into efficient implementations ought to be possible, we conjecture, but this is a different line of work. This is highly analogous to the problem of efficient compilation of dataflow programs (not very hard in the case of causal languages, but a real challenge in the case of languages that support anticipation).

We are not aware of earlier comonadic or arrow-based accounts of attribute evaluation. But functional attribute evaluation has been a topic of research for nearly 20 years, following on from the work of Johnsson [Joh87]. Some of this work, concerned with per-attribute compositional specification of attribute grammars, is mentioned in the related work section below.

The paper is organized as follows. In Section 10.2, we overview our comonadic approach to dataflow computation and processing of dataflow languages. In Section 10.3, we demonstrate that the attribute evaluation paradigm can also be analyzed comonadically, studying separately the simpler special case of purely synthesized attributed grammars and the general case. We also provide a discussion of the strengths and problems with the approach. Section 10.4 is a brief review of the related work whereas Section 10.5 summarizes. Most of the development is a carried out in the programming language Haskell, directly demonstrating that the approach is implementable (on the level of executable specifications). The code is Haskell 98 extended with multiparameter classes.

10.2 COMONADS AND DATAFLOW COMPUTATION

We begin by mentioning the basics about comonads to then quickly continue with a dense review of comonadic dataflow computation [UV05a, UV05b].

Comonads are the formal dual of monads, so a *comonad* on a category C is given by a mapping $D : |C| \to |C|$ (by $|C|$ we mean the collection of the objects of C) together with a $|C|$-indexed family ε of maps $\varepsilon_A : DA \to A$ (*counit*), and an operation $-^{\dagger}$ taking every map $k : DA \to B$ in C to a map $k^{\dagger} : DA \to DB$ (*coextension operation*) such that

1. for any $k : DA \to B$, $\varepsilon_B \circ k^{\dagger} = k$,

2. $\varepsilon_A^{\dagger} = \mathrm{id}_{DA}$,

3. for any $k : DA \to B$, $\ell : DB \to C$, $(\ell \circ k^{\dagger})^{\dagger} = \ell^{\dagger} \circ k^{\dagger}$.

Any comonad $(D, \varepsilon, -^{\dagger})$ defines a category C_D where $|C_D| = |C|$ and $C_D(A, B) = C(DA, B)$, $(\mathrm{id}_D)_A = \varepsilon_A$, $\ell \circ_D k = \ell \circ k^{\dagger}$ (*coKleisli category*) and an identity on objects functor $J : C \to C_D$ where $Jf = f \circ \varepsilon_A$ for $f : A \to B$.

CoKleisli categories make comonads relevant for analyzing notions of context-dependent function. If the object DA is viewed as the type of contextually situated values of A, a context-dependent function from A to B is a map $DA \to B$ in the base category, i.e., a map from A to B in the coKleisli category. The counit $\varepsilon_A : DA \to A$ discards the context of its input whereas the coextension $k^{\dagger} : DA \to DB$ of a function $k : DA \to B$ essentially duplicates it (to feed it to k and still have a copy left). The function $Jf : DA \to B$ is a trivially context-dependent version of a pure function $f : A \to B$.

In Haskell, we can define comonads as a type constructor class.

```
class Comonad d where
  counit :: d a -> a
  cobind :: (d a -> b) -> d a -> d b
```

Some examples are the following:

- $DA = A$, the identity comonad,

- $DA = A \times E$, the product comonad,

- $DA = \mathrm{Str}A = \nu X.A \times X$, the streams comonad ($\nu$ denoting the greatest fixed-point operator)

147

The stream comonad Str is defined as follows:

```
data Stream a = a :< Stream a                    -- coinductive

instance Comonad Stream where
  counit (a :< _) = a
  cobind k d@(_ :< as) = k d :< cobind k as
```

(Note that we denote the cons constructor of streams by :<.)

This comonad is the simplest one relevant for dataflow computation. Intuitively, it is the comonad of future. In a value of type $\mathsf{Str}A \cong A \times \mathsf{Str}A$, the first component of type A is the main value of interest while the second component of type $\mathsf{Str}A$ is its context. In our application, the first is the present and the second is the future of an A-signal. The coKleisli arrows $\mathsf{Str}A \to B$ represent those functions $\mathsf{Str}A \to \mathsf{Str}B$ that are anticausal in the sense only the present and future of an input signal can influence the present of the output signal. The interpretation of these representations as stream functions is directly provided by the coextension operation:

```
class SF d where
  run :: (d a -> b) -> Stream a -> Stream b

instance SF Stream where
  run k = cobind k
```

A very important anticausal function is unit anticipation (cf. the 'next' operator of dataflow languages):

```
class Antic d where
  next :: d a -> a

instance Antic Stream where
  next (_ :< (a' :< _)) = a'
```

To be able to represent general stream functions, where the present of the output can depend also on the past of the input, we must employ a different comonad LS. It is defined by $\mathsf{LS}A = \mathsf{List}A \times \mathsf{Str}A$ where $\mathsf{List}A = \mu X.1 + X \times A$ is the type of (snoc-)lists over A (μ denoting the least fixedpoint operator). The idea is that a value of $\mathsf{LS}A \cong \mathsf{List}A \times (A \times \mathsf{Str}A)$ can record the past, present and future of a signal. (Notice that while the future of a signal is a stream, the past is a list: it must be finite.) Note that, alternatively, we could have defined $\mathsf{LS}A = \mathsf{Str}A \times \mathsf{Nat}$ (a value in a context is the entire history of a signal together with a distinguished time instant). This comonad is Haskell-defined as follows. (Although in Haskell there is no difference between inductive and coinductive types, in the world of sets and functions the definition of lists below should be read inductively.)

```
data List a = Nil | List a :> a                  -- inductive
```

```
data LS  a = List a :=| Stream a

instance Comonad LS where
  counit (_ :=| (a :< _)) = a
  cobind k d = cobindL k d :=| cobindS k d
  where cobindL k (Nil      :=| _ ) = Nil
        cobindL k (az :> a :=| as) = cobindL k d' :> k d'
                                where d' = az :=| (a :< as)
        cobindS k d@(az :=| (a :< as)) = k d :< cobindS k d'
                                where d' = az :> a :=| as
```

(We denote the snoc constructor of lists by :> and pairing of a list and a stream by :=|. Now the visual purpose of the notation becomes clear: in values of type LS *A*, both the snoc constructors of the list (the past of a signal) and the cons constructors of the stream (the present and future) point to the present which follows the special marker :=|.)

The interpretation of coKleisli arrows as stream functions and the representation of unit anticipation are defined as follows:

```
instance SF LS where
  run k as = bs where (Nil :=| bs) = cobind k (Nil :=| as)

instance Antic LS where
  next (_ :=| (_ :< (a' :< _))) = a'
```

With the LS comonad it is possible to represent also the important parameterized causal function of initialized unit delay (the 'followed-by' operator):

```
class Delay d where
  fby :: a -> d a -> a

instance Delay LS where
  a0 'fby' (Nil      :=| _) = a0
  _  'fby' (_ :> a' :=| _) = a'
```

Relevantly for "physically" motivated dataflow languages (where computations input or output physical dataflows), it is also possible to characterize causal stream functions as a coKleisli category. The comonad LV is defined by $LV\,A = List\,A \times A$, which is obtained from $LS\,A \cong List\,A \times (A \times Str\,A)$ by removing the factor of future. This comonad is Haskell-implemented as follows.

```
data LV a = List a := a

instance Comonad LV where
  counit (_ := a) = a
  cobind k d@(az := _) = cobindL k az := k d
    where cobindL k Nil        = Nil
          cobindL k (az :> a) = cobindL k az :> k (az := a)
```

```
instance SF LV where
  run k as = run' k (Nil :=| as)
    where run' k (az :=| (a :< as))
                  = k (az := a) :< run' k (az :> a :=| as)

instance Delay LV where
  a0 `fby` (Nil        := _) = a0
  _   `fby` ((_ :> a') := _) = a'
```

Various stream functions are beautifully defined in terms of comonad operations and the additional operations of anticipation and delay. Some simple examples are the Fibonacci sequence, summation and averaging over the immediate past, present and immediate future:

```
fib :: (Comonad d, Delay d) => d () -> Integer
fib d = 0 `fby`
              cobind (\ e -> fib e + (1 `fby` cobind fib e)) d

sum :: (Comonad d, Delay d) => d Integer -> Integer
sum d = (0 `fby` cobind sum d) + counit d

avg :: (Comonad d, Antic d, Delay d) => d Integer -> Integer
avg d = ((0 `fby` d) + counit d + next d) `div` 3
```

In a dataflow language, we would write these definitions like this.

$$
\begin{aligned}
\textit{fib} &= 0 \text{ fby } (\textit{fib} + (1 \text{ fby } \textit{fib})) \\
\textit{sum } x &= (0 \text{ fby } \textit{sum } x) + x \\
\textit{avg } x &= ((0 \text{ fby } x) + x + \text{next } x)/3
\end{aligned}
$$

In [UV05b], we also discussed comonadic processors of dataflow languages, in particular the meaning of higher-order dataflow computation (the interpretation of lambda-abstraction); for space reasons, we cannot review this material here.

10.3   COMONADIC ATTRIBUTE EVALUATION

We are now ready to describe our comonadic approach to attribute evaluation. Attribute evaluation is similar to stream-based computation in the sense that there is a fixed (skeleton of a) datastructure on which computations are done. We will build on this similarity.

10.3.1   Attribute grammars

An attribute grammar as a specification of an annotation (attribution) of a syntax tree [Knu68] is a construction on top of a context-free grammar. To keep the presentation simple and to circumvent the insufficient expressiveness of Haskell's type system (to be discussed in Sec. 10.3.5), we consider here a fixed context-free grammar with a single nonterminal S with two associated production rules

$$S \longrightarrow E$$
$$S \longrightarrow SS$$

where E is a pseudo-nonterminal standing for some set of terminals.

An attribute grammar extends its underlying context-free grammar with attributes and semantic equations. These are attached to the nonterminals and the production rules of the context-free grammar. A semantic equation determines the value of an attribute at a node in a production rule application via the values of other attributes at other nodes involved. We explain this on examples. Let us use superscripts ℓ, b and subscripts L, R as a notational device to tell apart the different occurrences of the nonterminal S in the two production rules as follows:

$$S^\ell \longrightarrow E$$
$$S^b \longrightarrow S^b_L S^b_R$$

Now we can, for example, equip the nonterminal S with two boolean attributes *avl*, *locavl* and a natural-number attribute *height* and govern them by semantic equations

$$
\begin{aligned}
S^\ell.avl &= \text{tt} \\
S^b.avl &= S^b_L.avl \wedge S^b_R.avl \wedge S^b.locavl \\
S^\ell.locavl &= \text{tt} \\
S^b.locavl &= |S^b_L.height - S^b_R.height| \leq 1 \\
S^\ell.height &= 0 \\
S^b.height &= \max(S^b_L.height, S^b_R.height) + 1
\end{aligned}
$$

This gives us an attribute grammar for checking if an S-tree (a syntax tree whose root is an S-node) is AVL.

We can also, for example, equip the nonterminal S with natural-number attributes *numin*, *numout* and subject them to equations

$$
\begin{aligned}
S^b_L.numin &= S^b.numin + 1 \\
S^b_R.numin &= S^b_L.numout + 1 \\
S^\ell.numout &= S^\ell.numin \\
S^b.numout &= S^b_R.numout
\end{aligned}
$$

This is a grammar for pre-order numbering of the nodes of a tree. The attribute *numin* corresponds to the pre-order numbering, the attribute *numout* is auxiliary.

We can see that the value of an attribute at a node can depend on the values of that and other attributes at that node and the children nodes (as in the case of *avl*, *locavl*, *height*, *numout*) or on the values of that and other attributes at that

151

node, the parent node and sibling nodes (*numin*). Attributes of the first kind are called synthesized. Attributes of the second kind are called inherited. Attribute grammars are classified into purely synthesized attribute grammars and general attribute grammars (where there are also inherited attributes).

The problem of attribute evaluation is to compute the full attribution of a given grammatical tree (given the values of the inherited attributes at the root), but one may of course really care about selected attributes of selected nodes. E.g., in the case of AVLness, we are mostly interested in the value of *avl* at the root, while, in the case of pre-order numbering, our concern is the attribute *numin*.

The type of attributed grammatical *S*-trees is

$$\mathsf{Tree}\,E\,A \;=\; \mu X. A \times (E + X \times X)$$
$$\cong\; A \times (E + \mathsf{Tree}\,E\,A \times \mathsf{Tree}\,E\,A)$$

where A is the type of *S*-attributes of interest (aggregated into records). In Haskell, we can define:

```
data Tree e a = a :< Trunk e (Tree e a)

data Trunk e x = Leaf e | Bin x x
```

(Now :< is a constructor for making an attributed tree.)

An attribute evaluator in the conventional sense is a tree transformer of type $\mathsf{Tree}\,E\,1 \to \mathsf{Tree}\,E\,A$ where A is the type of records of all *S*-attributes of the grammar.

10.3.2   Comonadic purely synthesized attributed grammars

In the case of a purely synthesized attribute grammar, the local value of the defined attribute of an equation can only depend on the local and children-node values of the defining attributes. This is similar to anticausal stream-computation. The relevant comonad is the comonad structure on $\mathsf{Tree}\,E$. The idea that the second component of a value in $\mathsf{Tree}\,E\,A \cong A \times (E + \mathsf{Tree}\,E\,A \times \mathsf{Tree}\,E\,A)$ (the terminal at a leaf or the subtrees rooted by the children of a binary node) is obviously the natural datastructure to record the course of an attribute below a current node and in a purely synthesized grammar the local value of an attribute can only depend on the values of that and other attributes at the given node and below. The comonad structure is Haskell-defined as follows, completely analogously to the comonad structure on Str.

```
instance Comonad (Tree e) where
  counit (a :< _ ) = a
  cobind k d@(_ :< as) = k d :< case as of
            Leaf e       -> Leaf e
            Bin asL asR -> Bin (cobind k asL) (cobind k asR)
```

The coKleisli arrows of the comonad are interpreted as tree functions by the coextension operation as in the case of Str. Looking up the attribute values at the children of a node (which is needed to define the local values of synthesized attributes) can be done via an operation similar to 'next'.

```
class TF e d where
  run :: (d e a -> b) -> Tree e a -> Tree e b

instance TF e Tree where
  run = cobind

class Synth e d where
  children :: d e a -> Trunk e a

instance Synth e Tree where
  children (_ :< as) = case as of
                        Leaf e                    -> Leaf e
                        Bin (aL :< _) (aR :< _) -> Bin aL aR
```

10.3.3 Comonadic general attributed grammars

To be able to define attribute evaluation for grammars that also have inherited attributes (so the local value of an attribute can be defined through the values of other attributes at the parent or sibling nodes), one needs a notion of context that can store also store the upper-and-surrounding course of an attribute. This is provided by Huet's generic zipper datastructure [Hue97], instantiated for our tree type constructor. The course of an attribute above and around a given node lives in the type

$$
\begin{aligned}
\mathsf{Path}\,E\,A \;\; &= \;\; \mu X.\,1 + X \times (A \times \mathsf{Tree}\,E\,A + A \times \mathsf{Tree}\,E\,A) \\
&\cong \;\; 1 + \mathsf{Path}\,E\,A \times (A \times \mathsf{Tree}\,E\,A + A \times \mathsf{Tree}\,E\,A)
\end{aligned}
$$

of *path structures*, which are snoc-lists collecting the values of the attribute at the nodes on the path up to the root and in the side subtrees rooted by these nodes. A *zipper* consists of a tree and a path structure, which are the subtree rooted by a node and the path structure up to the root of the global tree, and records both the local value and lower and upper-and-surrounding courses of an attribute: we define

$$
\begin{aligned}
\mathsf{Zipper}\,E\,A \;\; &= \;\; \mathsf{Path}\,E\,A \times \mathsf{Tree}\,E\,A \\
&\cong \;\; \mathsf{Path}\,E\,A \times (A \times (E + \mathsf{Tree}\,E\,A \times \mathsf{Tree}\,E\,A))
\end{aligned}
$$

(Notice that $\mathsf{Zipper}\,E$ is analogous to the type constructor LS, which is the zipper datatype for streams.) In Haskell, we can define:

```
data Path e a = Nil | Path e a :> Turn a (Tree e a)
type Turn x y = Either (x, y) (x, y)

data Zipper e a = Path e a :=| Tree e a
```

(:> is a snoc-like constructor for path structures. := | is the pairing of a path structure and a tree into a zipper.)

The zipper datatype supports movements both up and sideways as well as down in a tree (*redoing* and *undoing* the zipper). The following upward focus shift operation in Haskell returns the zippers corresponding to the parent and the right or left sibling of the local node (unless the local node is the root of the global tree). (So we have put the parent and sibling functions into one partial function, as both are defined exactly when the local node is not the global root. This will be convenient for us.)

```
goParSibl :: Zipper e a
                -> Maybe (Turn (Zipper e a) (Zipper e a))

goParSibl (Nil :=| as) = Nothing
goParSibl (az :> Left  (a, asR) :=| as)
        = Just (Left  (az :=| (a :< Bin as asR),
                      (az :> Right (a, as) :=| asR)))
goParSibl (az :> Right (a, asL) :=| as)
        = Just (Right (az :=| (a :< Bin asL as),
                      (az :> Left  (a, as) :=| asL)))
```

The downward focus shift operation returns the terminal, if the local node is a leaf, and the zippers corresponding to the children, if the local node is binary. (We use a Trunk structure to represent this information.)

```
goChildren :: Zipper e a -> Trunk e (Zipper e a)

goChildren (az :=| (a :< Leaf e)) = Leaf e
goChildren (az :=| (a :< Bin asL asR))
          = Bin (az :> Left  (a, asR) :=| asL)
                (az :> Right (a, asL) :=| asR)
```

This does not seem to have been mentioned in the literature, but the type constructor Zipper E is a comonad (just as LS is; in fact, the same is true of all zipper type constructors). Notably, the central operation of coextension is beautifully definable in terms of the operations goParSibl and goChildren. This is only natural, since a function taking a tree with a focus to a local value is lifted to a tree-valued function by applying it to all possible refocussings of an input tree, and that is best organized with the help of suitable operations of shifting the focus.

```
instance Comonad (Zipper e) where
  counit (_ :=| (a :< _))  = a
  cobind k d = cobindP k d :=| cobindT k d
      where cobindP k d = case goParSibl d of
              Nothing -> Nil
              Just (Left  (d', dR)) ->
                cobindP k d' :> Left  (k d', cobindT k dR)
              Just (Right (d', dL)) ->
                cobindP k d' :> Right (k d', cobindT k dL)
```

154

```
cobindT k d = k d :< case goChildren d of
  Leaf e -> Leaf e
  Bin dL dR -> Bin (cobindT k dL) (cobindT k dR)
```

Of course, $Zipper\,E$ is the comonad that structures general attribute evaluation, similarly to LS in the case of general stream-based computation.

The interpretation of coKleisli arrows as tree functions and the operation for obtaining the values of an attribute at the children are implemented essentially as for $Tree\,E$.

```
instance TF e Zipper where
  run k as = bs where Nil :=| bs = cobind k (Nil :=| as)

instance Synth e Zipper where
  children (_ :=| (_ :< as)) = case as of
                    Leaf e                 -> Leaf e
                    Bin (aL :< _) (aR :< _) -> Bin aL aR
```

For the children operation, we might even choose to reuse the implementation we already had for $Tree\,E$:

```
instance Synth e Zipper where
  children (_ :=| d) = children d
```

But differently from $Tree\,E$, the comonad $Zipper\,E$ makes it possible to also query the parent and the sibling of the current node (or to see that it is the root).

```
class Inh e d where
  parSibl :: d e a -> Maybe (Turn a a)

instance Inh e Zipper where
  parSibl (Nil      :=| _) = Nothing
  parSibl (_ :> Left  (a, aR :< _) :=| _) =
                                Just (Left  (a, aR))
  parSibl (_ :> Right (a, aL :< _) :=| _) =
                                Just (Right (a, aL))
```

Notice that the locality aspect of general attribute grammars (attribute values at a node are defined in terms of values of this and other attributes at neighboring nodes) is nicely supported by the local navigation operations of the zipper datatype. What is missing in the navigation operations is support for uniformity (the value of an attribute is defined in the same way everywhere in a tree). But this is provided by the coextension operation of the comonad structure on the zipper datatype. Hence, it is exactly the presence of the comonad structure that makes the zipper datatype so fit for explaining attribute evaluation.

10.3.4 Examples

We can now implement the two example attribute grammars. This amounts to rewriting the semantic equations as definitions of coKleisli arrows from the unit type.

The first grammar rewrites to the following three (mutually recursive) definitions parameterized over a comonad capable of handling purely synthesized attribute grammars (so they can be instantiated for both $Tree\,E$ and $Zipper\,E$).

```
avl :: (Comonad (d e), Synth e d) => d e () -> Bool
avl d = case children d of
           Leaf _   -> True
           Bin _ _  -> bL && bR && locavl d
             where Bin bL bR = children (cobind avl d)

locavl :: (Comonad (d e), Synth e d) => d e () -> Bool
locavl d = case children d of
           Leaf _   -> True
           Bin _ _  -> abs (hL - hR) <= 1
             where Bin hL hR = children (cobind height d)

height :: (Comonad (d e), Synth e d) => d e () -> Integer
height d = case children d of
           Leaf _   -> 0
           Bin _ _  -> max hL hR + 1
             where Bin hL hR = children (cobind height d)
```

The second grammar is rewritten completely analogously, but the definitions require a comonad that can handle also inherited attributes (so that, of our two comonads, only $Zipper\,E$ qualifies). Notice that the definition of the root value of the inherited attribute *numin* becomes part of the grammar description here.

```
numin  :: (Comonad (d e), Synth e d, Inh e d)
                                  => d e () -> Int
numin  d = case parSibl d of
     Nothing -> 0
     Just (Left  _) -> ni  + 1
       where Just (Left  (ni, _ )) = parSibl (cobind numin  d)
     Just (Right _) -> noL + 1
       where Just (Right (_, noL)) = parSibl (cobind numout d)

numout :: (Comonad (d e), Synth e d, Inh e d)
                                  => d e () -> Int
numout d = case children d of
     Leaf e  -> numin d
     Bin _ _ -> noR
       where Bin _ noR = children (cobind numout d)
```

We can conduct some tests, which give the desired results:

```
> let t = () :< Bin
              (() :< Bin
                    (() :< Leaf 100)
                    (() :< Bin
                          (() :< Leaf 101)
```

156

```
                                    (()  :< Leaf 102)))
                    (()  :< Leaf 103)

> run (\ (d :: Tree Int ()) -> (avl d, height d)) t
(False,3) :< Bin
        ((True,2) :< Bin
                ((True,0) :< Leaf 100)
                ((True,1) :< Bin
                        ((True,0) :< Leaf 101)
                        ((True,0) :< Leaf 102)))
        ((True,0) :< Leaf 103)

> run (\ (d :: Zipper Int ()) -> (numin d, numout d)) t
(0,6) :< Bin
        ((1,5) :< Bin
                ((2,2) :< Leaf 100)
                ((3,5) :< Bin
                        ((4,4) :< Leaf 101)
                        ((5,5) :< Leaf 102)))
        ((6,6) :< Leaf 103)
```

We observe that the definitions of the coKleisli arrows match the semantic equations most directly. That is, a simple attribute evaluator is obtained just by putting together a tiny comonadic core and a straightforward rewrite of the semantic equations. It is obvious that the rewriting is systematic and hence one could easily write a generic comonadic attribute evaluator for attribute grammars on our fixed context-free grammar. We refrain from doing this here.

10.3.5 Discussion

We now proceed to a short discussion of our proposal.

1. Our approach to attribute evaluation is very denotational by its spirit and our code works thanks to Haskell's laziness. There is no need for static planning of the computations based on some analysis of the grammar, attribute values are computed on demand. In particular, there is no need for static circularity checking, the price being, of course, that the evaluator will loop when a computation is circular.

But this denotational-semantic simplicity has severe consequences on efficiency. Unless some specific infrastructure is introduced to cache already computed function applications, we get evaluators that evaluate the same attribute occurrence over and over. It is very obvious from our example of AVL-hood: evaluation of *localv* at some given node in a tree takes evaluation of *height* at all nodes below it. If we need to evaluate *localv* everywhere in the tree, we should evaluate *height* everywhere below the root just once, but our evaluator will compute the height of each node anew each time it needs it. The very same problem is present also in the comonadic approach to dataflow computation. Simple comonadic code illustrates the meaning of dataflow computation very well, but

157

to achieve efficiency, one has to put in more care. Luckily, there are methods for doing so, ranging from memoization infrastructures to total reorganization of the evaluator based on tupling and functionalization transformations. We refrain from discussing these methods in the present paper.

2. Instead of relying on general recursion available in Haskell, we could forbid circularity on the syntactic level (essentially saying that an attribute value at a node cannot be defined via itself). This is standard practice in attribute grammar processors, but for us it means we can confine ourselves to using structured recursion schemes only. For purely synthesized attribute grammars, where attribute evaluation reduces to upward accumulations, we presented a solution based on structured recursion in our SFP '01 paper [UV02]. Obviously here is an analogy to syntactic circularity prevention in dataflow languages, which is also standard practice.

3. In the examples, we used incomplete pattern matches (in the where-clauses). These are guaranteed to never give a run-time error, because the coextension operation and the operations children and parSibl remember if a focal node is leaf or parent, root, left child or right child. But the type system is unaware of this. This aesthetic problem can be remedied with the generalized algebraic datatypes (GADTs) of GHC [PJWW04] (in combination with rank-2 polymorphism). For example, trees and trunks can be classified into leaves and parents at the type level by defining

```
data Tree ty e a = a :<  Trunk ty e (UTree e a)
data UTree e a = forall ty . Pack (Tree ty e a)

data Leaf
data Bin

data Trunk ty e x where
    Leaf :: e -> Trunk Leaf e x
    Bin  :: x -> x -> Trunk Bin e x
```

An analogous refinement is possible for the path structure datatype. Under this typing discipline, our pattern matches are complete.

These finer datatypes do however not solve another aesthetic problem. When trees and trunks have been made leaves or parents at the type level, it feels unnatural to test this at the level of values, as is done in the case-constructs of our code. One would instead like a typecase construct. This situation arises because our types Leaf and Bin should really be values from a doubleton type, but in Haskell value-indexed types have to be faked by type-indexed types. A real solution would be to switch to a dependently typed language and to use inductive families.

4. We finish by remarking that GADTs or inductive families are also needed to deal with multiple nonterminals in a generic attribute grammar processor capable of handling any underlying context-free grammar. For a fixed context-free grammar, mutually recursive Haskell datatypes are enough (one attributed syntax tree datatype for every nonterminal). But in the case where the underlying context-free grammar becomes a parameter, these syntax tree datatypes must be indexed

by the corresponding nonterminals, whereby each datatype in the indexed family has different constructors. In this situation, GADTs become inevitable.

10.4 RELATED WORK

The uses of coKleisli categories of comonads to describe notions of computation have been relatively few. The idea has been put forward several times, e.g., by Brookes and Geva [BG92] and by Kieburtz [Kie99], but never caught on because of a lack of compelling examples. The example of dataflow computation seems to appear first in our papers [UV05a, UV05b].

The Freyd categories / arrow types of Power and Robinson [PR97] and Hughes [Hug00] have been considerably more popular, see, e.g., [Pat03, Hug05] for overviews. The main application is reactive functional programming.

From the denotational point of view, attribute grammars have usually been analyzed proceeding from the initial algebra structure of tree types. The central observation is that an attribute evaluator is ultimately a fold (if the grammar is purely synthesized) or an application of a higher-order fold (if it also has inherited attributes) [CM79, May81]; this definition of attribute evaluation is straightforwardly implemented in a lazy functional language [Joh87, KS86]. Gibbons [Gib93, Gib00] has specifically analyzed upward and downward accumulations on trees.

Finer functional attribute grammar processors depart from the denotational approach; an in-depth analysis of the different approaches to functional attribute grammar evaluation appears in Saraiva's thesis [Sar99]. Some realistic functional attribute grammar processors are Lrc [KS98] and UUAG [BSL03].

One of the salient features of our approach is the per-attribute organization of the evaluators delivered. This is not typical to functional attribute grammar evaluators. But decomposability by attributes has been identified as desirable in the works on "aspect-oriented" attribute grammar processors by de Moor, Peyton-Jones and Van Wyk [dMPJvW99] and de Moor, K. Backhouse and Swierstra [dMBS00]. These are clearly related to our proposal, but the exact relationship is not clear at this stage. We conjecture that use of the comonad abstraction is orthogonal to the techniques used in these papers, so they might even combine.

The zipper representation of trees with a distinguished position is a piece of folklore that was first documented by Huet [Hue97]. Also related are container type constructors that have been studied by McBride and his colleagues [McB00, AAMG05].

The relation between upward accumulations and the comonad structure on trees was described by in our SFP '01 paper [UV02]. In that paper, we also discussed a basic theorem about compositions of recursively specified upward accumulations. We are not aware of any work relating attribute evaluation to comonads or arrow types.

10.5 CONCLUSIONS AND FUTURE WORK

We have shown that attribute evaluation bears a great deal of similarity to dataflow computation in that computation happens on a fixed datastructure and that the result values are defined uniformly throughout the structure with the help of a few local navigation operations to access the contexts of the argument values. As a consequence, our previous results on comonadic dataflow computation and comonadic processing of dataflow languages are naturally transported to attribute evaluation. We are very pleased about how well comonads explicate the fundamental locality and uniformity characteristics of attribute definitions that initial algebras fail to highlight. In the case of the zipper datatype, we have seen that the only thing needed to make it directly useable in attribute evaluation is to derive an explicit coextension operation from the focus shift operations.

In order to properly validate the viability of our approach, we plan to develop a proof-of-concept comonadic processor of attribute grammars capable of interpreting attribute extensions of arbitrary context-free grammars. The goal is to obtain a concise generic reference specification of attribute evaluation. We predict that the limitations of Haskell's type system may force a solution that is not as beautiful than it should ideally be, but GADTs will provide some help.

We also plan to look into systematic ways for transforming the comonadic specifications into efficient implementations (cf. the problem of efficient compilation of dataflow languages). For purely synthesized attribute grammars, a relatively straightforward generic tupling transformation should solve the problem, but the general case will be a challenge.

Acknowledgments   We are very grateful to our anonymous referees for their constructive criticism and suggestions, especially in regards to related work and certain emphases of the paper.

The authors were partially supported by the Estonian Science Foundation under grant No. 5567.

REFERENCES

[AAMG05]   M. Abbott, T. Altenkirch, C. McBride and N. Ghani. δ for data: differentiating data structures. *Fund. Inform.*, 65(1–2):1–28, 2005.

[AW85]   E. A. Ashcroft, W. W. Wadge. *LUCID, The Dataflow Programming Language*. Academic Press, 1985.

[BG92]   S. Brookes, S. Geva. Computational comonads and intensional semantics. In M. P. Fourman, P. T. Johnstone, and A. M. Pitts, eds., *Applications of Categories in Computer Science*, v. 177 of *London Math. Society Lect. Note Series*, 1–44. Cambridge Univ. Press, 1992.

[BSL03]   A. Baars, S. D. Swierstra, A. Löh. UU AG system user manual. 2003.

[CM79]   L. M. Chirica, D. F. Martin. An order-algebraic definition of Knuthian semantics. *Math. Syst. Theory*, 13:1–27, 1979.

[CP96]   P. Caspi, M. Pouzet. Synchronous Kahn networks. In *Proc. of 1st ACM SIG-PLAN Int. Conf. on Functional Programming, ICFP '96*, 226–238. ACM Press, 1996. Also in *SIGPLAN Notices*, 31(6):226–238, 1996.

[dMBS00]   O. de Moor, K. Backhouse, S. D. Swierstra. First-class attribute grammars. *Informatica (Slovenia)*, 24(3):329–341, 2000.

[dMPJvW99] O. de Moor, S. Peyton Jones, E. Van Wyk. Aspect-oriented compilers. In K. Czarnecki, U. W. Eisenecker, eds., *Generative and Component-Based Software Engineering, GCSE '99 (Erfurt, Sept. 1999)*, vol. 1799 of *Lect. Notes in Comput. Sci.*, 121–133. Springer-Verlag, 1999.

[Gib93]   J. Gibbons. Upwards and downwards accumulations on trees. In R. S. Bird, C. C. Morgan, and J. C. P. Woodcock, eds., *Proc. of 2nd Int. Conf. on Math. of Program Construction, MPC '92 (Oxford, June/July 1992)*, vol. 669 of *Lect. Notes in Comput. Sci.*, 122–138. Springer-Verlag, 1993.

[Gib00]   J. Gibbons. Generic downward accumulation. *Sci. of Comput. Program.*, 37(1–3):37–65, 2000.

[HCRP91]   N. Halbwachs, P. Caspi, P. Raymond, D. Pilaud. The synchronous data flow programming language LUSTRE. *Proc. of the IEEE*, 79(9):1305–1320, 1991.

[Hue97]   G. Huet. The zipper. *J. of Funct. Program.*, 7(5):549–554, 1997.

[Hug00]   J. Hughes. Generalising monads to arrows. *Sci. of Comput. Program.*, 37(1–3):67–111, 2000.

[Hug05]   J. Hughes. Programming with arrows. In V. Vene, T. Uustalu, eds., *Revised Lectures from 5th Int. School on Advanced Functional Programming, AFP 2004*, vol. 3622 of *Lect. Notes in Comput. Sci.*, 73–129. Springer-Verlag, 2005.

[Joh87]   T. Johnsson. Attribute grammars as a functional programming paradigm. In G. Kahn, ed., *Proc. of 3rd Int. Conf. on Functional Programming and Computer Architecture, FPCA '87 (Portland, OR, Sept. 1987)*, vol. 274 of *Lect. Notes in Comput. Sci.*, 154–173. Springer-Verlag, 1987.

[Kie99]   R. Kieburtz. Codata and comonads in Haskell. Unpublished draft, 1999.

[Knu68]   D. Knuth. Semantics of context-free languages. *Math. Syst. Theory*, 2(2):127–145, 1968. Corrigendum, ibid., 51(1):95–96, 1971.

[KS86]   M. F. Kuiper, S. D. Swierstra. Using attributed grammars to derive efficient functional programs. Techn. report RUU-CS-86-16, Dept. of Comput. Sci., Univ. f Utrecht, 1986.

[KS98]   M. F. Kuiper, J. Saraiva. Lrc: a generator for incremental language-oriented tools. In K. Koskimies, ed., *Proc. of 7th Int. Conf. on Compiler Construction, CC '98 (Lisbon, March/Apr. 1998)*, vol. 1383 of *Lect. Notes in Comput. Sci.*, pp. 298–301. Springer-Verlag, 1998.

[May81]   B. Mayoh. Attribute grammars and mathematical semantics. *SIAM J. of Comput.*, 10(3):503–518, 1981.

[McB00]   C. McBride. The derivative of a regular type is the type of its one-hole contexts. Manuscript, 2000.

[Mog91]   E. Moggi. Notions of computation and monads. *Inform. and Comput.*, 93(1):55–92, 1991.

[Pat03]   R. Paterson. Arrows and computation. In J. Gibbons, O. de Moor, eds., *The Fun of Programming, Cornerstones of Computing*, 201–222. Palgrave Macmillan, 2003.

[PJWW04]   S. Peyton Jones, G. Washburn, S. Weirich. Wobbly types: practical type inference for generalized algebraic datatypes. Technical report MS-CIS-05-26, Comput. and Inform. Sci. Dept., Univ. of Pennsylvania, 2004.

[PR97]   J. Power, E. Robinson. Premonoidal categories and notions of computation. *Math. Structures in Comput. Sci.*, 7(5):453–468, 1997.

[Sar99]   J. Saraiva. Purely Functional Implementation of Attribute Grammars. PhD thesis, Dept. of Comput. Sci., Utrecht University, 1999.

[UV02]   T. Uustalu, V. Vene. The dual of substitution is redecoration. In K. Hammond, S. Curtis, eds., *Trends in Functional Programming 3*, 99–110. Intellect, 2002.

[UV05a]   T. Uustalu, V. Vene. Signals and comonads. *J. of Univ. Comput. Sci.*, 11(7):1310–1326, 2005.

[UV05b]   T. Uustalu, V. Vene. The essence of dataflow programming. In K. Yi, ed., *Proc. of 3rd Asian Symp. on Programming Languages and Systems, APLAS 2005 (Tsukuba, Nov. 2005)*, vol. 3780 of *Lect. Notes in Comput. Sci.*, 2–18. Springer-Verlag, 2005.

[Wad92]   P. Wadler. The essence of functional programming. In *Conf. Record of 19th Ann. ACM SIGPLAN-SIGACT Symp. on Principles of Programming Languages, POPL '92 (Albuquerque, NM, Jan. 1992)*, 1–12. ACM Press, 1992.

Chapter 11

Generic Generation of the Elements of Data Types

Pieter Koopman[1], Rinus Plasmeijer[1]

Abstract: An automatic test system for logical properties represents universal quantified properties by Boolean functions. Such a function is evaluated for a large number of values: the test suite. Automatic test systems generate a test suite of the desired size, evaluate the predicate for the values in this test suite, and generate a verdict based on the test results.

The automatic test system Gast uses a generic algorithm that generates test suites for arbitrary data types in a systematic way. Such a generic algorithm has as advantages that the generation of values of a new type can be derived automatically, instead of being hand coded. The systematic generation has as advantages that it allows proofs by exhaustive testing, and it is more efficient since test values are not duplicated.

In this paper we present a new generic algorithm for the systematic generation of elements of data types that is much more elegant, efficient and flexible than the existing algorithm. We also show a variant that yields the elements in pseudo-random order. Both algorithms are very efficient and lazy; only the elements actually needed are generated.

11.1 INTRODUCTION

In this paper we describe an elegant generic algorithm that yields a list of all elements of an arbitrary data type. Such an algorithm was needed in our model based test tool Gast [9, 10, 20]. Also in other application areas it is handy or necessary to be able to generate instances of an arbitrary type. For instance, data generation is used in Generic Editor Components [1] to create an instance for the

---

[1] Nijmegen Institute for Computing and Information Sciences,
Radboud University Nijmegen, Toernooiveld 1, Nijmegen, 6525 ED, The Netherlands;
Phone: +031 (0)24-3652643; Email: `pieter@cs.ru.nl`, `rinus@cs.ru.nl`

arguments of a chosen constructor. Such a constructor can be chosen interactively by the user as instance of an algebraic data type.

Automatic test systems like QuickCheck [3] and Gast represent a predicate of the form $\forall x \in T . P(x)$ by a function P :: T $\rightarrow$ Bool. The test systems evaluates this function for a fixed number N of elements of type T: the *test suite*. An automatic test system has to generate the test suite. If the system generates an element t_c of type T such that $P(t_c)$ yields False, the test system has found a counterexample: the property does not hold. When the property holds for all generated test data, the property passes the test. Properties can be proven by exhaustive testing if the list contains every instance of the type and the size of type (i.e. the number of elements in the type)

In this paper we concentrate on the generation of test suites. A popular way to generate test suites is by some pseudo-random algorithm. Experience shows that a well chosen pseudo-random generation and sufficient number of tests most likely covers all interesting cases and hence discovers counterexamples if they exists. Tools like QuickCheck and TorX [17] use pseudo-random generation of test suites. Drawbacks of pseudo-random test data generation are that one does not know when all elements of a finite type have been tested, and that elements might be duplicated in the test suite. This implies that proofs by exhaustive testing will pass unnoticed. Repetition of tests is useless in a referential transparent framework, the test result will always be identical.

In a functional programming context it is appealing to define a type class for the test suites. Based on the type of the predicate, the type system will select the appropriate instance of this class and hence the right test suite. This idea is used by QuickCheck. The test engineer has to provide an instance of this class for every type used in the tests. QuickCheck provides a special purpose test data generation language for defining test suites. Even with this language it is pretty tricky to define good test suites, especially for recursive data types. A proper test suite contains the nonrecursive instances of such a type, as well as finite recursive instances of the type.

Using generic programming techniques we can free the test engineer from the burden of defining a test suite for each type used in the tests. In generic programming manipulations of data types are specified on a general representation of the data types instead of the data types themselves. The generic system takes care of the conversion between the actual types and their generic representation and vice versa. Instead of specifying the manipulations for each and every data type, the manipulations are now specified once and for all on the generic representation of the data type. There are various variants of generic programming for functional programming described. Most implementations of generics in functional programming languages are based on the ideas of Ralf Hinze [6, 7]. There are various implementations in Haskell, like Generic Haskell [5] and the *scrap your boilerplate* approach [12, 13]. In this paper we will use generic programming in Clean [14] as introduced by Alimarine [2].

The automatic test system Gast has always contained a generic algorithm for the systematic generation of test suites [9], but here we present a new algorithm.

This algorithm is much more elegant than the old one, it is much easier for a test engineer to deviate from the default algorithm if that would be desired, and the new algorithm is orders of magnitude faster.

The advantages of systematic test data generation over pseudo-random data generation are: 1) all interesting boundary causes will occur, and will be used as one of the first test cases; 2) systematic generation indicates when all instances of a type are used and hence allows proofs by exhaustive testing; 3) since duplicates are avoided the testing process is more efficient. The advantages of a generic algorithm over a type class are that the generation of the elements of each new type can be derived rather than hand coded by the test engineer.

Data types that have semantic restrictions which cannot be imposed by the type system, like search trees and AVL-trees, cannot be handled by the generic algorithm alone. Since the data generation algorithm uses only the type information, it cannot cope with the additional semantic constraints. The test engineer has to specify how instances of such a type have to be constructed using the interface of the type. The generic algorithm can be used to generate the list of values to be inserted in the instance of the restricted type.

In section 11.2 we will review the basis of automatic testing. Thereafter we shortly review the original systematic data generation of Gast. In section 11.4 we introduce the new basic generic data generation algorithm. It is a widespread believe under testers that pseudo random testing finds counterexamples faster. In section 11.5 we show how the order of generated test data is pertubated in a pseudo-random way. Section 11.6 shows how instances of restricted types, like search trees, can be generated. Finally there are some conclusions. The reader is assumed to be familiar with generic programming in functional languages in general and in Clean in particular.

11.2 INTRODUCTION TO AUTOMATIC TESTING

In this section we will restrict ourselves to universally quantified predicates over a single variable: $\forall x \in T. P(x)$. The predicate will be represented by a boolean function in Clean: P :: T $\rightarrow$ Bool. Some simple examples representing the predicates $\forall c \in$ Char. isAlpha $c = ($isUpper $c \,\|\,$ isLower $c)$ and $\forall x \in$ Int. reverse $[x] = [x]$ are respectively:

```
propChar :: Char → Bool
propChar c = isAlpha c == (isUpper c || isLower c)

propRevUnit :: Int → Bool
propRevUnit x = reverse [x] == [x]
```

In fact this property of the reverse function holds for any type. We indicate a specific type instead of the more general propRevUnit :: x → Bool | Eq x to enable the test system to chose a specific test suite.

The result of testing will be represented by the data type Verdict:

```
:: Verdict = Proof | Pass | Fail
```

The function `testAll` implements the test process:

```
testAll :: Int (t→Bool) [t] → Verdict
testAll n p []    = Proof
testAll 0 p list = Pass
testAll n p [x:r]
    | p x        = testAll (n−1) p r
    | otherwise = Fail
```

The parameter n is the maximum number of tests, p is the predicate to be tested, and the list of values of type t is the test suite. For the purpose of explaining the test system we will define a class `testSuite` that generates the elements of a type in a very simple systematic way.

```
class testSuite a :: [a]
```

```
instance testSuite Bool where testSuite = [False,True]
instance testSuite Int  where testSuite = [0..]
instance testSuite Char where testSuite = map toChar [0..255]
```

Using this we define a function `doTest` that removes the burden of specifying the maximum number of tests and the appropriate test suite.

```
doTest :: (t→Bool) → Verdict | testSuite t
doTest p = testAll 1000 p testSuite
```

The property `propChar` can now be tested by executing:

```
Start = doTest propChar
```

The result of this test is `Proof`. In the same way the property `propRevUnit` can be tested. The result of this test is `Pass`, since there are more than 1000 values for the test value x. This merely indicates that this is a somewhat poorly designed test, it would be better to test this property for characters or Booleans. For such a finite type the test yields `Proof` rather than `Pass`.

With some effort we can also define instances of (polymorphic) recursive types. As example we show the instance for list.

```
instance testSuite [a] | testSuite a
where testSuite = l where l = [[]: [[h:t] \\ (h,t)←diag2 testSuite l]]
```

The function `diag2` from **Clean**'s standard library takes care of a fair choice between a new element for the head and tail of the generated lists. The cycle through l is inserted for efficiency reasons,

```
testSuite = [[]: [[h:t] \\ (h,t) ← diag2 testSuite testSuite]]
```

produces the same test suite. An initial part of the generated list of integers is:

```
[[],[0],[1],[0,0],[2],[1,0],[0,1],[3],[2,0],[1,1],[0,0,0],[4],[3,0],...
```

Using this test suite for lists we can state the property that reversing a list twice yields the original list, $\forall l \in [\text{Bool}]$. reverse (reverse l) = l. In Clean this is:

```
propRevRev :: [Bool] → Bool
propRevRev l = reverse (reverse l) == l
```

This property can be tested by executing `Start = doTest propRevRev`. The result is `Pass`. Since there are infinitely many lists of each type, it is impossible to do exhaustive testing for this property.

Note that this property only holds for finite and total lists. Testing it for infinite lists would cause nontermination. For these reasons all tests and properties in this paper are restricted to finite and total values.

The actual implementation of the test system Gast is somewhat more complicated since it has to cope with all operators of first order logic, predicates over an arbitrary number variables, and has to record information about the test values encountered. Also the number of test to perform can be specified. For instance, Gast mimics the operator $\exists x.P(x)$ by `Exists x. P x` (or `Exists P` using Currying). Gast will search for a single test value that makes property p true within the first 1000 test values, using an equivalent of `testAll` for the `Exists`-operator.

11.3   GENERIC TEST DATA GENERATION IN PREVIOUS WORK

One of the distinguishing features of Gast is that it is able to generate test data in a systematic way. This guarantees that test are never repeated. Repeating identical tests is useless in a referentially transparent language like Clean. For finite data types systematic test data generation enables proofs by exhaustive testing using a test system: a property is proven if it holds for all elements of the finite data type. Gast has used a generic systematic algorithm to generate test data from the very beginning. In this section we will review the original algorithm and the design decisions behind it.

In general it is impossible to test a property for all possible values. The number of values is simply too large (e.g. for the type `Int`), or even infinite (for recursive data types). Boundary value analysis is a well-known technique in testing that tells that not all values are equally interesting for testing. The values where the specification or implementation indicates a bound and the values very close to such a bound are interesting test values. For numbers, values like 0, 1, −1, *minint*, and *maxint* are the most frequently occurring test values. For recursive types the non-recursive constructor (`[]` for lists and `Leaf` for trees) and small instances are the obvious boundary values. Therefore, these values have to be in the beginning of the list of data values generated. Instances of recursive types can be arbitrarily large. Therefore there is no equivalent to the maximum values of integer in recursive types. When specific boundary values for some situations are known, it is easy to include these in the tests, see [10] for details.

The initial algorithm [9] was rather simple, but also very crude and inefficient. The basic approach of the initial data generation algorithm was to use a tree to record the generic representations of the values generated. For each new value to be generated the tree was updated to record the generation of the new value. In order to generate all small values early, the tree was extended in a breadth-first fashion. A somewhat simplified definition of the tree used is:

```
:: Trace = Empty
         | Unit
         | Pair [(Trace,Trace)] [(Trace,Trace)]
         | Either Bool Trace Trace
         | Int [Int]
         | Done
```

The constructor `Empty` is used to indicate parts of the tree that are not yet visited. Initially, the entire tree is not yet visited. The constructor `Unit` indicates that a constructor is generated here.

The two lists of tuples of traces in a `Pair` together implement an efficient queue [15] of new traces to be considered. This queue is used for a standard breath-first traversal of the tree, it contains the combinations of subtrees still to be considered in the generation of values. Elements are taken of the first list and enqueued by adding them to the front of the first list. When the first list is exhausted all elements from the second list are transferred to the first list in reversed order. In this way it is possible to enqueue and dequeue n elements in $O(n)$ steps. A naive implementation of a queue that appends each and every element to the end of a queue, represented as a single list, will use $O(n^2)$ operations.

The `Either` pairs the traces corresponding to the generic constructors LEFT and and RIGHT. The Boolean indicates the direction where the first extension has to be sought. For basic types, like integers, special constructors, like `Int`, are used to record the values generated. When the generation algorithm discovers that some part of the tree cannot be extended it is replaced by `Done`. This prevents fruitless traversals in future extensions of the tree. See [9] for more details.

11.4 GENERIC DATA GENERATION: BASIC APPROACH

The new generic data generation algorithm presented in this paper does not use a tree to record generated values. The use of the tree can be very time consuming. For instance the generation of all tuples of two characters takes nearly 20 minutes. All measurements in this paper are done on a basic 1 GHz AMD PC, running Windows XP, Clean 2.1.1. and Gast 0.51.

The generic function `gen` generates the lazy list of all values of a type by generating all relevant generic representations [2] of the members of that type.

generic gen a :: [a]

For the type UINT there is only one possibility: the constructor UNIT.

gen {|UNIT|} = [UNIT]

For a *PAIR* that combines two kinds of values, a naive definition using a list–comprehension would be [Pair a b \\ a←f, b←g]. However, we do not want the first element of f to be combined with all elements of g before we consider the second element of f, but some fair mixing of the values. This is also known as dovetailing. Suppose that f is the list $[a, b, c, ..]$ and g the list $[u, v, w, ..]$. The desired order of pairs is *PAIR a u, PAIR a v, PAIR b u, PAIR a w, PAIR b v, PAIR c u, ..* rather than *PAIR a u, PAIR a v, PAIR a w, .., PAIR b u, PAIR b v, PAIR b w, ...* The *diagonalizing list comprehensions* from Miranda[tm] [19] and the function `diag2` from the Clean standard library exactly do this job. The function `diag2` has type `[a] [b]` $\rightarrow$ `[(a,b)]`, i.e. it generates a list of tuples with the elements of the argument lists in the desired order. Using a list comprehension the tuples are transformed to pairs.

```
gen {|PAIR|} f g = [ PAIR a b \\ (a,b) ← diag2 f g ]
```

For the choice in the type `EITHER` we use an additional Boolean argument to merge the elements in an interleaved way. The definition of the function `merge` is somewhat tricky in order to avoid that it becomes strict in one of its list arguments. If the function `merge` becomes strict in one of its list arguments it generates all possible values before the current value is produced. This would cause the production of an infinite amount of intermediate data and hence a `Heap full` error.

```
gen {|EITHER|} f g = merge True f g
where
    merge :: !Bool [a] [b] → [EITHER a b]
    merge left as bs
      | left
         = case as of
              [] = map RIGHT bs
              [a:as] = [LEFT a: merge (not left) as bs]
      | otherwise
         = case bs of
              [] = map LEFT as
              [b:bs] = [RIGHT b: merge (not left) as bs]
```

In order to let this merge algorithm terminate for recursive data types we assume that the non recursive case (like `Nil` for lists, `Leaf` for trees) is listed first in the type definition. Using knowledge of the generic representation allows us to make the right initial choice in `gen {|EITHER|}`. In principle the generic representation contains sufficient information to find the terminating constructor dynamically, but this is more expensive and does not add any additional power. Since the order of constructors in a data type does not have any other significance in Clean, the assumption on the order of constructors is not considered to be a serious restriction. If it becomes necessary, this restriction can be removed at the cost of an runtime analysis of the structure of the generic representation of the type.

The actual implementation of generics in Clean uses some additional constructors in order to store additional information about constructors, fields in a record etcetera. The associated instances for the generic function `gen` are:

```
gen {|CONS|}   f = map CONS f
gen {|FIELD|}  f = map FIELD f
```

Finally we have to provide instances of `gen` for the basic types of Clean. Some examples are:

```
gen {|Int|}    = [0: [i \\ n←[1..maxint], i←[n, −n]]]
gen {|Bool|} = [False,True]
gen {|Char|} = map toChar ([32..126] ++ [9,10,13]) // the printable characters
gen {|String|} = map toString lists
```
where
```
    lists :: [[Char]]
    lists = gen {|*|}
```

In Clean a `String` is an array of characters rather than a list of characters as in Haskell. Strings are generated by generating list of characters by the generic algorithm, gen, and transforming the obtained lists of characters to strings by toString. The suffix {|*|} to gen indicates its kind. Generic functions of type {|*|} take no type arguments, functions of type {|*→*|} take one type argument etc. We will use a generator of kind {|*→*|} in the instance of the generator for lists, gen {| [] |} , below. These kinds are similar to Hinze's kind-indexed types [8].

After these preparations the generation of user defined types like

```
:: Color = Red | Yellow | Blue
:: Rec = { c :: Color, b :: Bool, i :: Int }
:: ThreeTree = ThreeLeaf | ThreeNode ThreeTree ThreeTree ThreeTree
:: Tree x = Leaf | Node (Tree x) x (Tree x)
```

and predefined types like two and three tuple can be derived by

derive gen Color, Rec, ThreeTree, Tree, (,), (,,)

If for one reason or another the test engineer wants to deviate from the default generic behavior, this can be done very easily. Using the **For**-operator the test engineer can specify a list of values for a specific test. See [9] for details.

If the test engineer decides to deviate from the default behavior for all tests, he can define a specific instance for that type instead of deriving one. For instance using only the colors Red and Blue and trees with exactly one Node in all tests is achieved by defining:

```
gen {|Color|}    = [ Red, Blue ]
gen {|Tree|} xs = [ Node Leaf x Leaf \\ x ← xs ]
```

instead of deriving the generation as shown above. In the examples below, generation is derived using the generic algorithm instead of using special definitions.

Unfortunately the order of elements in the predefined type list does not obey the given assumption on the order of the constructors. The predefined *Cons* constructor is defined before the *Nil* constructor. This implies that gen would always choose the *Cons* constructor if generic generation would be derived for lists.

Instead of changing the assumption, or the implementation of Clean, we supply a specific instance of gen for lists, instead of deriving one. A straightforward implementation is the direct translation of the general algorithm, where the order of constructors is reversed (first the empty list [ ]).

```
gen {| [] |} f = [ [] : [ [h:t] \\ (h,t)←diag2 f (gen {|*→*|} f) ]]
```

type	values
[Color]	[Red,Yellow,Blue]
[Int]	$[0,1,-1,2,-2,3,-3,4,-4,5,-5,6,-6,7,-7,8,-8,9,\cdots$
[(Color,Color)]	[(Red,Red),(Yellow,Red),(Red,Yellow) ,(Blue,Red),(Yellow,Yellow),(Red,Blue) ,(Blue,Yellow),(Yellow,Blue),(Blue,Blue)]
[[Color]]	[[] ,[Red], [Yellow], [Red,Red], [Blue] ,[Yellow,Red], [Red,Yellow], [Blue,Red] ,[Yellow,Yellow], [Red,Red,Red], $\cdots$
[[Int]]	$[[],[0],[1],[0,0],[-1],[1,0],[0,1],[2],[-1,0]$ $,[1,1],[0,0,0],[-2],[2,0],[-1,1],[1,0,0],\cdots$
[Rec]	[(Rec Red False 0) ,(Rec Yellow False 0) ,(Rec Red True 0) ,(Rec Blue False 0) ,(Rec Yellow True 0) ,(Rec Red False 1) ,(Rec Blue True 0) ,(Rec Yellow False 1), $\cdots$
[Tree Color]	[Leaf ,(Node Leaf Red Leaf) ,(Node (Node Leaf Red Leaf) Red Leaf) ,(Node Leaf Yellow Leaf) ,(Node(Node(Node Leaf Red Leaf)Red Leaf)Red Leaf) ,(Node (Node Leaf Red Leaf) Yellow Leaf) ,(Node Leaf Red (Node Leaf Red Leaf)), $\cdots$

TABLE 11.1. **Examples of lists of values generated by** gen

The parameter f holds the list of all elements to be placed in the generated lists. This list will be provided by the generic system. A more efficient implementation uses a cycle to use the generated lists as the tails of new lists.

gen $\{|\,[\,]\,|\}$ f = list **where** list = [[] : [[h:t] \\ (h,t)←diag2 f list]]

Here the function diag2 is used again to get the desired mix extending existing lists and generating new lists with elements that are not used until now.

11.4.1 Examples

In order to illustrate the behavior of this algorithm we show (a part of) the list of values generated for some of the example types introduced above in Table 11.1. The list of all values of type can be generated by an appropriate instance of gen. For instance the list of all elements of the type Color can be generated by:

```
list :: [Color]
list = gen {|*|}
```

For the type Tree Color the list of values is infinite, only an initial fragment of these lists is shown. Also for Int and Rec only an initial fragment of the list of values can be shown.

Note that the order of elements for parameterized types like (Color,Color) and [Color] reflects the dovetail behavior of the generation algorithm.

This algorithm is efficient. Generating 10^6 elements of a type takes typically 2 to 7 seconds, depending on the type of elements generated.

This algorithm generates all 9604 pairs of the 98 printable characters within 0.01 seconds, while the original algorithm outlined in section 11.3 needs 1136 seconds. This is five orders of magnitude faster.

11.5 PSEUDO-RANDOM DATA GENERATION

The actual algorithm used in Gast is slightly more complicated. It uses a stream of pseudo-random numbers to make small perturbations to the order of elements generated. Basically the choice between Left and Right in ggen {|Either|} becomes a pseudo-random one instead of strictly interleaved.

It is a widespread belief among testers that pseudo-random generation of test values is needed in order to find issues[2] quickly. This seems somewhat in contradiction with rule that boundary values should be tested first. When we consider a predicate with multiple universal quantified variables of the same type, it can make sense to try the elements of a type in a somewhat different order for the various variables. We have encountered a number of examples where this indeed raised issues faster. On the other hand it is very easy to create examples where any perturbation of the order of test data delays the finding of counterexamples. In order to achieve the best of both worlds Gast uses a systematic generation of data values with a pseudo-random perturbation of the order of elements discussed in section 11.4.

A simple solution would be to randomize the generated list of elements based on a sequence of pseudo-random numbers. This implies that test values will be generated (long) before they are actually used in the tests. This consumes just space and is considered undesirable in a lazy language like Clean.

The solution used in Gast is to replace the strict interleaved order of the choice in the instance of gen for EITHER by a pseudo-random choice. The change of selecting LEFT of Right deserves some attention. At first sight a chance of 50% seems fine. This works also very well for nonrecursive type like Color, and recursive types like list and Tree form section 11.4.

For a type like ThreeTree this approach fails. If we chose the constructor ThreeLeaf with probability 50% then the chance that all three arguments of the constructor ThreeNode terminate becomes too low. In practice such an algorithm generates too many huge or infinite data structures. QuickCheck has, for exactly this reason, a special language used by the test engineer to tune the relative frequency of constructors. With well chosen frequencies, the generated instances will be neither too small nor too large.

The problem of frequency of constructors can also be solved by an elaborated analysis of the generic representation of the types involved in the data generation. Due to the possibility of nested and mutually recursive data types this analysis is far from simple, but it can be done by a piece of generic Clean-code. Fortunately,

---

[2]A counterexample found by testing is called an *issue* until that it is clear that it is actually an error in the implementation. Other possible sources of counterexamples are for instance incorrect specifications and inaccuracies of the test system.

there is again a simple solution. We still assume that the nonrecursive constructor is the first constructor of a data type (if it exists). By increasing the probability of choosing the left branch in the recursive calls we can ensure that the small instance are near the beginning of the generated list of values. Since duplicates are never generated the algorithm cannot generate only the small elements.

In order to implement this we give the generic function ggen two arguments. The first is an integer indicating the recursion depth, the second one is a list of pseudo-random numbers guiding the choice between left and right.

generic ggen a :: Int [Int] → [a]

The instance of the generation for EITHER is the only one that changes significantly.

```
ggen {|EITHER|} f g n rnd = merge n r1 (f n r3) (g (n+1) r4)
where
    (r1,r2) = split rnd
    (r3,r4) = split r2

    merge :: Int RandomStream [a] [b] → [EITHER a b]
    merge n [i:r] as bs
     | (i rem n) ≠ 0
        = case as of
            [] = map RIGHT bs
            [a:as] = [LEFT a: merge n r as bs]
     | otherwise
        = case bs of
            [] = map LEFT as
            [b:bs] = [RIGHT b: merge n r as bs]
```

The function split splits a random stream into two independent random streams.

Also the order of elements in the predefined data types is changed in a pseudo-random way. For enumeration types like Bool and Char the given order of elements is randomized.

```
ggen {|Bool|} n rnd = randomize [False,True] rnd 2 (λ_.[])
ggen {|Char|} n rnd
 = randomize (map toChar [32..126]++[9,10,13]) rnd 98 (λ_.[])

randomize :: [a] [Int] Int ([Int] → [a]) → [a]
randomize list rnd n c = rand list rnd n []
where
    rand [] rnd n [] = c rnd
    rand [] rnd n [x] = [x:c rnd]
    rand [] rnd n l = rand l rnd n []
    rand [a:x] [i:rnd] n l
        | n == 0 || (i rem n) == 0
            = [a:rand x rnd (n–1) l]
        | otherwise
            = rand x rnd n [a:l]
```

For integers and reals we generate pseudo-random values after the common boundary values. This introduces the possibility that tests are repeated, but for these types it is usually less work than preventing duplicates. Due to the size of these types, proofs by exhaustive testing are impossible anyway.

```
ggen {|Int|} n rnd = randomize [0,1,−1,maxint,minint] rnd 5 id
```

This algorithm appears to be very effective in practice. It works also for some types that do not obey the rule that the nonrecursive constructor is the first one. Termination depends on the ratio between the number of points of recursion in the type and the number of constructors. One of the examples is the type list. This implies that the generation for lists can be derived form the general generic algorithm. In contrast to the previous algorithm, no hand coded definition is needed.

derive ggen []

The exact effect of the pseudo-random data generation depends on the pseudo-random numbers supplied as argument. By default the random numbers are generated by the function genRandInt from the Clean library MersenneTwister [18]. It generates pseudo-random numbers with period $2^{19937} − 1$, and the 623-dimensional equidistribution property is assured. A pseudo-random number generator is said to be k-dimensionally equidistributed if the generated numbers are uniformly distributed in a k-dimensional cube through a whole period, that is, if every consecutive k numbers have no relation. The 623-dimensional equidistribution of the Mersenne Twister algorithm is far higher than of most other widely used pseudo random generators. The seed of the pseudo random numbers can be fixed to obtain repeatable tests, or for instance be obtained from the clock to obtain different test values for each run.

11.5.1 Examples

The list of all pairs of colors with 42 as seed for the random number generation is generated by:

```
list :: [(Color,Color)]
list = ggen {|*|} 2 (genRandInt 42)
```

In Table 11.2 we show the effects using the default random stream of Gast.

Note that the generated lists of values contain the same elements as the lists generated by the algorithm gen in section 11.4.1. The property that all instances of a type occur exactly once is preserved[3]. This algorithm needs about 40% more time to generate the same number of elements for a type compared to the function gen, but it is still very efficient. The test system Gast spends it time on evaluating predicates and the administration of the test results, not on generating test data.

11.6 RESTRICTED DATA TYPES

Types like search trees, balanced trees, AVL-trees, red-black trees, and ordered lists have more restrictions than the type system can impose. Since the generic

---

[3]The shown instance for integers and the instance for reals are the only exceptions.

174

type	values
[Color]	[Red,Blue,Yellow]
[Int]	[0,−2147483648,2147483647,−1,1,684985474 ,862966190,−1707763078,−930341561,−1734306050 ,−114325444,−1262033632,−702429463,−913904323, ⋯
[(Color,Color)]	[(Red,Red),(Yellow,Red),(Red,Blue) ,(Blue,Red),(Yellow,Blue),(Red,Yellow) ,(Blue,Blue),(Yellow,Yellow),(Blue,Yellow)]
[[Color]]	[Red],[],[Yellow],[Red,Red],[Blue],[Yellow,Red] ,[Red,Yellow],[Blue,Red],[Yellow,Yellow] ,[Red,Red,Red,Red,Red],[Blue,Yellow],..
[[Int]]	[[1],[],[−2147483648],[1,1],[−1],[−2147483648,1] ,[1,−1],[0],[−1,1],[−2147483648,−1], ,[1,1,2147483647,−1,0],[1,−1],[0],[−1,1], ⋯
[Rec]	[(Rec Red False 2147483647) ,(Rec Yellow False 2147483647) ,(Rec Red True 2147483647) ,(Rec Blue False 2147483647), ⋯
[Tree Color]	[Leaf ,(Node (Node Leaf Red (Node (Node Leaf Yellow (Node Leaf Red Leaf)) Red Leaf)) Yellow (Node Leaf Red (Node (Node Leaf Red Leaf) Red Leaf))) ,(Node Leaf Yellow (Node Leaf Red (Node (Node Leaf Red Leaf) Red Leaf))), ⋯

TABLE 11.2. Examples of lists of values generated by ggen

algorithm does not know these restrictions, it cannot cope with them. The generic algorithm will generate instance that are type correct, but may or may not obey the additional constraints.

The interface of such a restricted type will contain functions to create an initial instance of the type, e.g. an empty tree, and to add elements to a valid instance of the restricted type. Using these constructor functions and the generic generation of elements to be included in the instance of the restricted type, we can easily generate instances of the generic type.

As example we will consider a search tree of integers. A typical interface to this abstract data type is:

```
:: SearchTree

empty  :: SearchTree
ins    :: Int SearchTree → SearchTree
delete :: Int SearchTree → SearchTree
occurs :: Int SearchTree → Bool
```

Using the functions ins and empty appropriate trees can be constructed. This can be used in the instance of gen or ggen by inserting lists of integers in the empty tree. These lists of integers are generated by the ordinary generic algorithm.

```
gen {|SearchTree|} = map (foldr ins empty) gen {|*|}
```

The initial part of the list of values is (using E for the empty tree and N as con-

175

structor for binary nodes):

```
[E, N E 0 E, N E 1 E, N E 0 E, N E −1 E, N E 0 (N E 1 E),N (N E 0 E) 1 E
,N E 2 E, N (N E −1 E) 0 E, N E 1 E, N E 0 E, N E −2 E, N E 0 (N E 2 E),
,N (N E −1 E) 1 E, N E 0 (N E 1 E), N E −1 (N E 0 E), N E 3 E, ⋯
```

For the algorithm with pseudo-random changes in the order, only the additional arguments of the function ggen have to be passed around.

This approach is applicable to every ordinary restricted recursive data type, since they all have an initial value and an insert operator. Depending on the restricted type it is possible that duplicated values are generated by an implementation following this scheme. For instance inserting the elements from the lists [0] and [0,0] in an empty tree yield the same search tree: [N E 0 E]. With additional effort one can prevent that identical trees will be generated, or remove the generated duplicates by filtering.

11.7   RELATED WORK

Any test tool that wants to do more than only executing predefined test scripts, needs to generate these suites. For any specification that contains variables, it is necessary to generate values for these variables. To the best of our knowledge this is the first approach to generate these values based on the type definition only.

The other tool that is able to test properties over types in a functional programming language is QuickCheck [3]. Its data generation is based on an ordinary type class instead of on generic programming. This implies that the user has to define an instance of the generation class for each type used as in an universal quantification. Moreover, the generation algorithm uses pseudo-random data generation without omitting duplicated elements. As a consequence QuickCheck is not able determine that all elements of a type are used in a test. Hence, QuickCheck cannot stop at that point, nor conclude that it has achieved a proof by exhaustive testing.

Claessen and Hughes give in [3, section 3.2] two reasons for their approach of test data generation based on an ordinary type class: .. ; *we don't want to oblige users to run their programs through a pre-processor between editing and testing them. But another strong reason is that it seems to be very hard to construct a generator for a type, without knowing something about the desired distribution of test cases.* In their Haskell implementation the separate pre-processor is needed for the generic code: Generic Haskell is implemented as a pre-processor. In Clean the generics are fully integrated in the language and handled by the compiler. No separate pre-processor is used. Our systematic generation from small to large solves the distribution of values problem effectively and elegantly.

In [11] we show how functions can be generated based on the grammar of the functions to be considered. This grammar is represented by a recursive algebraic data type. A very simple function transforms the data type to the corresponding function. The algorithm described here is used to generate instances of the data type representing the functions. This representing functions by data structures is similar to defunctionalization [4, 16]. Using the translation from data types to corresponding functions, the algorithm introduced here can also be used to generate functions in a generic and controlled way.

11.8   CONCLUSION

This paper introduces an efficient and elegant generic algorithm to generate the members of arbitrary data types. This list of values is an excellent test suite for a fully automatic test system. The elements are generated from small to large as required for effective testing based on boundary values. We show also a variant of this algorithm that imposes a pseudo-random perturbation of the order, but maintains the basic small to large order and avoids omissions or duplicates. This is believed to make finding counterexamples on average faster.

This algorithm is an essential component of the test tool Gast. The property that test data are not duplicated makes testing more efficient, evaluating a property two times for the same value will always yield an identical result in a functional context. The avoidance of omissions and duplicates makes it possible to prove properties for finite types by exhaustive testing. The advantages of a generic algorithm over an ordinary type class is that the generation for a new data type can be derived: the generic algorithm works for any type. Using a type class, the test engineer needs to specify an instance for each and every type used in the tests. Defining good instances is not easy. The advantages of this generic algorithm over the previous algorithm, outlined in sections 11.3, is that is is much more efficient, elegant, and comprehensible. As a consequence it is much easier for a test engineer to deviate from the default generic algorithm, if that would be desired.

The presented algorithms are efficient. Each of the algorithms is able to generate hundreds of thousands of elements of a type within one second on a fairly basic Windows PC.

Apart from a very useful algorithm in the context of an automatic test system, it is also an elegant application of generic programming. It has the beauty of a programming pearl. The test system Gast follows the trend towards constructing general usable algorithms by generic programming techniques also for more traditional applications as comparing, parsing and printing values.

REFERENCES

[1] Peter Achten, Marko van Eekelen, Rinus Plasmeijer. Compositional Model-Views with Generic Graphical User Interfaces. In Jayaraman, ed. Proceedings Practical Aspects of Declarative Programming, PADL04, LNCS 3057, 2004.

[2] Artem Alimarine, Rinus Plasmeijer. A Generic Programming Extension for Clean. In: Arts, Th., Mohnen M.: IFL 2001, LNCS 2312, pp 168–185, 2002.

[3] Koen Claessen, John Hughes. QuickCheck: A lightweight Tool for Random Testing of Haskell Programs. ICFP, ACM, pp 268–279, 2000. See also www.cs.chalmers.se/~rjmh/QuickCheck.

[4] Olivier Danvy and Lasse R. Nielsen. *Defunctionalization at Work*. PPDP '01 Proceedings, 2001, pp 162–174.

[5] Ralf Hinze, Johan Jeuring. *Generic Haskell: Practice and Theory*, In Backhouse and Gibbons, *Generic Programming*. LNCS 2793, pp 1–56, 2003. See also $http: //www.generic - haskell.org/$.

[6] Ralf Hinze, Simon Peyton Jones *Derivable Type Classes*, Proceedings of the Fourth Haskell Workshop, Montreal Canada, 2000.

[7] Ralf Hinze. *Polytypic values possess polykinded types*, Fifth International Conference on Mathematics of Program Construction, LNCS 1837, pp 2–27, 2000.

[8] Ralf Hinze, Johan Jeuring and Andres Löh. *Type-indexed data types*, In E. Boiten and B. Mller, *Proceedings of the 6th International Conference on Mathematics of Program Construction, MPC 2002* LNCS 2386, pp 148–174, 2002.

[9] Pieter Koopman, Artem Alimarine, Jan Tretmans, Rinus Plasmeijer. Gast: Generic Automated Software Testing. In R. Peña, *IFL 2002*, LNCS 2670, pp 84–100, 2002.

[10] Pieter Koopman, Rinus Plasmeijer. *Testing reactive systems with Gast.* In S. Gilmore, *Trends in Functional Programming 4*, pp 111–129, 2004.

[11] Pieter Koopman, Rinus Plasmeijer. *Testing Higher Order Functions*. Draft proceedings 17th International Workshop on Implementation and Application of Functional Languages, IFL05, 2005. See also https://www.cs.tcd.ie/ifl05/.

[12] Ralf Lämmel, Simon Peyton Jones *Scrap your boilerplate: a practical design pattern for generic programming*, ACM SIGPLAN Notices, **38**, 3, pp 26–37, mar, 2003, Proceedings of the ACM SIGPLAN Workshop on Types in Language Design and Implementation (TLDI 2003).

[13] Ralf Lämmel, Simon Peyton Jones, *Scrap more boilerplate: reflection, zips, and generalised casts*, Proceedings of the ACM SIGPLAN International Conference on Functional Programming (ICFP 2004), ACM Press, 2004, pp 244–25.

[14] Rinus Plasmeijer, Marko van Eekelen. *Clean language report version 2.1.* www.cs.ru.nl/ clean, 2005.

[15] Fethi Rabhi, Guy Lapalme. *Algorithms – A functional programming approach.* Addison–Wesley, 1999.

[16] John C. Reynolds. *Definitional interpreters for higher-order programming languages.* Higher-Order and Symbolic Computation, 11(4):363-397, 1998. Reprinted from the proceedings of the 25th ACM National Conference (1972).

[17] Jan Tretmans. *Testing Concurrent Systems: A Formal Approach.* In J. Baeten and S. Mauw, editors, $CONCUR'99 - 10^{th}$, LNCS 1664, pp 46–65, 1999.

[18] M. Matsumoto, T. Nishimura, *Mersenne Twister: A 623-dimensionally equidistributed uniform pseudorandom number generator*, ACM Trans. on Modeling and Computer Simulation, Vol. 8, No. 1, January pp 3–30 , 1998.

[19] David Turner *Miranda: a non-strict functional language with polymorphic types*, Proceedings FPLCA, LNCS 201, pp 1–16, 1985. Miranda is a trademark of Research Software Limited of Europe.

[20] Arjen van Weelden, Martijn Oostdijk, Lars Frantzen, Pieter Koopman, Jan Tretmans: *On-the-Fly Formal Testing of a Smart Card Applet*, In Sasaki et al: *Proceedings of the 20th IFIP TC11 International Information Security Conference* SEC 2005 2005.

Chapter 12

Extensible records with scoped labels

Daan Leijen[1]

Abstract: Records provide a safe and flexible way to construct data structures. We describe a natural approach to typing polymorphic and extensible records that is simple, easy to use in practice, and straightforward to implement. A novel aspect of this work is that records can contain duplicate labels, effectively introducing a form of scoping over the labels. Furthermore, it is a fully orthogonal extension to existing type systems and programming languages. In particular, we show how it can be used conveniently with standard Hindley-Milner, qualified types, and MLF.

12.1 INTRODUCTION

Tuples, or products, group data items together and are a fundamental concept to describe data structures. In ML and Haskell, we can construct a product of three integers as:

$(7, 7, 1973)$

Records are tuples where the individual components are labeled. Using curly braces to denote records, we can write the above product more descriptively as:

$\{day = 7, month = 7, year = 1973\}$

The record notation is arguably more readable than the plain product. It is also safer as we identify each component explicitly, preventing an accidental switch of the day and month for example.

Even though records are fundamental building blocks of data structures, most programming languages severely restrict their use: labels can not be reused at dif-

---

[1]Microsoft Research, Redmond, WA, USA. Email: `daan@microsoft.com`

ferent types, records must be explicitly declared and are not extensible, etc. This is surprising given the large amount of research that has gone into type systems and compilation methods for records. We believe that the complexity of the proposed systems is one of the most important reasons that they are not yet part of mainstream programming languages. Most systems require non-trivial extensions to a type system that are hard to implement, and, perhaps even more important, that are difficult to explain to the user.

For all systems described in literature, it is assumed that records do not contain duplicate labels. In this article we take a novel view at records where duplicate labels are allowed and retained, effectively introducing a form of scoping over the labels. This leads to a simple and natural system for records that integrates seamlessly with many other type systems. In particular:

- The types are straightforward and basically what a naïve user would expect them to be. The system is easy to use in practice, as the user is not confronted with artificial type system constructs. Of course, all operations are checked and the type system statically prevents access to labels that are absent.

- The records support scoped labels since fields with duplicate labels are allowed and retained. As records are equivalent up to permutation of distinct labels, all basic operations are still well-defined. The concept of scoped labels is useful in its own right and can lead to new applications of records in practice.

- The system is straightforward to implement using a wide range of implementation techniques. For predicative type systems, we can guarantee constant-time field selection.

- The system works with just about any polymorphic type system with minimal effort. We only define a new notion of equality between (mono) types and present an extended unification algorithm. This is all completely independent of a particular set of type rules. We show how it can be used specifically with MLF [15], a higher-ranked, impredicative type system. Building on MLF, we can model a form of first-class modules with records.

The entire system is implemented in the experimental language Morrow [16]. The type system of Morrow is based on MLF, and all the examples in this article, including the first-class modules, are valid Morrow programs.

The work described here builds on numerous other proposals for records, in particular the work of Wand [28], Remy [24], and Gaster and Jones [7]. One can view our work as just a small variation of the previous systems. However, we believe that our design is an important variation, as it leads to a record system with much less complexity. This makes our design more suitable for integration with existing type systems and programming languages.

In the next section we introduce the basic record operations. We explain the type rules and discuss what effect scoped labels have on programs. In Section 12.4 we show how our system can be used with MLF to encode a form of first-class modules. We formalize the type rules and inference in section 12.5 and 12.6. We conclude with an overview of implementation techniques and related work.

12.2 RECORD OPERATIONS

Following Cardelli and Mitchell [2] we define three primitive operations on records: *selection*, *restriction*, and *extension*. Furthermore, we add the constant $\{\}$ as the empty record.

Extension. We can extend a record r with a label l and value e using the syntax $\{l = e \mid r\}$. For example:

$$origin = \{x = 0 \mid \{y = 0 \mid \{\}\}\}$$

To reduce the number of braces, we abbreviate a series of extensions using comma separated fields, and we leave the extension of the empty record implicit. The above example can thus be written more conveniently as:

$$origin = \{x = 0, y = 0\}$$

The construction of the record is anonymous: we do not have to declare this record or its fields in advance. Furthermore, extension is polymorphic and not limited to records with a fixed type, but also applies to previously defined records, or records passed as an argument:

$$origin3 \quad = \{z = 0 \mid origin\}$$
$$named\ s\ r = \{name = s \mid r\}$$

Selection. The selection operation $(r.l)$ selects the value of a label l from a record r. For example, we can define a function *distance* that calculates the distance of a point to the origin:

$$distance\ p = sqrt\ ((p.x * p.x) + (p.y * p.y))$$

In contrast to many programming languages, the *distance* function works for any record that contains an x and y field of a suitable numeric type. For example, we can use this function on records with a different set of fields:

$$distance\ (named\ \texttt{"2d"}\ origin) + distance\ origin3$$

Restriction. Finally, the restriction operation $(r - l)$ removes a label l from a record r. Using our primitive operations, we can now define the common *update* and *rename* operations:

$$\{l := x \mid r\} \quad = \{l = x \mid r - l\} \qquad \text{-- update } l$$
$$\{l \leftarrow m \mid r\} = \{l = r.m \mid r - m\} \qquad \text{-- rename } m \text{ to } l$$

Here is an example of using update to change the x and y components of a point:

$$move\ p\ dx\ dy = \{x := p.x + dx,\ y := p.y + dy \mid p\}$$

Note that *move* works on any record containing an x and y field, not just points. Effectively, we use parametric polymorphism to model a limited form of subtyping [2].

12.2.1 Safe operations

The type system ensures statically that all record operations are safe. In particular, it ensures that record selection and restriction are only applied when the field is actually present. For example, the following expressions are both rejected by the type system:

$\{x = 1\}.y$

distance $\{x = 1\}$

Our type system accepts the extension of a record with a field that is already present, and the following example is accepted:

$\{x = 1 \mid origin\}$

We call this *free* extension. Many type systems in the literature require that a record can only be extended with a label that absent, which we call *strict* extension. We believe that strict extension unnecessarily restricts the programs one can write. For example, the function *named* extends *any* record with a new *name* field. In a system with strict extension, we need to write two functions: one for records without the label, and one for records that already contain the label. In this particular example this is easy to do, but in general we might want to extend records locally with helper fields. Without free extension, the local extensions would artificially restrict the use of the function.

There are two possible semantics we can give to free extension. If a duplicate label is encountered we can choose to overwrite the previous field with the new field, or we can choose to retain the old field. All previous proposals that allow free extension [28, 24, 1] use the first approach. In those systems, extension is really a mixture of update and extension: if a field is absent, the record is extended. If the field is already present, the previous value is overwritten, after which it is no longer accessible.

We take another approach to free extension where the previous fields are always retained, both in the value and in the type. In our system, we clearly separate the concepts of update and extension. To keep selection and restriction well-defined, we need to explicitly define these operations to work on the first matching label in a record. Therefore, we can always unambiguously select a particular label:

$\{x = 2, x = True\}.x$ -- select the first x field
$(\{x = 2, x = True\} - x).x$ -- select the second x field

Since previous fields are retained, our record system effectively introduces a form of scoping on labels. This is certainly useful in practice, where we can use scoped labels to model environments with access to previously defined values. For example, suppose we have an environment that includes the current text color:

$putText\ env\ s = putStr\ (ansiColor\ env.color\ s)$

We can define a combinator that temporarily changes the output color:

$warning\ env\ f = f\ \{color = red \mid env\}$

The function f passed to *warning* formats its output in a red color. However, it may want to format certain parts of its output in the color of the parent context. Using scoped labels, this is easily arranged: we can remove the first color field from the environment, thereby exposing the previous color field automatically (if present):

$f\ env = putText\ (env - color)\ \texttt{"parent color"}$

As we see in the next section, the type of the function f reflects that the environment is required to contain at least two *color* fields.

Another example of scoped labels occurs when encoding objects as records. Redefined members in a sub-class are simply extensions of the parent class. The scoped labels can now be used to access the overridden members in a parent class.

One can argue that free extension can lead to programming errors where one accidentally extends a record with a duplicate label. However, the type system can always issue a warning if a record with a fixed type contains duplicate labels, which could be attributed to a programmer mistake. This is comparable to a standard shadowed variable warning – and indeed, a warning is more appropriate here than a type error, since a program with duplicate labels can not go wrong!

12.3   THE TYPES OF RECORDS

We write the type of a record as a sequence of labeled types. To closely reflect the syntax of record values, we enclose record types in curly braces $\{\}$ too:

type $Point = \{x :: Int, y :: Int\}$

As we will see during the formal development, it makes sense to talk about a sequence of labeled types as a separate concept. We call such sequence a *row*. Following Gaster and Jones [7], we consider an extensible row calculus where a row is either empty or an extension of a row. The empty row is written as $(\!|\,|\!)$ and the extension of a row r with a label l and type τ is written as $(\!|\,l :: \tau \mid r\,|\!)$. The full unabbreviated type of a *Point* is written with rows as:

type $Point = \{(\!|\,x :: Int \mid (\!|\,y :: Int \mid (\!|\,|\!)\,|\!)\,|\!)\}$

Just like record extension, we abbreviate multiple extensions with a comma separated list of fields. Furthermore, we leave out the row brackets if they are directly enclosed by record braces.

12.3.1 Types of record operations

Using row types, we can now give the type signatures for the basic record operations:

$$
\begin{aligned}
(\_.l) &\quad :: \forall r\alpha.\ \{l :: \alpha \mid r\} \to \alpha \\
(\_ - l) &\quad :: \forall r\alpha.\ \{l :: \alpha \mid r\} \to \{r\} \\
\{l = \_ \mid \_\} &\quad :: \forall r\alpha.\ \alpha \to \{r\} \to \{l :: \alpha \mid r\}
\end{aligned}
$$

Note that we assume a distfix notation where argument positions are written as "_". Furthermore, we explicitly quantify all types in this paper, but practical systems can normally use implicit quantification. The selection operator $(\_.l)$ takes a record that contains a field l of type α, and returns the value of type α. Similarly, the restriction operator $(\_ - l)$ returns the record without the l field. The type of extension is very natural: it takes a value α and any record $\{r\}$, and extends it with a new field $l :: \alpha$. Here is for example the inferred type for *origin*:

$$
\begin{aligned}
origin &:: \{x :: Int, y :: Int\} \\
origin &= \{x = 0, y = 0\}
\end{aligned}
$$

The type of selection naturally ensures that a label is present when it is selected. For example, $origin.x$ is well-typed, since the type of the record, $\{x :: Int, y :: Int\}$, is an instance of the type of the expected argument $\{x :: \alpha \mid r\}$ of the selector function $(\_.x)$. Unfortunately, at this point, the type signatures are too strong: the valid expression $origin.y$ is still rejected as $\{x :: Int, y :: Int\}$ is just not an instance of $\{y :: \alpha \mid r\}$.

To accept the above selection, we need a new notion of equality between types where the rows are considered equal *up to permutation of distinct labels*. The new equality relation ($\cong$) is formalized in Figure 12.1. The first three rules are standard. Rule (*eq-trans*) defines equality as a transitive relation. The last two rules define equality between rows. Rule (*eq-head*) defines two rows as equal when their heads and tails are equal. The rule (*eq-swap*) is the most interesting: it states that the first two fields of a row can be swapped if (and only if) their labels are different. Together with transitivity (*eq-trans*) and row equality (*eq-head*), this effectively allows us to swap a field repeatedly to the front of a record, but not past an equal label. With the new notion of equality, we can immediately derive that:

$$
\{x :: Int, y :: Int\} \cong \{y :: Int, x :: Int\}
$$

The expression $origin.y$ is now well-typed since the isomorphic type $\{y :: Int, x :: Int\}$ is an instance of $\{y :: \alpha \mid r\}$. The new notion of equality is the only addition needed to integrate our notion of records with a specific type system. Since no other concepts are introduced, the types of the primitive operations are basically what a naïve user would expect them to be. The same holds for the inferred types of derived operations such as update and rename:

$$
\{l := \_ \mid \_\} :: \forall r\alpha\beta.\ \alpha \to \{l :: \beta \mid r\} \to \{l :: \alpha \mid r\}
$$

$(eq\text{-}var)$	$\alpha \cong \alpha$
$(eq\text{-}const)$	$c \cong c$
$(eq\text{-}app)$	$\dfrac{\tau_1 \cong \tau_1' \quad \tau_2 \cong \tau_2'}{\tau_1\, \tau_2 \cong \tau_1'\, \tau_2'}$
$(eq\text{-}trans)$	$\dfrac{\tau_1 \cong \tau_2 \quad \tau_2 \cong \tau_3}{\tau_1 \cong \tau_3}$
$(eq\text{-}head)$	$\dfrac{\tau \cong \tau' \quad r \cong s}{(\!| l :: \tau \mid r |\!) \cong (\!| l :: \tau' \mid s |\!)}$
$(eq\text{-}swap)$	$\dfrac{l \neq l'}{(\!| l :: \tau, l' :: \tau' \mid r |\!) \cong (\!| l' :: \tau', l :: \tau \mid r |\!)}$

FIGURE 12.1. **Equality between (mono) types**

$$\{l := x \mid r\} = \{l = x \mid r - l\}$$

$$\{l \leftarrow m \mid \_\} :: \forall r\alpha.\, \{m :: \alpha \mid r\} \rightarrow \{l :: \alpha \mid r\}$$
$$\{l \leftarrow m \mid r\} = \{l = r.m \mid r - m\}$$

We see that the type of update is very natural: given a record with an l field of type β, we can assign it a new value of a possibly different type α.

12.3.2 Scoped labels

As remarked before, the type signature for record extension is free and does not reject duplicate labels. For example, both of the following expressions are well-typed:

$$\{x = 2, x = True\} :: \{x :: Int, x :: Bool\}$$
$$\{x = True, x = 2\} :: \{x :: Bool, x :: Int\}$$

Note that the types of the two expressions are not equivalent though. Since rule $(eq\text{-}swap)$ only applies to distinct labels, selection and restriction are still well-defined operations. For example, the following expression selects the second field, as signified by the derived type:

$$(\{x = 2, x = True\} - x).x :: Bool$$

This example shows that it is essential to retain duplicate fields not only in the runtime value, but also in the static type of the record.

12.4 HIGHER-RANKED IMPREDICATIVE RECORDS

Since the type signatures for record operations are so general, we can conveniently package related functions together. Together with a mechanism for local type declarations, we can view these packages as a form of first-class modules. However, records should be able to contain polymorphic values in order to encode more complicated modules. Take for example the following type signature for a *Monad* module:

$$\textbf{type } \textit{Monad } m = \{ \textit{unit} :: \forall \alpha. \;\; \alpha \to m\, \alpha$$
$$, \textit{bind} :: \forall \alpha \beta. \; m\, \alpha \to (\alpha \to m\, \beta) \to m\, \beta$$
$$\}$$

In this signature, the monad implementation type *m* is polymorphic over the monad record. Furthermore, the types of *unit* and *bind* members are itself polymorphic, and thus use impredicative higher-rank polymorphism since the quantifiers are nested inside the record structure. Unfortunately, type inference for impredicative rank-n polymorphism is a notoriously hard problem [15, 22, 19].

When we move to more complicated type systems, our framework of records proves its value, since it only relies on a new notion of equality between (mono) types and no extra type rules are introduced. This means that it becomes relatively easy to add our system to just about any polymorphic type system. In particular, it integrates seamlessly with MLF, an elegant impredicative higher-ranked type inference system by Le Botlan and Remy [15]. We have a full implementation of this system in the experimental Morrow compiler [16] and all the examples in this article are valid Morrow programs.

The combination of MLF with anonymous polymorphic and extensible records (and variants) leads to a powerful system where fields can have full polymorphic type signatures. For example, we can for example give an implementation of an identity monad:

$$\textbf{newtype } \textit{Id } \alpha = \textit{Id } \alpha$$
$$\textit{idm} :: \textit{Monad Id}$$
$$\textit{idm} = \{ \textit{unit } x \qquad = \textit{Id } x$$
$$, \textit{bind } (\textit{Id } x)\, f = f\, x$$
$$\}$$

Since Morrow uses the MLF type system, the (higher-ranked) type for *idm* is automatically inferred and the type annotation is not necessary. Neither is it necessary to declare the *Monad* type; we can just construct an anonymous record. Indeed, we can use the *unit* member polymorphically without any type declaration:

$$\textit{twice} :: \forall \alpha. \; \alpha \to \textit{Id } (\textit{Id } \alpha)$$
$$\textit{twice } x = \textit{idm.unit } (\textit{idm.unit } x)$$

Apart from abstract types, these examples are very close to the goals of the XHM system, described by Jones [14] as an approach to treat modules as first-class citizens. We believe that our notion of records in combination with higher-order polymorphic MLF is therefore a significant step towards a realistic implementation of polymorphic and extensible first-class modules.

12.5   TYPE RULES

In this section, we formalize the concept of rows and define the structure of types. First, we have to make some basic assumptions about the structure of types. This structure is needed as not all types are well-formed. For example, a row type can not extend an integer and a *Maybe* type needs a parameter:

$$(\!| l = Maybe \mid Int |\!)$$

Following standard techniques [13, 24] we assign *kinds* to types to exclude ill-formed types. The kind language is very simple and given by the following grammar:

$$
\begin{array}{llll}
\kappa & ::= & * & \text{kind of term types} \\
& \mid & \mathsf{row} & \text{kind of row types} \\
& \mid & \kappa_1 \to \kappa_2 & \text{kind of type constructors}
\end{array}
$$

All terms have types of kind $*$. The arrow kind is used for type constructors like *Maybe* and function types. Furthermore, the special kind row is the kind of row types. We assume that there is an initial set of type variables $\alpha \in A$ and type constants $c \in C$. Furthermore, the initial set of type constants C should contain:

$$
\begin{array}{lll}
Int & ::: * & \text{integers} \\
(\to) & ::: * \to * \to * & \text{functions} \\
(\!|\,|\!) & ::: \mathsf{row} & \text{empty row} \\
(\!| l = \_ \mid \_ |\!) & ::: * \to \mathsf{row} \to \mathsf{row} & \text{row extension} \\
\{\_\} & ::: \mathsf{row} \to * & \text{record constructor} \\
\langle\_\rangle & ::: \mathsf{row} \to * & \text{variant constructor}
\end{array}
$$

For each kind κ, we have a collection of types τ^κ of kind κ described by the following grammar:

$$
\begin{array}{llll}
\tau^\kappa & ::= & c^\kappa & \text{constants} \\
& \mid & \alpha^\kappa & \text{type variables} \\
& \mid & \tau_1^{\kappa_2 \to \kappa} \tau_2^{\kappa_2} & \text{type application}
\end{array}
$$

Note how the above grammar rules for well-kinded types exclude the previous ill-formed type example. The set of type schemes σ is described by quantification of types of kind $*$:

$$
\begin{array}{llll}
\sigma & ::= & \forall \alpha^\kappa.\, \sigma & \text{polymorphic types} \\
& \mid & \tau^* & \text{monotypes}
\end{array}
$$

Using a simple process of kind inference [13] the kinds of all types can be automatically inferred and no explicit annotations are necessary in practice. In the rest of this article, we therefore leave out most kind annotations when they are apparent from the context. Note that we assume higher-order polymorphism [13, 12] where variables in type expressions can quantify over types of an arbitrary kind. This is necessary since our primitive operations quantify over row kinds. For example, here is the kind annotated type for selection:

$$(\_.l) :: \forall r^{\text{row}} \alpha^* . \{l :: \alpha \mid r\} \rightarrow \alpha$$

As we remarked before, our framework makes just few assumptions about the actually type rules and can be embedded in any higher-order polymorphic type system. To use our framework with standard Hindley-Milner type rules [8, 18] we need to make the implicit syntactic equality between mono types explicit with our equality relation defined in Figure 12.1. We do not repeat all the Hindley-Milner type rules here, but just give the application rule as a typical example:

$$(app) \quad \frac{\Gamma \vdash e_1 : \tau_1 \rightarrow \tau \quad \Gamma \vdash e_2 : \tau_2 \quad \tau_1 \cong \tau_2}{\Gamma \vdash e_1\, e_2 : \tau}$$

Exactly the same approach can be used to use our notion of records with qualified types [10] and Haskell. To use our framework with the MLF type rules is even easier as we only need to extend the rule (*eq-refl*) of the MLF equality relation on poly types ($\equiv$) to include our notion of equality on mono types ($\cong$):

$$(eq\text{-}refl\text{-}mono) \quad \frac{\tau \cong \tau'}{\tau \equiv \tau'}$$

No change is necessary to the actual type rules of MLF as those are already defined in terms of the standard MLF equality relation on type schemes.

12.6 TYPE INFERENCE

This section describes how our system supports type inference, where the most general type of an expression is automatically inferred. Central to type inference is the unification algorithm.

12.6.1 Unification

To support higher-order polymorphism, we use *kind preserving* substitutions in this article. A kind preserving substitution always maps type variables of a certain kind to types of the same kind. Formally, a substitution θ is a *unifier* of two types τ and τ' iff $\theta\tau \cong \theta\tau'$. We call such unifier a most general unifier of these types if every other unifier can be written as the composition $\theta' \circ \theta$, for some substitution θ'. Figure 12.2 gives an algorithm for calculating unifiers in the presence of rows. We write $\tau \sim \tau' : \theta$ to calculate the (most general) unifier θ for two types τ and τ'.

(*uni-const*)	$c \sim c : []$
(*uni-var*)	$\alpha \sim \alpha : []$
(*uni-varl*)	$\dfrac{\alpha \notin \mathsf{ftv}(\tau)}{\alpha^{\kappa} \sim \tau^{\kappa} : [\alpha \mapsto \tau]}$
(*uni-varr*)	$\dfrac{\alpha \notin \mathsf{ftv}(\tau)}{\tau^{\kappa} \sim \alpha^{\kappa} : [\alpha \mapsto \tau]}$
(*uni-app*)	$\dfrac{\tau_1 \sim \tau_1' : \theta_1 \quad \theta_1 \tau_2 \sim \theta_1 \tau_2' : \theta_2}{\tau_1 \, \tau_2 \sim \tau_1' \, \tau_2' : \theta_2 \circ \theta_1}$
(*uni-row*)	$\dfrac{s \simeq (\!\!|\, l :: \tau' \mid s' \,|\!\!) : \theta_1 \quad \mathsf{last}(r) \notin \mathsf{dom}(\theta_1) \quad \theta_1 \tau \sim \theta_1 \tau' : \theta_2 \quad \theta_2(\theta_1 r) \sim \theta_2(\theta_1 s') : \theta_3}{(\!\!|\, l :: \tau \mid r \,|\!\!) \sim s : \theta_3 \circ \theta_2 \circ \theta_1}$

FIGURE 12.2.   Unification between (mono) types

(*row-head*)	$(\!\!|\, l :: \tau \mid r \,|\!\!) \simeq (\!\!|\, l :: \tau \mid r \,|\!\!) : []$
(*row-swap*)	$\dfrac{l \neq l' \quad r \simeq (\!\!|\, l :: \tau \mid r' \,|\!\!) : \theta}{(\!\!|\, l' :: \tau' \mid r \,|\!\!) \simeq (\!\!|\, l :: \tau \mid l' :: \tau' \mid r' \,|\!\!) : \theta}$
(*row-var*)	$\dfrac{\mathsf{fresh}(\beta) \quad \mathsf{fresh}(\gamma)}{\alpha \simeq (\!\!|\, l :: \gamma \mid \beta \,|\!\!) : [\alpha \mapsto (\!\!|\, l :: \gamma \mid \beta \,|\!\!)]}$

FIGURE 12.3.   Isomorphic rows

The first five rules are standard Robinson unification [26], slightly adapted to only return kind-preserving unifications [13]. The last rule (*uni-row*) deals with unification of rows. When a row $(\!\!|\, l :: \tau \mid r \,|\!\!)$ is unified with some row s, we first try to rewrite s in the form $(\!\!|\, l :: \tau' \mid s' \,|\!\!)$ using the rules for type equality defined in Figure 12.1. If this succeeds, the unification proceeds by unifying the field types and the tail of the rows.

Figure 12.3 gives the algorithm for rewriting rows where the expression $r \simeq (\!\!|\, l :: \tau \mid s \,|\!\!) : \theta$ asserts that r can be rewritten to the form $(\!\!|\, l :: \tau \mid s \,|\!\!)$ under substitution θ. Note that r and l are input parameters while τ, s, and θ are synthesized. The first two rules correspond to the rules (*eq-head*) and (*eq-swap*) of type equality in Figure 12.1. The last rule unifies a row tail that consist of a type variable. Note that this rule introduces fresh type variables which might endanger termination of the algorithm. This is the reason for the side condition in rule (*uni-row*): $\mathsf{last}(r) \notin \mathsf{dom}(\theta_1)$.

If we look closely at the rules in Figure 12.3 there are only two possible substitutions as the outcome of a row rewrite. When a label l can be found, the substitution will be empty as only the rules (*row-swap*) and (*row-head*) apply. If a label is not present, the rule (*row-var*) applies and a singleton substitution $[\alpha \mapsto (\!|l::\gamma \,|\, \beta|\!)]$ is returned, where α is the tail of s. Therefore, the side-condition $\mathsf{last}(r) \notin \mathsf{dom}(\theta_1)$ prevents us from unifying rows with a common tail but a distinct prefix[2]. Here is an example where unification would not terminate without the side condition:

$$\backslash r \rightarrow \textbf{if } \textit{True} \textbf{ then } \{x = 2 \,|\, r\} \textbf{ else } \{y = 2 \,|\, r\}$$

During type inference, the rows in both **if** branches are unified:

$$(\!|x::\textit{Int} \,|\, \alpha|\!) \sim (\!|y::\textit{Int} \,|\, \alpha|\!) : \theta_3 \circ \theta_2 \circ \theta_1$$

Which implies that $(\!|y::\textit{Int} \,|\, \alpha|\!)$ is rewritten as:

$$(\!|y::\textit{Int} \,|\, \alpha|\!) \simeq (\!|x::\gamma \,|\, y::\textit{Int} \,|\, \beta|\!) : \theta_1$$

Where $\theta_1 = [\alpha \mapsto (\!|x::\gamma \,|\, \beta|\!)]$. After unification of γ and $\textit{Int}$, the unification of the row tails is now similar to the initial situation and thus loops forever:

$$\theta_2(\theta_1\alpha) \sim \theta_2(\theta_1((\!|y::\textit{Int} \,|\, \beta|\!))) : \theta_3$$
$$=$$
$$(\!|x::\textit{Int} \,|\, \beta|\!) \sim (\!|y::\textit{Int} \,|\, \beta|\!) : \theta_3$$

However, with the side condition in place, no such thing will happen since $\mathsf{last}(r) = \alpha \in \{\alpha\} = \mathsf{dom}(\theta_1)$. Not all record systems described in literature correctly ensure termination of record unification for this class of programs. For example, the unification rules of TREX fail to terminate for this particular example [7].

The reader might be worried that the side condition endangers the soundness or completeness of unification, but such is not the case, as asserted by the following theorems.

Theorem 1. *Unification is sound. If two types unify they are equal under the resulting substitution:* $\tau \sim \tau' : \theta \Rightarrow \theta\tau \cong \theta\tau'$.

Proof. Proved by straightforward induction over the cases of the unification algorithm. A full proof can be found in [17].

Theorem 2. *Unification is complete. If two types are equal under some unifier, unification will succeed and find a most general unifier:* $\theta\tau \cong \theta\tau' \Rightarrow \tau \sim \tau' : \theta_1 \wedge \theta_1 \sqsubseteq \theta$.

Proof. Standard proof of completeness over the structure of types. A constructive proof is given in a separate technical report [17].

As most type inference algorithms reduce to a set of unification constraints, soundness and completeness results carry over directly with the above results for row

---

[2]In practice, this side condition can also be implemented by passing $\mathsf{last}(r)$ to the ($\simeq$) function and checking in (*row-var*) that $\alpha \neq \mathsf{last}(r)$

unification. In particular, the proofs for Hindley-Milner, qualified types [11], and MLF[15] are easily adapted to hold in the presence of row unification.

12.7 IMPLEMENTING RECORDS

Providing an efficient implementation for extensible and polymorphic records is not entirely straightforward. In this section we discuss several implementation techniques and show in particular how standard compilation techniques can be used to provide constant-time access for label selection.

Association lists. A naïve implementation of records uses a simple association list of label-value pairs. Selection becomes a linear operation, and this is probably too inefficient for most practical applications.

Labeled vectors. A more efficient representation for label selection is a vector of label-value pairs where the fields are sorted on the label according to some order on the labels. Label selection can now use a binary search to select a particular label and becomes an $O(log(n))$ operation. When labels can be compared efficiently, for example by using a Garrigue's hashing scheme [4], the binary search over the vector can be implemented quite efficiently. It is also possible to improve the search time for small and medium sized records by using a partially evaluated header [25], but at the price of a potentially more expensive extension operation.

Labeled vectors + constant folding. Label selection can be divided into two separate operations: looking up the index of the label (*lookup*), and selecting the value using that index (*select*). When the labels of the record are known it is possible to partially evaluate the *lookup* operation using standard compiler techniques. The expression $\{l = expr\}.l$ is translated with *lookup* and *select* as:

let $r = \{l = expr\}; i = lookup\ r\ l$ **in** *select r i*

Since the type of r is known, the compiler can statically evaluate *lookup r l* and replace it by 0, avoiding a binary search at runtime:

let $r = \{l = expr\}$ **in** *select r* 0

This optimization by itself guarantees constant-time label selection for all records with a fixed set of labels (like in C or ML).

If the record type is open, the *lookup* operation can not be evaluated statically. However, techniques like the worker-wrapper transformation in GHC [21] can often expose known offsets. An aggressive compiler can also push the lookup operation through extensions in order to float properly, where offsets are adjusted along the lines of the evidence translation of Gaster and Jones [7].

Vectors. One of the most efficient representation for records is a plain vector without labels. Gaster and Jones [7, 6] showed how to this representation can be used with polymorphic extensible records using standard evidence translation of qualified types [10, 11]. We can apply this technique to our system in the context of qualified types by adding an *extension* predicate $l|r$, that asserts that row r is extended with a label l. For example, the type of selection becomes:

$$(\_.l) :: \forall r\alpha.\ (l|r) \Rightarrow \{l :: \alpha \mid r\} \rightarrow \alpha$$

Standard evidence translation turns each predicate $l|r$ into a runtime parameter that corresponds to the offset of l in the extended row r [7] It may seem that we have sacrificed the simplicity of our system as the type signatures now show an artificial predicate, that is just used for compilation. The crucial observation here is that, in contrast to lacks predicates, extension predicates can always be solved and never lead to an error. This means that the type system can use these predicates under the hood without ever showing them to the user.

12.8   RELATED WORK

An impressive amount of work has been done on type systems for records and we necessarily restrict ourselves to short overview of the most relevant work.

The label selective calculus [5, 3] is a system that labels function parameters. Even though this calculus does not describe records, there are many similarities with our system and the unification algorithm contains a similar side condition to ensure termination. One of the earliest and most widely used approaches to typing records is subtyping [2, 23]. The type of selection in such system becomes:

$$(\_.l) :: \forall \alpha.\ \forall r \leqslant \{l :: \alpha\}.\ r \rightarrow \alpha$$

That is, we can select label l from any record r that is a subtype of the singleton record $\{l :: \alpha\}$. Unfortunately, the information about the other fields of a record is lost, which makes it hard to describe operations like row extension. Cardelli and Mitchell [2] introduce an overriding operator on types to overcome this problem.

Wand [28, 29] was the first to use row variables to capture the subtype relationship between records using standard parametric polymorphism. However, since his notion of free extension can overwrite previous labels, not all programs have a principal type. The work of Wand is later refined by Berthomieu and Sagazan [1] where a polynomial unification algorithm is presented. Remy [24] extended the work of Wand with a flexible system of extensible records with principle types, where flags are used to denote the presence or absence of labels and rows. For example, the type of free extension becomes:

$$\{l = \_ \mid \_\} :: \forall r\varphi\alpha.\ \alpha \rightarrow \{l :: \varphi \mid r\} \rightarrow \{l :: pre(\alpha) \mid r\}$$

The type variable φ ranges over field types that can be either absent *abs* or present $pre(\tau)$ with a type τ. The type of Remy's extension encodes that a field that is already present is overwritten, while an absent field becomes present. This is a very flexible system, but the resulting types can be somewhat confusing since absent labels in the value can be present in the type (with an absent flag *abs*).

Ohori [20] was the first to present an efficient compilation method for polymorphic records with constant time label selection, but only for non-extensible rows. Subsequently, Gaster and Jones [7, 6] presented an elegant type sytem for records and variants based on the theory of qualified types [10, 11]. They use strict extension with special *lacks* predicates to prevent duplicate labels.

$$\{l = \_ \mid \_\} :: \forall r\alpha.\ (r\backslash l) \Rightarrow \alpha \rightarrow \{r\} \rightarrow \{l :: \alpha \mid r\}$$

The predicates correspond to runtime label offsets, and standard evidence translation gives a straightforward compilation scheme with constant time label selection. A drawback is that this system relies on a type system that supports qualified types, and that each use of a label leads to a lacks predicate, which in turn can lead to large types that are hard to read or expensive to implement [9]. Sulzmann [27] gives a general constraint based formulation of record operations, but it does not lead directly to an efficient compilation scheme [6].

12.9 CONCLUSION

We believe that polymorphic and extensible records are a flexible and fundamental concept to program with data structures, but that the complexity of type systems for such records prevents widespread adoption in mainstream languages. We presented polymorphic and extensible records based on scoped labels, which is unconvential but also a simpler alternative to existing solutions.

We would like to thank François Pottier for pointing out the similarities between our system and the label selective calculus of Jaques Garrigue.

REFERENCES

[1] B. Berthomieu and C. de Sagazan. A calculus of tagged types, with applications to process languages. In *TAPSOFT Workshop on Types for Program Analysis*, 1995.

[2] L. Cardelli and J. Mitchell. Operations on records. *Journal of Mathematical Structures in Computer Science*, 1(1):3–48, Mar. 1991.

[3] J. P. Furuse and J. Garrigue. A label-selective lambda-calculus with optional arguments and its compilation method. RIMS 1041, Kyoto University, Oct. 1995.

[4] J. Garrigue. Typing deep pattern-matching in presence of polymorphic variants. In *The JSSST Workshop on Programming and Programming Languages*, Mar. 2004.

[5] J. Garrigue and H. Aït-Kaci. The typed polymorphic label selective calculus. In *21th ACM Symp. on Principles of Programming Languages (POPL'94)*, Jan. 1994.

[6] B. R. Gaster. *Records, Variants, and Qualified Types*. PhD thesis, Dept. of Computer Science, University of Nottingham, July 1998.

[7] B. R. Gaster and M. P. Jones. A polymorphic type system for extensible records and variants. Technical Report NOTTCS-TR-96-3, University of Nottingham, 1996.

[8] J. Hindley. The principal type scheme of an object in combinatory logic. *Transactions of the American Mathematical Society*, 146:29–60, Dec. 1969.

[9] M. Jones and S. Peyton Jones. Lightweight extensible records for Haskell. In *The Haskell Workshop*, 1999.

[10] M. P. Jones. A theory of qualified types. In *4th. European Symposium on Programming (ESOP'92)*, volume 582 of *LNCS*, pages 287–306. Springer-Verlag, Feb. 1992.

[11] M. P. Jones. *Qualified types in Theory and Practice*. Distinguished Dissertations in Computer Science. Cambridge University Press, 1994.

[12] M. P. Jones. From Hindley-Milner types to first-class structures. In *Proceedings of the Haskell Workshop*, June 1995. Yale University report YALEU/DCS/RR-1075.

[13] M. P. Jones. A system of constructor classes: overloading and implicit higher-order polymorphism. *Journal of Functional Programming*, 5(1):1–35, Jan. 1995.

[14] M. P. Jones. Using parameterized signatures to express modular structure. In *23th ACM Symp. on Principles of Programming Languages (POPL'96)*, pages 68–78. ACM Press, 1996.

[15] D. Le Botlan and D. Rémy. MLF: Raising ML to the power of System-F. In *Proceedings of the International Conference on Functional Programming (ICFP 2003), Uppsala, Sweden*, pages 27–38. ACM Press, aug 2003.

[16] D. Leijen. Morrow: a row-oriented programming language. `http://www.equational.org/morrow`, Jan. 2005.

[17] D. Leijen. Unqualified records and variants: proofs. Technical Report UU-CS-2005-00, Dept. of Computer Science, Universiteit Utrecht, 2005.

[18] R. Milner. A theory of type polymorphism in programming. *Journal of Computer and System Sciences*, 17:248–375, Aug. 1978.

[19] M. Odersky and K. Läufer. Putting type annotations to work. In *23th ACM Symp. on Principles of Programming Languages (POPL'96)*, pages 54–67, Jan. 1996.

[20] A. Ohori. A polymorphic record calculus and its compilation. *ACM Transactions on Programming Languages and Systems*, 17(6):844–895, 1995.

[21] S. Peyton Jones and A. Santos. A transformation-based optimiser for Haskell. *Science of Computer Programming*, 32(1–3):3–47, Sept. 1998.

[22] S. Peyton-Jones and M. Shields. Practical type inference for arbitrary-rank types. Submitted to the Journal of Functional Programming (JFP), 2004.

[23] B. C. Pierce and D. N. Turner. Simple type theoretic foundations for object-oriented programming. *Journal of Functional Programming*, 4(2):207–247, Apr. 1994.

[24] D. Rémy. Type inference for records in a natural extension of ML. In C. A. Gunter and J. C. Mitchell, editors, *Theoretical Aspects Of Object-Oriented Programming. Types, Semantics and Language Design*. MIT Press, 1993.

[25] D. Rémy. Efficient representation of extensible records. INRIA Rocquencourt, 2001.

[26] J. A. Robinson. A machine-oriented logic based on the resolution principle. *Journal of the ACM*, 12(1):23–41, Jan. 1965.

[27] M. Sulzmann. Designing record systems. Technical Report YALEU/DCS/RR-1128, Dept. of Computer Science, Yale University, Apr. 1997.

[28] M. Wand. Complete type inference for simple objects. In *Proceedings of the 2nd. IEEE Symposium on Logic in Computer Science*, pages 37–44, 1987. Corrigendum in LICS'88, page 132.

[29] M. Wand. Type inference for record concatenation and multiple inheritance. *Information and Computation*, 93:1–15, 1991.

Chapter 13

Project Start Paper: The EmBounded Project

Kevin Hammond*, Roy Dyckhoff*, Christian Ferdinand**, Reinhold Heckmann**, Martin Hofmann***, Steffen Jost*, Hans-Wolfgang Loidl***, Greg Michaelson†, Robert Pointon†, Norman Scaife‡, Jocelyn Sérot‡ and Andy Wallace†

Abstract This paper introduces the EU Framework VI **EmBounded** project, a €1.3M project that will develop static analyses for resource-bounded computations (both space and time) in real-time embedded systems using the domain-specific language Hume,a language that combines functional programming for computations with finite-state automata for specifying reactive systems.

> **embound**, *v.*
> *poet. arch.*
>
>   *trans.* To set bounds to; to confine, contain, hem in.
>
>   Hence **embounded** *ppl. a.*
>
>   1595 SHAKESPEARE *The Life and Death of King John* IV. iii. 137
>   That sweete breath which was *embounded* in this beauteous clay.

*School of Computer Science, University of St Andrews, North Haugh, St Andrews, Scotland, KY16 9SX. **email:** {kh,rd,jost}@dcs.st-and.ac.uk.

AbsInt GmbH, Saarbrücken, Germany. **email: {cf,heckmann}@absint.com

***Ludwig-Maximilians-Universität, München.
email: {mhofmann,hwloidl}@informatik.uni-muenchen.de

†Depts. of Comp. Sci. and Elec. Eng., Heriot-Watt University, Riccarton, Edinburgh, Scotland. **email:** {G.Michaelson, A.M.Wallace}@hw.ac.uk

‡LASMEA, Université Blaise-Pascal, Clermont-Ferrand, France
email: {Jocelyn.SEROT,Norman.Scaife}@univ-bpclermont.fr
This work is partially funded by EU Framework VI grant IST-2004-510255, EmBounded.

195

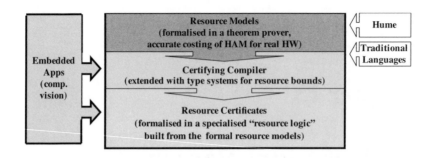

FIGURE 13.1. Schematic Diagram of the Embounded Project Objectives

13.1 PROJECT OVERVIEW

EmBounded is a 3-year Specific Targeted Research Project (STREP) funded by the European Commission under the Framework VI Future and Emerging Technology Open (FET-OPEN) programme. It commenced in June 2005 and involves 5 partners from 3 European countries, providing expertise in high-level resource prediction (Ludgwig-Maximilians-Universität, Germany and St Andrews, UK); precise costing of low-level hardware instructions (AbsInt GmbH, Germany); domain-specific languages and implementation (Heriot-Watt University, UK and St Andrews); and the design and implementation of real-time embedded systems applications, in particular in the area of computer vision algorithms for autonomous vehicles (LASMEA, France and Heriot-Watt). Further details of the project may be found at http://www.embounded.org.

The Embounded Vision

We envisage future real-time embedded system software engineers programming in very high-level functionally-based programming notations, whilst being supported by automatic tools for analysing time and space behaviour. These tools will provide *automatically verifiable certificates* of resource usage that will allow software to be built in a modular and compositional way, whilst providing strong guarantees of overall system cost. In this way, we will progress towards the strong standards of mathematically-based engineering that are present in other, more mature, industries, whilst simultaneously enhancing engineering productivity and reducing time-to-market for embedded systems.

Project Objectives

The primary technical *objectives* of the EmBounded project are (Figure 13.1):

196

a) to produce *formal models of resource consumption* in real-time embedded systems for functional programming language constructs;

b) to develop *static analyses* of upper bounds for these resources based on the formal models of resource consumption;

c) to provide independently and cheaply verifiable automatically generated *resource certificates* for the space and time behaviour of software/firmware components that can be used to construct embedded software/firmware in a compositional manner;

d) to validate our analyses against complex real-time embedded *applications* taken from computer vision systems for autonomous vehicle control;

e) to investigate how these technologies can be applied in the short-to-medium term in more *conventional language frameworks* for embedded systems.

Overall Research Methodology

Our work is undertaken in the context of Hume [12], a functionally-based domain-specific high-level programming language for real-time embedded systems. The project will combine and extend our existing work on source-level static analyses for space [18, 16] and time [26] with machine-code level analyses for time [20]. This will yield static analyses capable of deriving generic time and space resource bounds from source-level programs that can be accurately targeted to concrete machine architectures. Our source-level analyses will exploit a standard *type-and-effect systems* approach [2] and will model bounds on resource consumption for higher-order, polymorphic and recursive expressions. The analyses will be combined with the generation of resource certificates that can be checked against concrete resource prediction models using standard automatic theorem-proving techniques. We will also prove the correctness of our analyses for the same theorem-proving technology by extending the proofs we have developed as part of an earlier EU-funded project (IST-2001-33149, Mobile Resource Guarantees – MRG). Our resource model will be phrased in terms of the Hume abstract machine architecture, HAM; will extend our earlier work by considering time and other resources in addition to space usage and by handling advanced features of the expression language including timeouts and exceptions; and will be related to a concrete architecture specifically designed for real-time embedded systems used, the Renesas M32C. The work will be evaluated in the context of a number of applications taken from the embedded systems sphere, primarily real-time computer vision.

Novelty and Progress Beyond the State-of-the-art

EmBounded is novel in attempting to i) construct *formal upper bounds for space and time* on recursive, polymorphic and higher-order functions; ii) bring automatic memory management techniques to a hard real-time, real-space domain;

iii) apply functional programming design to hard real-time and tightly bounded space settings; and iv) produce formally verifiable and compositional *certificates of resource usage* for real-time embedded programs. These are all open research problems, for which at best partial solutions have so far been found. Novelty also comes from the combination of static analyses at both high and low levels; from the integration of hard real-time program analyses with certificate verification; and from the applications domain. Finally, we anticipate developing new cost analyses that will allow the analysis of more forms of recursive program and/or the production of more accurate cost information than can presently be obtained.

If successful, we anticipate that the EmBounded project will enable several research advances to be made:

- it will develop compositional resource certificates for embedded systems;

- it will allow safe use of features such as recursion, polymorphism and automatic memory management in real-time systems, so allowing the in-principle use of functional programming technology under real-time conditions;

- it will synthesise resource cost models from both source and machine levels, so enabling more accurate modelling than is possible individually;

- it will extend theoretical cost modelling technology to recursive, higher-order and polymorphic functions;

- it will characterise software development using constructs with well defined formal and analytic properties in the context of realistic applications;

- it will represent the first serious attempt to apply modern functional programming language technology to hard real-time systems, including complex industrially-based applications.

As a minimum outcome, we expect to produce a set of certified models and analyses that will determine upper bounds on time and space costs for a range of useful primitive recursive function forms. We should also have determined the accuracy of these models both against some representative computer vision algorithms that have been adapted to the analyses, and against some representative, simple real-time control applications that have been written in Hume. In this way we will have made a step towards ensuring the practical application of functional programming technology in a real-time, hard-space setting.

13.2 THE HUME LANGUAGE

Our research uses Hume as a "virtual laboratory" for studying issues related to time and space cost modelling. Hume is designed as a layered language where the *coordination layer* is used to construct reactive systems using a finite-state-automata based notation; while the *expression layer* is used to structure computations using a purely functional rule-based notation that maps patterns to expressions. Expressions can be classified according to a number of levels (Figure 13.2),

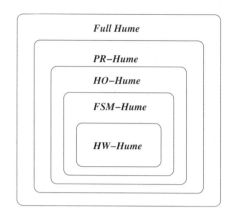

Full Hume
Full recursion

PR–Hume
Primitive Recursive functions

HO–Hume
Non–recursive higher–order functions
Non–recursive data structures

FSM–Hume
Non–recursive first–order functions
Non–recursive data structures

HW–Hume
No functions
Non–recursive data structures

FIGURE 13.2.   Expression Levels in the Hume Language

where lower levels lose abstraction/expressibility, but gain in terms of the properties that can be inferred. For example, the bounds on costs inferred for primitive recursive functions (PR-Hume) will usually be less accurate than those for non-recursive programs, while cost inference for Full Hume programs is undecidable in general (and we therefore restrict our attention in the **EmBounded** project to PR-Hume and below). A previous paper has considered the Hume language design in the general context of programming languages for real-time systems [11].

We have previously developed prototype stack and heap cost models for FSM-Hume [13], based on a simple formal operational semantics derived from the Hume Abstract Machine, and have also developed a prototype stack and heap analysis for a subset of PR-Hume. During the course of the **EmBounded** project, these analyses will be extended to cover time issues and the full range of Hume language constructs. We must also explore issues of quality, compositionality and the cost of the analysis in order to reach a good balance between theoretical coverage and practicality.

13.3   PROJECT WORK PLAN

Formal Models of Resource Consumption

Our first technical objective is to produce formal models of the exact time and space consumption of Hume programs. Space properties of interest include both dynamic stack and heap allocations and static global data allocations. Time must be measured in real, absolute time units at the granularity of the hardware clock for each target architecture. In order to ensure accurate modelling of time consumption, the models will reflect domain-specific compiler optimisations and important architectural characteristics such as cache behaviour.

Conceptually the formal cost models will be based on a formal operational se-

	Semantics	Cost Model
Hume	code $\xrightarrow{\text{evaluation}}$ cost	
	$\downarrow$ translation	$\parallel$ correspondence
HAM	code $\xrightarrow{\text{evaluation } \mathbf{D4}}$ cost	

FIGURE 13.3. Cost Modelling Methodology

mantics, extended in order to make explicit the intensional properties of program execution, such as time and space consumption. So as to achieve the desired level of accuracy, low-level architectural issues will be integrated in the description of state in the operational semantics. Accurate modelling of the compilation process is also required, in order to retain a close relationship between information that can be obtained from the concrete architecture and the results from the static analyses. This will link the resource consumption models with the static analyses. Finally, a *correspondance proof* determines the soundness of the Hume cost model against the HAM seamtics. Our approach is shown in Figure 13.3.

The resulting formal models will form the basis for defining and automatically verifying resource certificates. They will be novel in their accurate and rigorous modelling of time and space. In particular, they will model low-level processor characteristics such as cache behaviour and instruction-level-parallelism (ILP) using the techniques developed by Absint.

At the time of writing, we have largely completed this objective, having constructed formal operational semantics for both Hume and the HAM that have been extended to expose explicit stack, heap and time information. We are now proceeding to incorporate time information derived from abstract interpretation of binary code fragments using the AbsInt tool.

A Cost Model for Hume Expressions   We illustrate our approach by showing how a cost model can be constructed to expose time, heap and stack costs for Hume expressions. The statement

$$\mathcal{V},\eta \vdash^{t \mid p \mid m}_{t' \mid p' \mid m'} e \rightsquigarrow \ell,\eta'$$

may be read as follows: expression e evaluates under the environment, heap configuration $\mathcal{V},\eta$ in a finite number of steps to a result value stored at location ℓ in heap η', provided that there were t time, p stack and m heap units available before computation. Furthermore, at least t' time, p' stack and m' heap units are unused after the evaluation is finished. We illustrate the approach by showing a few sample rules. Integers are constructed as boxed values, and a pointer to the new value saved on the stack. The time cost is given by Tmkint.

$$\frac{n \in \mathbb{Z} \qquad \text{NEW}(\eta) = \ell \qquad w = (\text{int},n)}{\mathcal{V},\eta \vdash^{t' + \text{Tmkint} \mid p' + 1 \mid m' + \text{SIZE}(w)}_{t' \mid p' \mid m'} n \rightsquigarrow \ell,\eta[\ell \mapsto w]} \quad (\text{CONST INT})$$

Variables are simply looked up from the environment and the corresponding value pushed on the stack. The time cost of this is the cost of the `PushVar` instruction, shown here as Tpushvar. There is no heap cost.

$$\frac{\mathcal{V}(x) = \ell}{\mathcal{V}, \eta \vdash^{t' + \text{Tpushvar}}_{t'} \; ^{p' + }_{p'} \; ^{m}_{m} \; x \rightsquigarrow \ell, \eta} \qquad \text{(VARIABLE)}$$

There are three cases for conditionals: two symmetric cases where the condition is true or false, respectively; and a third case to deal with exceptions. We show here only the false case. In the case of a true/false condition the time cost is the cost of evaluating the conditional expression, plus the cost of evaluating an `If` instruction `Tiftrue`/`Tiffalse` plus the cost of executing the true/false branch, plus the cost of a goto if the condition is false.

$$\frac{\mathcal{V}, \eta \vdash^{t_1 \; p_1 \; m}_{t'_1 \; p' \; m'} \; e_1 \rightsquigarrow \ell, \eta' \quad 0 \notin \text{dom}(\eta') \qquad \eta'(\ell) = (\text{bool}, \text{ff}) \qquad \mathcal{V}, \eta' \vdash^{t'_1 - \text{Tiffalse}}_{t'_3} \; ^{p' + }_{p''} \; ^{m'}_{m''} \; e_3 \rightsquigarrow \ell'', \eta''}{\mathcal{V}, \eta \vdash^{t_1}_{t'_3 - \text{Tgoto}} \; ^{p}_{p'} \; ^{m}_{m''} \; \text{if } e_1 \text{ then } e_2 \text{ else } e_3 \rightsquigarrow \ell'', \eta''} \quad \text{(CONDITIONAL FALSE)}$$

The remaining rules are constructed similarly. The main technical difficulties are dealing correctly with higher-order functions and exceptions and capturing the costs of pattern-matching and scheduling. For reasons of brevity we will not consider these issues here.

Static Analyses

The cost models we have outlined above can now be used as the basis for static analyses. Our second objective is the development of static analyses corresponding to these formal models. The analyses will predict upper bounds on both worst-case execution time (WCET) and maximum space (both static and dynamic memory) usage for (a subset of) Hume programs as previously identified. They will work on the Hume source level to produce conservative estimates of worst-case behaviour based on the target architecture (whether abstract machine or concrete hardware implementation).

Our analyses will build on our theoretical work on costing higher-order and recursive definitions [26, 33, 16, 18], applied work on first-order programs [14, 24], and the static analyses of low-level code developed by AbsInt [10, 22, 15]. Combining these analyses will lead to a hybrid analysis that should yield considerably more accurate results than can be obtained using either kind of analysis alone, and that should be capable of analysing very high-level language constructs.

Our high-level analyses will be constructed using a type-and-effect system approach. This approach allows our analyses to be scaled to consider higher-order functions and complex data structures in a common framework. In order to support automatic memory management, we will include mechanisms to support limited forms of compile-time garbage collection based on Tofte-style *memory regions* [32] and/or *usage annotations* [4]. This will enable effective and accurate prediction of run-time memory usage without compromising the required real-time program properties. We will also investigate the application of our analyses to implicit memory allocation.

Our low-level analyses use abstract interpretation of machine-code instructions to provide time and space analyses for a complete program. They exploit detailed models of the hardware architecture including cache logic and the instruction scheduler, pipeline, and branch prediction.

At the time of writing, construction of the static analyses is the main focus of work at St Andrews and LMU.

Formal, Verifiable Resource Certificates

Our third objective is the automatic generation of certificates of bounded resource consumption. Such certificates can be attached to code fragments for the target machines, and composed to provide overall guarantees of bounded resource consumption. In an embedded system context, once a program is linked and the resource bounds verified, there is no further need for a certificate and it may be discarded. An additional benefit from certificate generation is the enhancement of confidence in the behavioural correctness of the program.

Formally defining the structure of certificates will amount to first defining an assertion language that defines which statements can be made for HAM programs. The structure of certificates will be a suitably simplified representation of a formal proof of statements in the assertion language. The proof will be relative to the resource-aware program logic for the HAM. This program logic has to accurately model resources, but still be simple enough to enable automated reasoning on these certificates. We will draw on our program logic, the Grail Logic [3], for a JVM-like low-level language, in deciding on the style of the logic and the embedding of the assertion language into the logic. In contrast to the Grail Logic, the HAM Logic will have to model costs incurred at assembler level, for the particular hardware. Bridging this gap in abstraction levels on the low level will be a major focus of this work, and we will investigate methods of reflecting this level of detail without making the program logic prohibitively expensive.

At the time of writing, we have started work on encoding the formal cost models we have now developed in a form that can be used by the Isabelle theorem prover. This will form the basis for our subsequent work on certification.

Embedded Applications

Our fourth objective is the development of testbed applications in Hume that can be costed using our new analyses. We need to develop three kinds of applications: simple exemplars, isolating single issues; more complex *cost benchmarks*; and realistic applications. The simple exemplars will provide underpinning components for the subsequent applications. They will also enable us to explore principled approaches to developing embedded software that exploit program constructs with well characterised properties and analyses. The more complex cost benchmarks will build on the simple exemplars and enable exploration of integration of different analyses. The realistic applications will serve as proofs of concept, demonstrating that our approach can deal with complex real-time applications with hard space requirements.

EmBounded will build on Heriot-Watt and LASMEA expertise in formally motivated development of vision and control software using functional languages, through a series of closely linked stages of application software development. Initially, we will revisit classic vision algorithms for low-, intermediate- and high-level vision, focusing on the Hume expression layer. We will investigate the degree to which such algorithms can be formulated using strongly finite-state, higher-order or primitive recursive constructs. We will empirically evaluate these algorithms for direct comparison with predictions from the analyses, embodying the cost models developed above. We will then look at composing classic vision algorithms to form a complete mono-source vision system and a high-level stereoscopic vision system. Again we will empirically measure these systems to enable evaluation of compositional cost-model based analyses. Next, we will explore real-time tracking, again using composed components developed at earlier stages. This is where we will first introduce concurrency at the Hume coordination layer, enabling initial evaluation of cost modelling of full Hume programs. Finally, we intend to develop a real-time control system for the *CyCab* autonomous vehicle, incorporating real-time tracking and multiple sensor monitoring. Whilst the focus will be on evaluation of cost models and analyses applied to a substantive, complex system, we would also seek to incorporate the control system in a CyCab vehicle for on-road trials.

At the time of writing, we have produced some simple exemplars of computer vision algorithms that exploit recursion and dynamic data structures, and are considering how these can best be analysed. We have also successfully produced and analysed space usage for a simple real-time computer game, based on the commercial Simple Simon system. This application runs on a simple Renesas M32C development board in less than 2KB of dynamic memory for Hume stack and heap, plus 7KB of flash memory for the Hume program code and runtime system, including interfaces to the physical buttons and LED outputs supported by the board. We are now working on obtaining analytical time costs for this architecture.

Application to Traditional Languages

Our final objective is the determination of how our formal models and analyses could be applied to present-generation languages and application frameworks that are in widespread use for the development of embedded systems. A number of common language features, such as assignment, unrestricted exception handling or dynamic method dispatch, are known to both complicate static analyses and to reduce the quality of analytical results. This has motivated our use of Hume as a "virtual laboratory" in the first instance: by eliminating such features it is possible to make more rapid progress on the key issues related to the analysis. In order to extend our work, we will therefore first identify generic language features that are amenable to analysis using our techniques. We will subsequently explore how the analyses can be extended to the other language constructs of interest. Despite the lack of good formal semantics for many traditional languages, we anticipate being able to demonstrate that the use of a suitably restricted, but still powerful, subset of the language will permit the construction of good-quality static analyses for determining bounds on time- and space-resource usage.

13.4   THE STATE OF THE ART IN PROGRAM ANALYSES FOR REAL-TIME EMBEDDED SYSTEMS

Static analysis of *worst-case execution time* (WCET) in real-time systems is an essential part of the analyses of over-all response time and of quality of service [27]. However, WCET analysis is a challenging issue, as the complexity of interaction between the software and hardware system components often results in very pessimistic WCET estimates. For modern architectures such as the PPC755, for example, WCET prediction based on simple weighted instruction counts may result in an over-estimate of time usage by a factor of 250. Obtaining high-quality WCET results is important to avoid seriously over-engineering real-time embedded systems, which would result in considerable and unnecessary hardware costs for the large production runs that are often required.

Memory management is another important issue in real-time and/or embedded systems with their focus on restricted memory settings. Some languages provide automatic dynamic memory management without strong guarantees on time performance (e.g. Java [25]), whilst others rely on more predictable but error-prone explicit memory management (e.g. C, C^{++}, RTSj or Ada). One recent approach [8] is to exploit memory *regions* for some or all allocation and to combine annotations with automatic inference. Such approaches do not, however, provide real-time guarantees, and typically require manual intervention in the allocation process. Moreover, static region analysis can be overly pessimistic [8] for long-lived allocations. Regardless of the memory management method, there is a strong need for static guarantees of memory utilisation bounds.

Three competing technologies can be used for worst-case execution time analysis: experimental or testing-based approaches, probabilistic measures and static analysis. Experimental approaches determine worst-case execution costs by (repeated and careful) measurement of real executions, using either software or hardware monitoring. However, they cannot guarantee upper bounds on execution cost. Probabilistic approaches similarly do not provide absolute guaranteed upper bounds, but are cheap to construct, deliver more accurate costs, and can be engineered to deliver high levels of trust in their results. Finally, existing static analyses based on low-level machine models can provide guaranteed upper bounds on execution time, but are time-consuming to construct, and may be unduly pessimistic, especially for recent architectures with complex cache behaviour.

Experimental Approaches to WCET Analysis

Cache memories and pipelines usually work very well, but under some circumstances minimal changes in the program code or program input may lead to dramatic changes in the execution time. For (hard) real-time systems such as a flight-control computer, this is undesirable and possibly even hazardous. The widely used classical methods of predicting execution times are not generally applicable. Software monitoring changes the code, which in turn impacts the cache behaviour. Hardware simulation, emulation, or direct measurement with logic analysers can only determine the execution times for some inputs and cannot be used to infer the execution times for all possible inputs in general.

Some producers of time-critical software have thus developed their own method, which is based on strict design and coding rules, the most deterministic usage of the internal speed-up mechanisms of the microprocessor, and measurements of code fragments whose limited size makes it possible to obtain a WCET for all their possible inputs. This method allows the computation of a safe WCET for the whole program by combining the WCETs of the individual fragments. An appropriate combination formula exists thanks to the design and coding rules. However, this method poses the following drawbacks: it limits the effective power of the CPU, requires manual effort for the measurements and related intellectual analysis, and cannot be performed too early during software development, since the target hardware has to be available for measurement purposes. Moreover, in order to ensure that an upper bound of the WCET is really being observed, complex extensive verification and justification of the measurement process is required. It is also possible that this measurement-based method might not scale up to future projects. Therefore major industries depending on time-critical software are actively studying and evaluating new approaches to WCET determination based on static program analysis, as they are pursued by AbsInt.

Probabilistic WCET Analysis

Probabilistic WCET analysis provides distribution functions, rather than absolute upper bounds, for the execution time. This approach is valid even in the hard-real-time environment, if it can provide a guarantee that the probability of deadline over-run by any mission-critical task is within the accepted safety levels (e.g., less than 10^{-9} per flight hour for avionics applications).

Existing implementations of probabilistic WCET analysis tend to be rather low-level: for example, in [6], the program units used are basic blocks (instruction sequences with one entry and one exit) of either Java byte-code, or machine code compiled from C. The difficulty with this approach is that the information about high-level program structure, which is essential for combining the distribution functions of individual basic blocks into "larger" functions, is then lost, and needs to be re-constructed from specifically-designed program annotations. The analysis is performed in the "bottom-up" direction.

Static Analyses for Execution Cost

There has been a significant amount of work on analyzing general execution costs, typically focusing on time usage, since the pioneering work on *automatic complexity analysis* for first-order Lisp programs undertaken by Wegbreit [34]. There has been progress on automatically costing higher-order functions, and recent work has begun to tackle the many problems surrounding costing recursion (e.g. Amadio et al. [1, 7] consider synthesis of polynomial time bounds for first-order recursive programs). The static analyses for real-time systems of which we are aware (e.g. Verilog's SCADE or stack analysers such as that of Regehr et al. [28] or AbsInt's `StackAnalyzer` tool) are, however, highly conservative in limiting their attention to first-order non-recursive systems with statically allocated data structures. Typically, languages used for real-time systems do not support features such as recursion or higher-order functions because of costing difficulties, and cost analyses that might deal with such features are not applied to real-time systems because the mostly widely-employed languages do not possess the requisite features.

Le Métayer [23] uses *program transformation* via a set of rewrite rules to derive complexity functions for FP programs. A database of known recurrences is used to produce closed forms for some recursive functions. However, the language is restricted to a particular set of higher-order combinators for expressing functions and the analysis is not *modular* as the transformation can only be applied to complete programs.

Rosendahl [30] also uses *program transformation* to obtain a step counting version of first-order Lisp programs; this is followed by abstract interpretation to obtain a program giving an upper bound on the cost. Again this abstract interpretation requires a complete program, limiting both its scalability and its applicability to systems with e.g. compiled libraries. Finally, Benzinger [5] obtains worst-case complexity analysis for NuPrl-synthesized programs by "*symbolic execution*" followed by recurrence solving. The system supports first-order functions and lazy lists but higher-order functions must be annotated with complexity information. Moreover, only a restricted and awkward primitive recursion syntax is supported.

13.5   EXISTING WORK BY THE CONSORTIUM

High-Level Static Analyses for Real-Time, Hard Space Systems

St Andrews and LMU have developed complementary formal models for determining upper bounds on space usage [18, 14] and time usage [26]. LMU has focused on determining formally verified space models for first-order languages [16], whilst St Andrews has focused on models that allow inference of time usage for higher-order, polymorphic and (primitive) recursive programs [33]. The combination of this work will lead to a powerful formal model capable of allowing inference of both time and space bounds for a language supporting modern language technologies, including higher-order definitions, polymorphism, recursion and automatic memory management. Our work is influenced by that of Reistad and Gifford [29] for the cost analysis of higher-order Lisp expressions, by the "time system" of Dornic et al. [9], and by Hughes, Pareto and Sabry's *sized types* [19], for checking (but *not* inferring) *termination* for recursion and *productivity* for reactive streams in a higher-order, recursive, and non-strict functional language. Both St Andrews and LMU have produced automatic analyses [18, 14, 26] based on these resource prediction models using standard *type-and-effect* system technology to automatically *infer* costs from source programs.

Low-Level Static Analyses

Motivated by the problems of measurement-based methods for WCET estimation, AbsInt has investigated a new approach based on static program analysis [22, 15]. This has been evaluated by Airbus France [31] within the Framework V RTD project "DAEDALUS" (IST-1999-20527). The approach relies on the computation of abstract cache and pipeline states for every program point and execution context using *abstract interpretation*. These abstract states provide safe approximations for all possible concrete cache and pipeline states, and provide the basis for an accurate timing of hardware instructions, which leads to safe and precise WCET estimates valid for all executions of the application.

Resource Certification

In the Framework V MRG project we aimed to develop certificates for bounded resource consumption for higher-level JVM programs, and to use these certificates in a proof-carrying-code infrastructure for mobile systems. In this infrastructure a certifying compiler automatically generates certificates for (linear) bounds on heap space consumption for a strict, first-order language with object-oriented extensions. These certificates can be independently checked when composing software modules. Novel features in the reasoning infrastructure are the use of a hiearchy of programming logics, using high-level type systems to capture information on heap consumption, and the use of tactic-based certificates in the software infrastructure. The latter drastically reduces the size of the certificates that are generated. In the context of embedded systems, the cost model (and thus the certificates built on them) must reflect lower-level architecture features. The bounds for the resource consumption that are expressed in these certificates will be provided by our static analyses, and may also incorporate information gained by measurement on the concrete hardware.

Linear Types for Memory Allocation

LFPL [16, 18] uses linear types to determine resource usage patterns. A special resource type called "*diamond*" is used to count constructors. First-order LFPL definitions can be computed in linearly bounded space, even in the presence of

207

general recursion. More recently, Hofmann and Jost have introduced [18] automatic inference of these resource types, and thus of heap-space consumption, using linear programming. At the same time, the linear typing discipline is relaxed to allow analysis of programs typable in a usage type system such as [21, 4]. Extensions of LFPL to higher-order functions have been studied in [17] where it was shown that such programs can be evaluated using dynamic programming in time $O(2^{p(n)})$ where n is the size of the input and p is a fixed polynomial. It has been shown that this is equivalent to polynomial space plus an unbounded stack.

13.6 CONCLUSIONS

In the **EmBounded** project, we are trying to push back the boundaries of applicability for functional programming by considering hard real-time, hard space systems. We believe that functional programming notations have a great deal to offer to modern software engineering practices, through the twin advantages of abstraction and compositionality. By tackling the long-standing behavioural bugbears of time and space usage through careful language design in conjunction with state-of-the-art static analysis techniques, we hope to show that functional languages can also be highly practical and deliver real benefits in terms of automated support for the development of complex programs in the real-time embedded systems domain.

Having constructed cost models for Hume and the HAM, our immediate challenge in the project is to construct sound resource analyses to determine good upper bounds for recursive higher-order functions. In particular, we need to extend our work on space to also deal with time information and we must also study the integration between time information at the source and binary levels. We must also develop convincing real-time applications that exploit recursion and higher-order functions in an essential way. In order to do this, we are studying applications from the computer vision domain that may be used for real-time object tracking, or direction of autonomous vehicles. Finally, we must demonstrate that functional languages are suitable for use in time- and space-constrained settings. We have constructed one realistic demonstrator based on the Simple Simon game, and will now consider additional.

REFERENCES

[1] R. Amadio. Max-plus Quasi-Interpretations. In *Proc Typed Lambda-Calculi and Applications (TLAC '03), Springer-Verlag LNCS 2701*, 2003.

[2] T. Amtoft, F. Nielson, and H. Nielson. *Type and Effect Systems: Behaviours for Concurrency*. Imperial College Press, 1999.

[3] D. Aspinall, L. Beringer, M. Hofmann, H-W. Loidl, and A. Momigliano. A Resource-aware Program Logic for Grail. In *Proc. ESOP'04 — European Symposium on Programming*, 2004.

[4] D. Aspinall and M. Hofmann. Another Type System for In-Place Update. In D. Le Metayer, editor, *Programming Languages and Systems (Proc. ESOP'02)*, volume Springer LNCS 2305, 2002.

[5] R. Benzinger. Automated Complexity Analysis of Nuprl Extracted Programs. *Journal of Functional Programming*, 11(1):3–31, 2001.

[6] G. Bernat, A. Burns, and A. Wellings. Portable Worst-Case Execution Time Analysis Using Java Byte Code. In *Proc. 12th Euromicro International Conference on Real-Time Systems*, Stockholm, June 2000.

[7] G. Bonfante, J.-Y. Marion, and J.-Y. Moyen. On Termination Methods with Space Bound Certifications. In *Proc Perspectives of System Informatics, Springer-Verlag LNCS 2244*, 2001.

[8] M. Deters and R.K. Cytron. Automated Discovery of Scoped Memory Regions for Real-Time Java. In *Proc. ACM Intl. Symp. on Memory Management, Berlin, Germany*, pages 132–141, June 2002.

[9] V. Dornic, P. Jouvelot, and D.K. Gifford. Polymorphic Time Systems for Estimating Program Complexity. *ACM Letters on Programming Languages and Systems*, 1(1):33–45, March 1992.

[10] C. Ferdinand, R. Heckmann, M. Langenbach, F. Martin, M. Schmidt, H. Theiling, S. Thesing, and R. Wilhelm. Reliable and precise WCET determination for a real-life processor. In *Proc. EMSOFT 2001, First Workshop on Embedded Software*, volume 2211 of *Lecture Notes in Computer Science*, pages 469–485. Springer-Verlag, 2001.

[11] K. Hammond. Is it Time for Real-Time Functional Programming? In *Trends in Functional Programming, volume 4*. Intellect, 2004.

[12] K. Hammond and G.J. Michaelson. The Hume Language Definition and Report, Version 0.3. Technical report, Heriot-Watt University and University of St Andrews.

[13] K. Hammond and G.J. Michaelson. Predictable Space Behaviour in FSM-Hume. In *Proc. Implementation of Functional Langs.(IFL '02), Madrid, Spain*, number 2670 in Lecture Notes in Computer Science. Springer-Verlag, 2003.

[14] K. Hammond and G.J. Michaelson. Predictable Space Behaviour in FSM-Hume. In *Proc. Implementation of Functional Langs.(IFL '02), Madrid, Spain*, number 2670 in Lecture Notes in Computer Science. Springer-Verlag, 2003.

[15] R. Heckmann, M. Langenbach, S. Thesing, and R. Wilhelm. The influence of processor architecture on the design and the results of WCET tools. *Proceedings of the IEEE*, 91(7):1038–1054, July 2003. Special Issue on Real-Time Systems.

[16] M. Hofmann. A type system for bounded space and functional in-place update. *Nordic Journal of Computing*, 7(4):258–289, 2000.

[17] M. Hofmann. The strength of non size-increasing computation. In *Proc. ACM Symp. on Principles of Prog. Langs. (POPL), Portland, Oregon*. ACM Press, 2002.

[18] M. Hofmann and S. Jost. Static Prediction of Heap Space Usage for First-Order Functional Programs. In *POPL'03 — Symposium on Principles of Programming Languages*, New Orleans, LA, USA, January 2003. ACM Press.

[19] R.J.M. Hughes, L. Pareto, and A. Sabry. Proving the Correctness of Reactive Systems using Sized Types. In *Proc 1996 ACM Symposium on Principles of Programming Languages – POPL '96*, St Petersburg, FL, January 1996.

[20] D. Kästner. TDL: a Hardware Description Language for Retargetable Postpass Optimisations and Analyses. In *Proc. 2003 Intl. Conf. on Generative Programming and Component Engineering, – GPCE 2003, Erfurt, Germany*, pages 18–36. Springer-Verlag LNCS 2830, September 2003.

[21] N. Kobayashi and A. Igarashi. Resource Usage Analysis. In *POPL '02 — Principles of Programming Languages*, Portland, Oregon, January 2002.

[22] M. Langenbach, S. Thesing, and R. Heckmann. Pipeline modeling for timing analysis. In *Proc. 9th International Static Analysis Symposium SAS 2002*, volume 2477 of *Lecture Notes in Computer Science*, pages 294–309. Springer-Verlag, 2002.

[23] D. Le Métayer. ACE: An Automatic Complexity Evaluator. *ACM Transactions on Programming Languages and Systems*, 10(2):248–266, April 1988.

[24] K MacKenzie and N. Wolverson. Camelot and Grail: Compiling a Resource-Aware Functional Language for the Java Virtual Machine. In *TFP'03 — Symposium on Trends in Functional Programming*, Edinburgh, Scotland, Sep 11–12, 2003, 2003.

[25] K. Nilsen. Issues in the Design and Implementation of Real-Time Java. *Java Developers' Journal*, 1(1):44, 1996.

[26] A.J. Rebón Portillo, K. Hammond, H.-W. Loidl, and P. Vasconcelos. A Sized Time System for a Parallel Functional Language (Revised). In *Proc. Implementation of Functional Langs.(IFL '02), Madrid, Spain*, number 2670 in Lecture Notes in Computer Science. Springer-Verlag, 2003.

[27] P. Puschner and A. Burns. A Review of Worst-Case Execution-Time Analysis. *Real-Time Systems*, 18(2/3):115–128, 2000.

[28] J. Regehr, A.J. Reid, and K. Webb. Eliminating Stack Overflow by Abstract Interpretation. In *Proc 3rd Intl. Conf. on Embedded Software (EMSOFT 2003*.

[29] B. Reistad and D.K. Gifford. Static Dependent Costs for Estimating Execution Time. In *LFP'94 — Conference on Lisp and Functional Programming*, pages 65–78, Orlando, Florida, June 27–29, June 1994. ACM Press.

[30] M. Rosendahl. Automatic Complexity Analysis. In *Proc. FPCA'89 — Intl. Conf. on Functional Prog. Langs. and Comp. Arch.*, pages 144–156, 1989.

[31] S. Thesing, J. Souyris, R. Heckmann, F. Randimbivololona, M. Langenbach, R. Wilhelm, and C. Ferdinand. An abstract interpretation-based timing validation of hard real-time avionics software. In *Proc. 2003 Intl. Conf. on Dependable Systems and Networks (DSN 2003)*, pages 625–632. IEEE Computer Society, 2003.

[32] M. Tofte and J.-P. Talpin. Region-based Memory Management. *Information and Computation*, 132(2):109–176, 1997.

[33] P.B. Vasconcelos and K. Hammond. Inferring Costs for Recursive, Polymorphic and Higher-Order Functional Programs. In *Proc. Implementation of Functional Languages (IFL 2003)*, 2004.

[34] B. Wegbreit. Mechanical Program Analysis. *Communications of the ACM*, 18(9):528–539, 1975.

Chapter 14

Project Evaluation Paper: Mobile Resource Guarantees

Donald Sannella[1], Martin Hofmann[2], David Aspinall[1], Stephen Gilmore[1], Ian Stark[1], Lennart Beringer[1], Hans-Wolfgang Loidl[2], Kenneth MacKenzie[1], Alberto Momigliano[1], Olha Shkaravska[2]

Abstract: The Mobile Resource Guarantees (MRG) project has developed a proof-carrying-code infrastructure for certifying resource bounds of mobile code. Key components of this infrastructure are a certifying compiler for a high-level language, a hierarchy of program logics, tailored for reasoning about resource consumption, and an embedding of the logics into a theorem prover. In this paper, we give an overview of the project's results, discuss the lessons learnt from it and introduce follow-up work in new projects that will build on these results.

14.1 INTRODUCTION

The Mobile Resource Guarantees (MRG) project was a three year project funded by the EC under the FET proactive initiative on Global Computing. The aim of the MRG project was to *develop an infrastructure needed to endow mobile code with independently verifiable certificates describing its resource behaviour.* These certificates are condensed and formalised mathematical proofs of resource-related properties which are by their very nature self-evident, unforgeable, and independent of trust networks. This "proof-carrying-code" (PCC) approach to security (19) has become increasingly popular in recent years (13; 1; 20).

Typical application scenarios for such an infrastructure include the following.

- A provider of a distributed computational power, for example a node in a computational Grid, may only be willing to offer this service upon receiving dependable guarantees about the required resource consumption.

---

[1]Laboratory for Foundations of Computer Science, School of Informatics, University of Edinburgh, Edinburgh EH9 3JZ, Scotland
[2]Inst. f. Informatik, Ludwig-Maximilians Universität, D-80538 München, Germany

- A user of a handheld device or another embedded system might want to know that a downloaded application will definitely run within the limited amount of memory available.

Our PCC infrastructure combines techniques from several different research areas. Most notably, we present a novel approach to PCC of building a hierarchy of logics and of translating high-level language properties into a specialised program logic (see Section 14.3). This approach combines the idea of minimising the proof infrastructure as promoted by foundational PCC (1) with exploiting high-level program properties in the certificates. The properties are expressed in an extended type system and type inference is used for static program analysis. Thus we combine work on program logics in the automated theorem proving community with type-system-based analyses in the programming language community. We also show how the embedding of this hierarchy of logics into the Isabelle/HOL theorem prover yields an executable formalisation that can be directly used in the infrastructure. Since soundness and completeness between the levels are established within the prover, the specialised logic does not enter the trusted code base.

In the following section we will outline the initial objectives of the project (Section 14.2) and then give an overview of the key techniques used, and newly developed, to meet these objectives. We provide an overview of the design of our proof and software infrastructure (Sections 14.3 and 14.4). We summarise the main results in Section 14.5, and discuss future work which builds on these results.

14.2 PROJECT OBJECTIVES

The objectives outlined in our initial proposal strike a balance between foundational and more applied work. The foundational work develops a proof infrastructure built on type systems and program logics. The applied work creates a software infrastructure in a PCC prototype which covers the entire path of mobile code in a distributed system. A general overview of the project, developed about half-way through the project, is presented in (5).

Objective 1   is the development of a framework in which certificates of resource consumption exist as formal objects. This consists of a cost model and a program logic for an appropriate virtual machine and run time environment.

Objective 2   consists of the development of a notion of formalised and checkable proofs for this logic playing the role of certificates.

Objective 3   is the development of methods for machine generation of such certificates for appropriate high-level code. Type systems are used as an underlying formalism for this endeavour. Since resource related properties of programs are almost always undecidable, we aim — following common practice — for a conservative approximation: there will be programs for which no certificate can be obtained although they may abide by the desired resource policy.

Objective 4 While proof-like certificates are generally desirable, they may sometimes be infeasible to construct or too large to transmit. We therefore study relaxations based on several rounds of negotiation between supplier and user of code leading to higher and higher confidence that the resource policy is satisfied.

We have fully achieved Objectives 1–3, and we started work on Objective 4, which is now being picked up in follow-up projects (see Section 14.5).

14.3   AN INFRASTRUCTURE FOR RESOURCE CERTIFICATION

Developing an efficient PCC infrastructure is a challenging task, both in terms of foundations and engineering. In this section we present the foundational tools needed in such an infrastructure, in particular high-level type-systems and program logics. In terms of engineering, the main challenges are the size of the certificates, the size of the trusted code base (TCB) and the speed of validation.

14.3.1   Proof Infrastructure

In this section we describe the proof infrastructure for certification of resources. This is based on a *multi-layered logics approach* (shown in Figure 14.1), where all logics are formalised in a proof assistant, and meta-theoretic results of soundness and completeness provide the desired confidence.

As the basis we have the (trusted) *operational semantics* which is extended with general "effects" for encoding the basic security-sensitive operations (for example, heap allocation if the security policy is bounded heap consumption). Judgements in the operational semantics have the form $E \vdash h, e \Downarrow h', v, \rho$, where E maps variables to values, h represents the pre-heap and h' the post-heap, and v is the result value, consuming ρ resources. The foundational PCC approach (1) performs proofs directly on this level thereby reducing the size of the TCB, but thereby increasing the size of the generated proofs considerably. To remedy this situation more recent designs, such as the Open Verifier Framework (12) or Certified Abstract Interpretation (10), add untrusted, but provably sound, components to a foundational PCC design.

On the next level there is a general-purpose *program logic* for partial correctness (2; 3). Judgements in this logic have the form $\Gamma \rhd e : A$, where the context Γ maps expressions to assertions, and A, an assertion, is a predicate over the parameters of the operational semantics. The role of the program logic is to serve as a platform on which various higher level logics may be unified. The latter purpose makes logical completeness of the program logic a desirable property, which has hitherto been mostly of meta-theoretic interest. Of course, soundness remains mandatory, as the trustworthiness of any application logic defined at higher levels depends upon it. Our soundness and completeness results establish a strong link

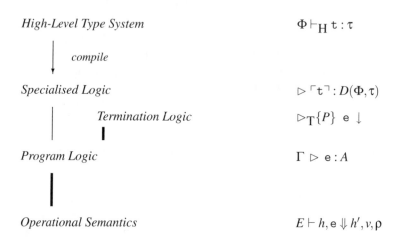

FIGURE 14.1.   A family of logics for resource consumption

between operational semantics and program logic, shown as thick lines in Figure 14.1. Note that, since we formalise the entire hierarchy of logics and prove soundness, we do not need to include any of these logics in the TCB.

Whereas assertions in the core logic make statements about partial program correctness, the *termination logic* is defined on top of this level to certify termination. This separation improves modularity in developing these logics, and allows us to use judgements of partial correctness when talking about termination. Judgements in this logic have the form $\triangleright_T \{P\}\ e \downarrow$, meaning an expression e terminates under the precondition P.

On top of the general-purpose logic, we define a *specialised logic* (for example the heap logic of (8)) that captures the specifics of a particular security policy. This logic uses a restricted format of assertions, called *derived assertions*, which reflects the judgement of the high-level type system. Judgements in the specialised logic have the form $\triangleright \ulcorner t \urcorner : D(\Phi, \tau)$, where the expression $\ulcorner t \urcorner$ is the result of compiling a high-level term t down to a low-level language, and the information in the high-level type system is encoded in a special form of assertion $D(\Phi, \tau)$ that relies on the context Φ and type τ associated to t. Depending on the property of interest, this level may be further refined into a hierarchy of proof systems, for example if parts of the soundness argument of the specialised assertions can be achieved by different type systems. In contrast to the general-purpose logic, this specialised logic is not expected to be complete, but it should provide support for automated proof search. In the case of the logic for heap consumption, we achieve this by inferring a system of derived assertions whose level of granularity is roughly similar to the high-level type system. However, the rules are expressed in terms of code fragments in the low-level language. Since the side conditions of the typing rules are computationally easy to validate, automated proof search is supported by the syntax-directedness of the typing rules. At points where syntax-directedness fails — such as recursive program structures — the necessary invariants are provided by the type system.

On the top level we find a *high-level type system* that encodes information on resource consumption. In the judgement $\Phi \vdash_H t : \tau$, the term t has an (extended) type τ in a context Φ. This in an example of increasingly complex type systems that have found their way into main-stream programming as a partial answer to the unfeasibility of proving general program correctness. Given this complexity, soundness proofs of the type systems become subtle. As we have seen, our approach towards guaranteeing the absence of bad behaviour at the compiled code level is to translate types into proofs in a suitably specialised program logic.

The case we have worked out in (3) is the Hofmann-Jost type system for heap usage (14) and a simpler instance is given in the rest of this section. In our work, however, we give a general framework for tying such analyses into a fully formalised infrastructure for reasoning about resource consumption.

14.3.2   An Example of a Specialised Program Logic

We now elaborate our approach on a simple static analysis of heap-space consumption based on (11). The idea is to prove a constant upper bound on heap allocation, by showing that no function allocates heap in a loop. The goal is to detect such non-loop-allocating cases and separate them from the rest, for which no guarantees are given.

It should be emphasised that the heap space analysis in the MRG infrastructure (as shown in Figure 14.5) can handle recursive functions with allocations as long as the consumption can be bounded by a linear function on the input size (14). We choose this simpler analysis in this section to explain the principles of our approach without adding too much complexity in the logics.

We use the expression fragment of a simple first-order, strict language similar to Camelot (18) (see later in 14.4.1), with lists as the only non-primitive datatype and expressions in administrative-normal-form (ANF), meaning arguments to functions must be variables (k are constants, x variables, f function names):

$$e \in expr \quad ::= \quad k \mid x \mid \mathtt{nil} \mid \mathtt{cons}(x_1, x_2) \mid f(x_1, \ldots, x_{n_f}) \mid \mathtt{let}\ x = e_1\ \mathtt{in}\ e_2$$
$$\mid \mathtt{match}\ x\ \mathtt{with}\ \mathtt{nil} \Rightarrow e_1; \mathtt{cons}(x_1, x_2) \Rightarrow e_2$$

We now define a non-standard type system for this language, where $\Sigma(f)$ is a pre-defined type signature mapping function names to $\mathbb{N}$, as follows:

$$\frac{\vdash_H e : n \qquad n \leq m}{\vdash_H e : m} \text{ (WEAK)} \qquad \frac{}{\vdash_H k : 0} \text{ (CONST)} \qquad \frac{}{\vdash_H x : 0} \text{ (VAR)}$$

$$\frac{}{\vdash_H f(x_1,\dots,x_{n_f}) : \Sigma(f)} \text{(APP)} \qquad \frac{}{\vdash_H \mathtt{nil} : 0} \text{(NIL)} \qquad \frac{}{\vdash_H \mathtt{cons}(x_1,x_2) : 1} \text{(CONS)}$$

$$\frac{\vdash_H e_1 : m \quad \vdash_H e_2 : n}{\vdash_H \mathtt{let}\, x = e_1 \,\mathtt{in}\, e_2 : m+n} \text{(LET)} \qquad \frac{\vdash_H e_1 : n \quad \vdash_H e_2 : n}{\vdash_H \mathtt{match}\, x \,\mathtt{with}\, \mathtt{nil} \Rightarrow e_1 ; \mathtt{cons}(x_1,x_2) \Rightarrow e_2 : n} \text{(MATCH)}$$

Let us say that a function is *recursive* if it can be found on a cycle in the call graph. Further, a function *allocates* if its body contains an allocation, i.e, a subexpression of the form $\mathtt{cons}(x_1,x_2)$. One can show that a program is typeable iff no recursive function allocates. Moreover, in this case the type of a function bounds the number of allocations it can make.

In order to establish correctness of the type system and, more importantly, to enable generation of certificates as proofs in the program logic, we will now develop a derived assertion and a set of syntax-directed proof rules that mimic the typing rules and permit the automatic translation of any typing derivation into a valid proof.

Recall that $\Gamma \rhd e : A$ is the judgement of the core logic, and that A is parameterised over variable environment, pre- and post-heap (see (2) for more details on encoding program logics for these kinds of languages). Based on this logic, we can now define a *derived assertion*, capturing the fact that the heap h' after the execution is at most n units larger than the heap h before execution[2]:

$$D(n) \equiv \lambda E\, h\, h'\, v\, \rho.\ |dom(h')| \le |dom(h)| + n$$

We can now prove *derived rules* of the canonical form $\rhd e : D(n)$ to arrive at a program logic for heap consumption:

$$\frac{\rhd e : D(n) \quad n \le m}{\rhd e : D(m)} \text{(DWEAK)} \qquad \frac{}{\rhd k : D(0)} \text{(DCONST)} \qquad \frac{}{\rhd x : D(0)} \text{(DVAR)}$$

$$\frac{}{\rhd f(x_1,\dots,x_{n_f}) : \Sigma(f)} \text{(DAPP)} \qquad \frac{}{\rhd \mathtt{nil} : D(0)} \text{(DNIL)} \qquad \frac{}{\rhd \mathtt{cons}(x_1,x_2) : D(1)} \text{(DCONS)}$$

$$\frac{\rhd e_1 : D(m) \quad \rhd e_2 : D(n)}{\rhd \mathtt{let}\, x = e_1 \,\mathtt{in}\, e_2 : D(m+n)} \text{(DLET)} \qquad \frac{\rhd e_1 : D(n) \quad \rhd e_2 : D(n)}{\rhd \mathtt{match}\, x \,\mathtt{with}\, \mathtt{nil} \Rightarrow e_1 ; \mathtt{cons}(x_1,x_2) \Rightarrow e_2 : D(n)} \text{(DMATCH)}$$

---

[2]We do not model garbage collection here, so the size of the heap always increases. This restriction will be lifted in the next section.

We can now automatically construct a proof of bounded heap consumption, by replaying the type derivation for the high-level type system $\vdash_H$, and using the corresponding rules in the derived logic. The verification conditions coming out of this proof will consist only of the inequalities used in the derived logic. No reasoning about the heaps is necessary at all at this level. This has been covered already in the soundness proof of the derived logic w.r.t. the core program logic.

14.3.3 Modelling Reusable Memory

To tackle the issue of reusable memory, we introduce the model of a global "free-list". Heap allocations are fed from the freelist. Furthermore, Camelot provides a destructive pattern `match` operator, which returns the heap cell matched against to the freelist. This high-level memory model is the basis for extending the type system and the logic to a language where memory can be reused.

We can generalise the type system to encompass this situation by assigning a type of the form $\Sigma(f) = (m,n)$ with $m,n \in \mathbb{N}$ to functions and, correspondingly, a typing judgement of the format $\vdash_\Sigma e : (m,n)$. The corresponding derived assertion $D(m,n)$ asserts that if in the pre-heap the global freelist has a length greater than or equal to m, then the freelist in the post-heap has a length greater than or equal to n. Since the freelist, as part of the overall heap, abstracts the system's garbage collection policy, we have the invariant that the size of the post-heap equals the size of the pre-heap.

Now the type of an expression contains an upper bound on the space needed for execution as well as the space left over after execution. If we know that, say, $e : (5,3)$ then we can execute e after filling the freelist with 5 freshly allocated cells, and we will find 3 cells left-over, which can be used in subsequent computations.

The typing rules for this extended system are as follows. Corresponding derived rules are provable in the program logic.

$$\frac{\vdash_H e : (m,n) \quad m' \geq m+q \quad n' \leq n+q}{\vdash_H e : (m',n')} \text{(WEAK)} \qquad \frac{}{\vdash_H k : (0,0)} \text{(CONST)} \qquad \frac{}{\vdash_H x : (0,0)} \text{(VAR)}$$

$$\frac{}{\vdash_H f(x_1,\ldots,x_{n_f}) : \Sigma(f)} \text{(APP)} \qquad \frac{}{\vdash_H \texttt{nil} : (0,0)} \text{(NIL)} \qquad \frac{}{\vdash_H \texttt{cons}(x_1,x_2) : (1,0)} \text{(CONS)}$$

$$\frac{\vdash_H e_1 : (m,n) \quad \vdash_H e_2 : (n,k)}{\vdash_H \texttt{let } x = e_1 \texttt{ in } e_2 : (m,k)} \text{(LET)} \qquad \frac{\vdash_H e_1 : (m,n) \quad \vdash_H e_2 : (m+1,n)}{\vdash_H \texttt{match } x \texttt{ with nil} \Rightarrow e_1; \texttt{cons}(x_1,x_2)@\_ \Rightarrow e_2 : (m,n)} \text{(MATCH)}$$

Notice that this type system does not prevent deallocation of live cells. Doing so would compromise functional correctness of the code but not the validity of the derived assertions which merely speak about freelist size.

In (8) we extend the type system even further by allowing for input-dependent freelist size using an amortised approach. Here it is crucial to rule out "rogue programs" that deallocate live data. There are a number of type systems capable of doing precisely that; among them we choose the admittedly rather restrictive linear typing that requires single use of each variable.

14.4 A PCC INFRASTRUCTURE FOR RESOURCES

Having discussed the main principles in the design of the MRG infrastructure, we now elaborate on its main characteristic features (a detailed discussion of the operational semantics and program logic is given in (2)).

14.4.1 Proof Infrastructure

As an instantiation of our multi-layered logics approach, the proof infrastructure realises several program logics, with the higher-level ones tailored to facilitate reasoning about heap-space consumption. While we focus on heap-space consumption here, we have in the meantime extended our approach to cover more general resources in the form of resource algebras (4).

Low-level language: JVM bytecode In order to use the infrastructure in an environment for mobile computation, we focus on a commonplace low-level language: a subset of JVM bytecode. This language abstracts over certain machine-specific details of program execution. Being higher-level than assembler code facilitates the development of a program logic as basis for certification, but also somewhat complicates the cost modelling. For the main resource of interest, heap consumption, allocation is still transparent enough to allow accurate prediction (as shown by the evaluation of our cost model for the JVM). For other resources, in particular execution time, cost modelling is significantly more complicated.

The unstructured nature of JVM code usually gives rise to fairly awkward rules in the operational semantics and in the program logic. We have therefore decided to introduce a slight abstraction over JVM bytecode, *Grail* (9), an intermediate language with a functional flavour, which is in a one-to-one correspondence with JVM bytecode satisfying some mild syntactic conditions. Thus, we can perform certification on the Grail level, and retrieve the Grail code from the transmitted JVM bytecode on the consumer side.

The *operational semantics* for Grail is a resource-aware, big-step semantics over this functional language. Resources are modelled in general terms by specifying a resource algebra over constructs of the language. Separating the rules of the semantics from the propagation of resources makes it easy to model new resources on top of this semantics.

The *program logic* for Grail is a VDM-style partial correctness logic. Thus, it can make meaningful statements about heap consumption, provided that a program terminates. To assure termination, we have also developed a separate termination logic, built on top of the core program logic. It should be emphasised that the program logic does not rely in any way on the Grail code being compiled from a particular high level language. It can be seen as a uniform language for

```
val fac: int -> int -> int          val fac: int -> int
let rec fac n b =                    let rec fac n =
   if n < 1 then b                      if n < 1 then 1
           else fac (n - 1) (n * b)             else n * fac (n - 1)
```

FIGURE 14.2.   Tail-recursive (left) and recursive (right) Camelot code of factorial

phrasing properties of interest as discussed in the previous section. The benefit
of compiling down from a higher-level language is that its additional structure
can be used to automatically generate the certificates that prove statements in this
program logic.

High-level language: Camelot   As high-level language we have defined a variant of OCAML: Camelot (18). It is a strict functional language with object-
oriented extensions and limited support for higher-order functions. Additionally,
it has a destructive match statement to model heap deallocation, and it uses a
freelist-based heap model that is implemented on top of the JVM's heap model.
Most importantly, it is endowed with an inference algorithm for heap-space consumption (14), based on this internal freelist heap model. This inference can
derive linear upper bounds for Camelot programs fulfilling certain linearity constraints. Based on this inference, the compiler can also generate a certificate for
bounded heap consumption, and it emits a statement in the Grail program logic,
expressing this bound for the overall program.

As an example let us examine a tail-recursive and a genuinely recursive Camelot
program implementing the factorial function, shown in Figure 14.2. The Java
Bytecode corresponding to the tail-recursive Camelot program is given in the first
column of Figure 14.3. Recall that many JVM commands refer to the operand
stack. If we explicitly denote the items on this stack by $0, $1, $2,..., starting
from the top, then we obtain a beautified bytecode of the tail-recursive version
given in the right column of Figure 14.3. In Grail we take this one step further
by removing the stack altogether and allowing arithmetic operations on arbitrary
variables. Moreover, we use a functional notation for jumps and local variables
as exemplified by the code in the left column of Figure 14.4. In contrast, the
genuinely recursive version uses JVM method invocation in the recursive call.

With this functional notation of Grail it is possible to develop a program logic
that is significantly simpler compared to other JVM-level logics such as (7). However, in our work we do not tackle issues such as multi-threading nor do we aim
to cover a full high-level language such as Java. We rather focus on the automatic
generation of resource certificates.

Meta Logic: Isabelle/HOL   In order to realise our infrastructure, we have to
select and use a logical framework in the implementation of the hierarchy of pro-

```
static int fac(int);              static int fac(int);
  Code:                             Code:
    0:  iconst_1                      0:  $0 = 1
    1:  istore_1                      1:  b = $0
    2:  iload_0                       2:  $0 = n
    3:  iconst_1                      3:  $1 = 1
    4:  if_icmplt 18                  4:  if ($0<$1) then 18 else 5
    7:  iload_1                       5:  $0 = b
    8:  iload_0                       8:  $1 = n
    9:  imul                          9:  $0 = $0 * $1
   10:  istore_1                     10:  b = $0
   11:  iload_0                      11:  $0 = n
   12:  iconst_1                     12:  $1 = 1
   13:  isub                         13:  $0 = $0 - $1
   14:  istore_0                     14:  n = $0
   15:  goto    2                    15:  goto 2
   18:  iload_1                      18:  $0 = b
   19:  ireturn                      19:  ireturn $0
```

FIGURE 14.3. Java bytecode in ordinary (left) and beautified (right) form

gram logics. Here we have chosen a very powerful system, Isabelle/HOL, and to definitionally realise the program logic as an inductive definition in the meta logic. To avoid the specification of a separate assertion language, we use a shallow embedding for assertions, which are simply meta-logical predicates over the components of the operational semantics. This simplified approach comes at the expense of an increased trusted code base, since we now have to use an entire instance of Isabelle/HOL in the certificate validation phase, as we will see below. However, we found this choice to be adequate for a prototype system in a scenario of global computing with fairly powerful compute nodes. This choice also enables us to use a very succinct representation of certificates as fragments of Isabelle proof scripts. Even without any semantic compression we achieve a certificate size of about 22-32% of the code size, close to the commonly quoted 20% as an acceptable size for a certificate.

14.4.2 Software Infrastructure

The overall structure of the software infrastructure is depicted in Figure 14.5 and is an instance of a general PCC infrastructure (19) with a code producer (left hand side) and a code consumer (right hand side). The main components on the producer side are a *certifying compiler*, which translates high-level Camelot programs into the Grail intermediate code and additionally generates a certificate of its heap consumption. The latter is formalised as a lemma in the heap space logic for the Grail language (8). The Grail code is processed by an assembler, the Grail

```
method static int fac (int n) =
  let
    val b = 1
    fun f(int n, int b) =              method static int fac (int n) =
        if n<1 then b                    let
               else f_else(n,b)            fun f_else(n) =
                                           let
    fun f_else(int n, int b) =                val n' = sub n 1
    let                                       val n' =
        val b = mul b n             invokestatic <Fac Fac.fac(int)>(n')
        val n = sub n 1               in mul n n'
    in                                 end
       f(n,b)                        in
    end                                if n<1 then 1
  in                                         else f_else(n)
    f(n,b)                           end
  end
```

FIGURE 14.4. Tail-recursive (left) and recursive (right) Grail code of factorial

de-functionaliser (gdf), to generate JVM bytecode. This bytecode is transmitted together with the Isabelle proof script as the certificate of its heap consumption to the code consumer. On the consumer side, the Grail code is retrieved via a disassembler, the Grail functionaliser (gf). Then Isabelle/HOL is used in batch mode to automatically check that the resource property expressed in the attached certificate is indeed fulfilled for this program. Once this has been confirmed the code can be executed on the consumer side.

It should also be noted that the current infrastructure does not represent a closed system, in which all mobile code has to be compiled with the same compiler. While the preferred way of generating a code/certificate pair is to write the program in Camelot and have the compiler automatically produce a certificate, it is also possible to use another high-level language such as Java or Scheme that compiles into JVM bytecode, and to then manually generate a proof for the desired resource property. Since the logic has been formalised in Isabelle/HOL, the entire development infrastructure for this prover is available in generating the certificates. As a mixture of both scenarios, it is also possible to write the top level program in Camelot, and call foreign language code from Camelot. This is particularly useful for accessing Java library functions, e.g. for GUI parts of the code. In (21) an extension of Camelot with object-oriented features is described. These extensions have been used in implementing a directory lookup application to be executed on a PDA, based on the MIDP standard for small devices, which provides a restricted set of Java libraries and is partially based on Sun's KVM.

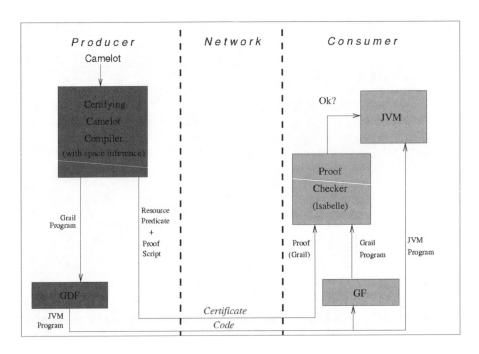

FIGURE 14.5. PCC infrastructure for MRG

14.5 RESULTS

The most visible result of the project is a complete working infrastructure for generating and checking certificates describing the resource behaviour of programs written in a high-level functional programming language. Although the nature of the project was foundational, we emphasised from the start the importance of producing prototypes for the components of the PCC infrastructure — partly as a testbed for experimentation, but also as an on-line test of our techniques in a realistic, distributed setting.

The main novel techniques in the development of the infrastructure are our *multi-layered logics approach* for providing reasoning support tuned to, but not restricted to, the automatic verification of resource properties, and the use of *tactic-based certificates* in order to reduce the size of the certificate, albeit at the cost of increasing the TCB size. However, since we have established soundness of all logics in the prover, of these only the operational semantics needs to be trusted and as validation engine the prover could be replaced by a proof checker with support for a subset of the proof scripting language.

More specifically we have produced the following:

- A *completely formalised virtual machine and cost model* (9) for a JVM-like language. We have used Isabelle/HOL as the theorem proving platform for this formalisation and for encoding the logics.

222

- A *resource aware program logic* (2; 3) for the bytecode language of the above virtual machine.

- A *specialised logic for heap consumption* (8) that is built on top of the program logic.

- A *certifying compiler* for the strict, first-order functional, object-oriented language Camelot (18), integrated into a prototype PCC infrastructure.

- *Advanced reasoning principles* (14; 17) for resources, based on high-level type systems.

Our particular conclusions on the design of a PCC infrastructure are as follows:

- For automatic certificate generation it is crucial to make use of high-level structural information and to propagate this information down to the program logic. In our design we have realised this as several layers of logics, with the heap logic being tailored to the high-level type-system used to infer information on heap space consumption. In particular, we deliberately depart from the standard approach of splitting certificate validation into verification condition generation and simplification. In our experience, the verification conditions even for simple properties become too complex to be automatically solved by a proof assistant. In contrast, by drawing on information from the high level type inference, we can perform simplifications "on the fly" and thus can keep proofs more manageable.

- The program logic serves as a common language in which to phrase program properties. Thus, program logics over low-level languages can be seen as the "assembler code" for proofs of program properties and as the target language for a compiler that realises high-level type systems to express such properties.

- Encoding the program logic in a proof assistant is not only useful for developing the logic and enforcing formal rigour; it can also serve as an immediate platform for realising the required software infrastructure. While in terms of the size of the TCB and interoperability with other systems a more general format of certificates as proof objects would be favourable, a direct embedding into a proof assistant also yields certificates of small size.

- We found the VDM-style version of the program logic (for partial correctness), with judgements of the form $\Gamma \rhd e : A$, significantly easier to use than an earlier Hoare-style version we had developed, with judgements of the form $\Gamma \rhd \{A\}\ e\ \{A'\}$. This confirms earlier observations on how the need for *auxiliary variables* in a Hoare setting complicates its practical usability (16; 19).

New projects that build on the MRG infrastructure are:

- MOBIUS, an Integrated Project of the FET-GC2 proactive initiative (http://mobius.inria.fr/), deals with innovative trust management for global computing, where the resources can be as diverse as network access

223

and the secure flow of information. In contrast to MRG, this project focuses on Java as a high-level language, and thus will bring the results of our research to a broader community.

- EmBounded, a FET-Open STREP project (`http://www.embounded.org/`), which aims to provide resource bounded computation for embedded systems, using Hume as the high-level programming language. Here we can draw on our amortised costs approach for developing inferences on resource consumption (heap, stack and time) for Hume.

- ReQueST, an EPSRC-funded project (`https://wiki.inf.ed.ac.uk/ReQueST`), aims to develop methods, invent algorithms, and engineer software to equip each request for a Grid service with an irrefutable and accurate certificate which specifies the quantity and type of resources which will be consumed if the request is serviced.

Since the end of MRG, several extensions to the infrastructure as described in this paper have been developed. Related to Objective 4 of the project, on ways of reducing the size of the certificates, we are now studying the use of two forms of resource policies to arrive at a more flexible system without the need of additional communication. In this setup, a guaranteed resource policy is sent together with the certificate. On the consumer side validation of a certificate now involves two steps: a check that the guaranteed resource policy implies the target resource policy on the consumer and validation of the certificate w.r.t. the guaranteed resource policy. Typically, the guaranteed resource policy will contain information about the high-level program, such as the space consumption depending on the input size, and local side-conditions on the consumer are captured in the target resource policy. This approach is discussed in more detail in (6).

Overall we conclude that the project has been very successful in developing the foundations for a novel PCC approach for resources and in producing a prototype infrastructure demonstrating the principles. Finally, visit our project web pages, where you can find project summaries, published papers, and a tutorial (15) with on-line exercises: `http://groups.inf.ed.ac.uk/mrg/`. An on-line demo is directly available at: `http://projects.tcs.ifi.lmu.de/mrg/pcc/`.

ACKNOWLEDGEMENTS

This document summarises work in the MRG project (IST-2001-33149) which was funded by the EC under the FET proactive initiative on Global Computing. We would like to thank the many researchers who contributed to MRG, in particular R. Amadio, R. Atkey, B. Campbell, S. Jost, B. Klin, M. Konečný, M. Prowse, U. Schöpp, and N. Wolverson.

REFERENCES

[1] A.W. Appel. Foundational Proof-Carrying Code. In *Symposium on Logic in Computer Science (LICS'01)*, pages 247–258. IEEE Computer Society, June 2001.

[2] D. Aspinall, L. Beringer, M. Hofmann, H-W. Loidl, and A. Momigliano. A Program Logic for Resource Verification. In *International Conference on Theorem Proving in Higher Order Logics (TPHOLs2004)*, LNCS 3223, pages 34–49. Springer, September 2004.

[3] D. Aspinall, L. Beringer, M. Hofmann, H-W. Loidl, and A. Momigliano. A Program Logic for Resources. *Theoretical Computer Science*, 2006. Special Issue on Global Computing. To appear.

[4] D. Aspinall, L. Beringer, and A. Momigliano. Optimisation Validation. In *Workshop on Compiler Optimization Meets Compiler Verification (COCV06)*, Vienna, Austria, April 2, 2006. To appear in ENTCS.

[5] D. Aspinall, S. Gilmore, M. Hofmann, D. Sannella, and I. Stark. Mobile Resource Guarantees for Smart Devices. In *Construction and Analysis of Safe, Secure, and Interoperable Smart Devices (CASSIS'04)*, LNCS 3362, pages 1–26. Springer, 2005.

[6] D. Aspinall and K. MacKenzie. Mobile Resource Guarantees and Policies. In *Construction and Analysis of Safe, Secure, and Interoperable Smart Devices (CASSIS'05)*, LNCS 3956, Nice, March 8–11, 2005. Springer. To appear.

[7] F. Y. Bannwart and P. Müller. A Logic for Bytecode. In *Bytecode Semantics, Verification, Analysis and Transformation (BYTECODE)*, volume 141(1) of *ENTCS*, pages 255–273. Elsevier, 2005.

[8] L. Beringer, M. Hofmann, A. Momigliano, and O. Shkaravska. Automatic Certification of Heap Consumption. In *Logic for Programming, Artificial Intelligence, and Reasoning (LPAR'04)*, LNCS 3452, pages 347–362, Montevideo, Uruguay, March 14–18, Feb 2005. Springer.

[9] L. Beringer, K. MacKenzie, and I. Stark. Grail: a Functional Form for Imperative Mobile Code. In *Workshop on Foundations of Global Computing*, volume 85(1) of *ENTCS*. Elsevier, June 2003.

[10] F. Besson, T. Jensen, and D. Pichardie. Proof-Carrying Code from Certified Abstract Interpretation and Fixpoint Compression. *Theoretical Computer Science. Special Issue on Applied Semantics*, 2006. Also: Tech. Report INRIA-5751. To appear.

[11] D. Cachera, T. Jensen, D. Pichardie, and G. Schneider. Certified Memory Usage Analysis. In *International Symposium on Formal Methods (FM'05)*, LNCS 3582, pages 91–106, Newcastle, July 18–22, 2005. Springer.

[12] Bor-Yuh Evan Chang, A. Chlipala, G. Necula, and R. Schneck. The Open Verifier Framework for Foundational Verifiers. In *Workshop on Types in Language Design and Implementation (TLDI'05)*. ACM, January 2005.

[13] C. Colby, P. Lee, G.C. Necula, F. Blau, M. Plesko, and K. Cline. A Certifying Compiler for Java. In *Conference on Programming Language Design and Implementation (PLDI'00)*, pages 95–107. ACM Press, 2000.

[14] M. Hofmann and S. Jost. Static Prediction of Heap Space Usage for First-Order Functional Programs. In *Symposium on Principles of Programming Languages (POPL'03)*, pages 185–197, New Orleans, LA, USA, January 2003. ACM Press.

[15] M. Hofmann, H-W. Loidl, and L. Beringer. Certification of Quantitative Properties of Programs. In *Logical Aspects of Secure Computer Systems*, Marktoberdorf, Aug 2-13, 2005. IOS Press. Lecture Notes of the Marktoberdorf Summer School 2005. To appear.

[16] T. Kleymann. *Hoare Logic and VDM: Machine-Checked Soundness and Completeness Proofs*. PhD thesis, LFCS, University of Edinburgh, 1999.

[17] M. Konečný. Functional In-Place Update with Layered Datatype Sharing. In *Intl. Conf. on Typed Lambda Calculi and Applications (TLCA'03)*, LNCS 2701, pages 195–210. Springer, June 2003.

[18] K. MacKenzie and N. Wolverson. Camelot and Grail: Resource-aware Functional Programming on the JVM. In *Trends in Functional Programing*, volume 4, pages 29–46. Intellect, 2004.

[19] G. Necula. Proof-carrying Code. In *Symposium on Principles of Programming Languages (POPL'97)*, pages 106–116, Paris, France, January 15–17, 1997. ACM Press.

[20] M. Wildmoser, T. Nipkow, G. Klein, and S. Nanz. Prototyping Proof Carrying Code. In *Exploring New Frontiers of Theoretical Informatics*, pages 333–347. Kluwer, 2004.

[21] N. Wolverson and K. MacKenzie. O'Camelot: Adding Objects to a Resource Aware Functional Language. In *Trends in Functional Programing*, volume 4, pages 47–62. Intellect, 2004.